STALIN IN OCTOBER

STALIN IN OCTOBER

The Man Who
Missed the Revolution
Robert M. Slusser

The Johns Hopkins University Press

Baltimore and London

This book has been brought to publication with the generous
assistance of the Andrew W. Mellon Foundation.

Hardcover edition originally published 1987
Softshell Books edition, 1990

The Johns Hopkins University Press
701 West 40th Street
Baltimore, Maryland 21211
The Johns Hopkins Press Ltd., London

The paper used in this publication meets the minimum requirements of American
National Standard for Information Sciences—Permanence of Paper for Printed
Library Materials, ANSI Z39.48-1984.

Library of Congress Catalog Card Number 87-3666
ISBN 0-8018-4112-7

Library of Congress Cataloging in Publication data
will be found on the last page of this book.

This one is for the children:
Ginny and Big Jim; Paul Eric; and Jim

CONTENTS

PREFACE &
ACKNOWLEDGMENTS

This book concerns what Isaac Deutscher called "the queer and undeniable fact" of Joseph Stalin's "absence or inactivity at the [Bolshevik] headquarters during the rising" of October 1917, known to history as the October Revolution. I cannot claim to have solved the problem definitively—I am not sure a definitive solution is possible at present—but I have tried to put it in its historical context.

My thanks go to R. Carter Elwood, who first encouraged me to undertake the study. For basic data on the Russian Revolution I have relied primarily on the work of Alexander Rabinowitch. For an understanding of Stalin's complex psychology, one of the principal elements in the case, I have followed Robert C. Tucker's pioneering analysis of the tension between Stalin's grandiose self-image and the often harsh reality that threatened to undermine that image.

A third scholar whose work has guided me is the late Charles Duval, Jr. Duval's still unpublished biography of Sverdlov is required reading for an understanding of the formative years of Soviet power. Holland Hunter and John N. Westwood provided useful data on the train that brought Stalin to Petrograd in March 1917. Robert Himmer generously shared with me his wide-ranging work in progress on Stalin.

For helping to make possible conditions in which I could work, I am grateful to a number of my colleagues in the Department of History at Michigan State University, especially Kwan-wai So, Warren Cohen, Don Lammers, Harold Marcus, and Bill McCagg. For reading the manuscript, offering some valuable comments, and recommending its publication I thank Robert V. Daniels.

Indispensable help was rendered by the staff of the Michigan State University Library, especially Henry Koch and Robert Runser.

Financial support was provided by the Earhart Foundation; my thanks especially to the executive secretary, Dr. Antony T. Sullivan. Jack Goellner, director of the Johns Hopkins University Press, showed exemplary patience during the work's long gestation and chose the title. Carol Ehrlich, my editor at the Press, combined tact and critical acumen for which I am grateful. Jo Grandstaff was a top-notch typist and valued friend.

Portions of the work were presented at the Department of History, Yale University, and the Center for Russian and East European Studies, University of Michigan; my thanks to both institutions. Peter Clement, Mary Rohrkemper, and other members of a seminar on Stalin at Michigan State University contributed valuable insights.

The bottom line belongs to Elizabeth. Without her love and support, neither this book nor its author would be in existence.

NOTE TO THE READER

All dates are given Old Style, thirteen days behind the Western calendar.

Transliteration is based on the Library of Congress system, with modifications.

STALIN IN OCTOBER

I // MARCH

Arrival

Among the passengers who got off the Trans-Siberian express on its arrival in Petrograd on Sunday morning, March 12, 1917, were three prominent figures in the Bolshevik party: Matvei K. Muranov, who had served as one of five Bolshevik deputies in the Fourth State Duma; Lev B. Kamenev (Rozenfel'd), editor of the Bolshevik newspaper, *Pravda*, in 1913–14; and Joseph V. Stalin (Dzhugashvili), since 1912 a member of the party's Central Committee and its Russian Bureau. All three were returning from the Siberian exile to which they had been sentenced by tsarist authorities and from which they had just been freed under an amnesty that was one of the first official acts carried out by the new Provisional Government established shortly after the collapse of the tsarist regime and the abdication of Nicholas II on March 2.

Revolutionary politics and the winds of chance had brought the three men together briefly. For the first weeks after their return the three would cooperate closely in pursuit of their common interests; thereafter their careers would develop along divergent paths. For Kamenev, the path of life would lead ultimately to disgrace and execution on the orders of his 1917 comrade, Stalin. Muranov, in contrast, would live to see Stalin buried and would die in peaceful old age as a state pensioner.

As for Stalin, in March 1917 he was a comparatively young man (thirty-seven) in search of a greatness to which he felt destined but who had yet to discover the role and function in the world which would earn him the recognition to which he believed himself entitled. It would have seemed bizarre in the extreme had some bystander with the gift of prophecy recognized in the pockmarked, swarthy, short (five-foot four-inch) Georgian of March 1917 the man who would one day inspire awe, reverence, and terror as the most powerful despot Russia had ever known. Only in a time of revolutionary transformation would a meteoric rise to power like that of Stalin be possible, and even for Stalin the road to the summit was to be long, arduous, and dangerous. The eight months of the revolution, from February to October 1917, proved far from adequate as the launching base for his ascent; for Stalin, the year 1917 was to constitute such a mixed record of partial achievements and outright failures, missed opportunities and foolish blunders, that he could never afterwards contemplate it without acute discomfort. For that reason he devoted much of his energy in later years to the never-ending task of revising the record of his activities in 1917, correcting it, touching it up, or simply blotting it out from the collective memory of history.

In March 1917 Stalin had lived just over half of his allotted span; thirty-seven years old on December 21, 1916, he died a little over thirty-six years later, on March 5, 1953. Behind him lay years of struggle as an obscure, ambitious, and unscrupulous professional revolutionary; ahead lay the road to unlimited power, but power achieved at a staggering cost in human suffering.

At the time it seemed a stroke of luck for Stalin that he was one of the first political exiles to return to the capital after the overthrow of the autocracy. Ironically, the tsarist government had made an unwitting contribution to Stalin's seeming good fortune. In October 1916, in an act of desperation, government authorities had decided to help meet the army's insatiable demand for cannon fodder by inducting political prisoners and exiles. The order did not explicitly exclude Bolsheviks, despite the well-known antiwar stance of the party's leader, Vladimir Il'ich Lenin. A convinced Leninist in the ranks of the tsarist army could do more harm to the national war effort than a platoon of enemy soldiers. By including Stalin's name in the list of those to be called to the colors, the tsarist authorities in effect certified him to be nondangerous to the war effort—a useful clue to the questions that will confront us shortly of Stalin's attitude toward Lenin's stand on the war and toward Lenin himself.

Not all the Bolshevik exiles in Siberia were called up: Yakov M. Sverdlov, for example, a prominent party member who for a time shared quarters with Stalin in his Siberian exile, received no induction order. But Sverdlov had been an outspoken supporter of Lenin's stand on the war, a fact the tsarist authorities may have taken into account.

The induction order found Stalin in Kureika, a remote settlement north of the Arctic Circle in the forbidding and nearly inaccessible Turukhansk region. To reach Krasnoyarsk, a regional center where the medical examinations for call-ups were held, Stalin had to make a six-week journey across frozen tundra and along icebound rivers, reaching his destination only at the end of December 1916. As far as the stated purpose of his trip was concerned he could have saved himself the trouble, for the army doctors rejected him—not, as later hagiographers maintained, because he was regarded as politically dangerous, but because he had a withered left arm that prevented him from handling a rifle or a bayonet effectively. Stalin's future military glory, including self-appointment as Supreme Commander of the Soviet Armed Forces and the title of Generalissimo in the course of World War II, would have seemed sheer fantasy to the medical board that examined him in January 1917.

Rejection by the army was a stroke of luck, but the real gain for Stalin lay in the time advantage the call-up gave him. His four-year sentence of exile had only a few more months to run; taking advantage of the laxness of police surveillance in the waning days of tsarist power, Stalin simply remained near Krasnoyarsk, finding temporary shelter in the nearby town of Achinsk. From Achinsk it was only a few hours' trip to Krasnoyarsk, where he could catch the train for Petrograd, a four-days' journey. News of the tsar's abdication reached Stalin and other exiles in Achinsk early in March, and on the eighth a group including the three Bolshevik leaders boarded the train for the capital. En route some of the exiles sent a telegram to the ex-tsar's brother, Michael Romanoff, congratulating him on his decision not to assume the title of tsar in a last-ditch effort to save the dynasty. Kamenev was among those who signed the telegram, but not Stalin.

Stalin's early return to Petrograd and the advantages it gave him can usefully be contrasted with the experience of his friend and fellow Georgian G. K. Ordzhonikidze, who was languishing in the even more remote Siberian region of Yakutia at the time of the February Revolution and who remained there through May. As a result, in the words of biographers Georges Haupt and Jean-Jacques Marie, Ordzhonikidze played "only a minor role in the Revolution and Civil War."[1]

Stalin's early arrival in Petrograd gave him a head start over Lenin, who came into the city on April 3. For some three weeks, therefore,

Stalin enjoyed the experience of being one of the top-ranking Bolsheviks at the center of a rapidly changing revolutionary situation. How effectively did he make use of his opportunity? The answer is provided by his later determination to suppress, distort, or obliterate the record of that period of his career and to silence or destroy the surviving witnesses to it. It is only thanks to the failure of some careless or remarkably brave and stubborn archivist to purge the files that one of the most damning records of Stalin's activities in this first phase of the revolution lay undetected during all the years of his supreme power, emerging intact only in 1962.

The Local Situation

When Stalin arrived in Petrograd he found that the major lines along which the revolution would develop had already been set, lines to which he could react and which he could hope to influence but which he was in no position to define, let alone to originate. There already existed a number of freshly minted political organizations established in the first flush of revolutionary enthusiasm, as well as some Bolshevik party bodies that had survived the final convulsions of expiring tsarism.

There was, first of all, the Petrograd Soviet of Workers' Deputies, established on February 27 on the initiative of the local Mensheviks and their rivals and allies, the Socialist Revolutionaries (SR's). A few Bolsheviks had also joined the Executive Committee of the Soviet, but it was dominated by the Mensheviks and SR's. In keeping with their interpretation of Marxist theory, the Mensheviks regarded the fall of tsarism as Russia's long-awaited bourgeois revolution, which would lead in the fullness of time to a liberal democratic republic and the flowering of Russian capitalist industrialization. Only when that process had run its course, with the growth of a large-scale working class, would Russia be ready for the proletarian revolution which, in Menshevik eyes, Marx had foretold. Until that time, which might lie decades in the future, the task of the workers' parties and their political organs such as the Soviet was to defend the interests of the workers against the bourgeois state and its capitalist allies. Under no conditions, the Mensheviks held, should a workers' party attempt to assume political power before the objective socioeconomic conditions capable of providing the basis for a socialist regime had been established. In support of this position the Mensheviks could invoke the authority of Friedrich Engels, who had specifically warned of the dangers a socialist government would face if it were set up before its time. Since Russia in 1917 manifestly had not attained the conditions described by Engels as essential for a successful proletarian revolution, the Mensheviks reasoned that the Soviet must abstain from exercising power, even though there were militant workers in Petrograd who were anxious to set up a provisional revolutionary government. Reluctantly, the SR's accepted the Mensheviks' self-denying logic, all the more readily since their own program provided guidance only up to the revolution, not beyond it.

Although in theory an expression of grass-roots initiative on the part of the factory workers, the Soviet was in fact built from the top down, owing its genesis to a self-chosen executive committee of ranking Menshevik and SR leaders who came together at a time when the troops of the Petrograd garrison had already broken with their tsarist commanders. It was the Executive Committee that organized the election of deputies in the plants and factories of Petrograd, and it was the same Executive Committee that continued thereafter to speak in the name of the Soviet as representative of the workers.

In apparent confirmation of the Menshevik-SR theory of the revolution, a new provisional government manifestly bourgeois in character appeared almost simultaneously. It emerged in the final days of tsarism out of the Provisional Committee of the Fourth State Duma, a committee that had been called into existence in a desperate effort to maintain a modicum of continuity in the exercise of state power. The Duma, in turn, was a quasi-legislative body that had been elected in the far-off prewar year of 1912 by an electorate deliberately restricted by the tsarist government in such a way as to give preponderant influence to the propertied and well-to-do classes. Thus it was the unmistakably middle- and upper-class Provisional Government that took a rather shaky grip on power at the time of the collapse of the tsarist regime, while the Petrograd Soviet contented itself with exercising a wary supervision over the government's behavior in the name of the workers.

A formula expressing this "dual power" relationship soon emerged in the speeches and publications of the Soviet: the Soviet would support the Provisional Government "insofar as" it defended the achievements of the revolution.

On one point the Soviet leaders drew the line: none of them must sully their socialist virtue by accepting a position in the Provisional Government. For its part, the latter was eager to draw in some of the moderate socialists as a means of broadening its base and strengthening its authority. The Mensheviks and SR's stood firm, however; a leading Menshevik, the Georgian Nikolai Chkheidze, refused a tempting invitation to join the Provisional Government as minister of justice. Less scrupulous and more ambitious, a rising young socialist

5

lawyer from Lenin's home town of Simbirsk, Alexander Kerensky, accepted the offer when it was addressed to him, justifying his action on the ground that the socialists needed their own spokesman in the bourgeois camp.

The local Petrograd Bolsheviks took only a small part in the formation of the Soviet, and none at all in that of the Provisional Government. The February Revolution found them in some disarray, for as one of its final efforts the Okhrana (tsarist security police) had arrested the Petersburg Committee (PK) of the Bolshevik party on February 26. (The committee insisted on calling itself the "Petersburg" rather than "Petrograd" committee, to indicate its disapproval of the renaming of the capital in 1914, on the ground that the change was an expression of national chauvinism.) It was not until March 2 that a group of local Petrograd Bolsheviks came together in the attic of the Central Labor Exchange Building to hold their first formal session after the February Revolution.

During the interval while the Petersburg Committee was in limbo, its authority was assumed by the nominally subordinate *raion* (district) committee of the Vyborg *raion*, one of the sections of the capital with a predominantly working-class population, and one where the workers held a particularly strong faith in the capacity of their class to make their own revolution, without the aid of party intellectuals. Even after the reestablishment of the Petersburg Committee, the Vyborg *Raion* Committee continued to exert a strong influence on Bolshevik policy, usually throwing its weight to the more radical end of the political spectrum.

Even without the timely initiative of the Vyborg *Raion* Committee, the temporary eclipse of the Petersburg Committee would not have meant the total absence of a Bolshevik voice in the February Revolution, thanks to the existence of yet another body, the Russian Bureau of the Central Committee of the party. In its origins this body went back to the prerevolutionary years—Stalin had at one time been one of its members—but its presence in Petrograd in February 1917 reflected the hard work and revolutionary zeal of three young men who had joined the party before the war and who had somehow avoided arrest by the Okhrana. Two of the young men were from a working-class background: Aleksandr Gavrilovich Shlyapnikov, whose detailed and all-too-candid memoirs of this period would later earn for him Stalin's murderous hostility, and Pyotr A. Zalutsky, who never wrote his memoirs but who nonetheless fell victim to Stalin's wrath because of his outspoken criticism of Stalin's policies in 1917 and subsequently.

The third member of the Russian Bureau was an intellectual of middle-class background, Vyacheslav M. Skryabin, soon to make a name for himself under his party pseudonym, Molotov (from *molot*, "hammer," presumably as a gesture of self-identification with the workers). Under the leadership of Shlyapnikov, who had worked in close contact with Lenin and who had been co-opted to the Central Committee in September 1915, these three young and still inexperienced men did their best to speak in the name of the party and to define its position on the urgent problems arising out of the revolution.

Their first action was the publication of a manifesto on February 27, "To All the Citizens of Russia," which called on the workers and soldiers to elect representatives to a provisional revolutionary government. Though issued in the name of the Russian Bureau, the manifesto was in fact the work of a group of members of the Vyborg *Raion* Committee, who wanted to head off an intellectual-led socialist revolution by preempting the ground through the establishment of their own worker-led provisional government. The effort failed, primarily because it lacked a broad base of support in the Petrograd proletariat, but in part because it was overtaken and thrust aside by the better-organized movement to set up the citywide Soviet of Workers' Deputies. In any case the February 27 manifesto, which reflected Bolshevik policy as it had been worked out during the Revolution of 1905, was little more than a stopgap measure, a quick improvisation designed to assert the party's continuing existence and its determination to make its voice heard.

It soon became apparent to the members of the Russian Bureau, however, that there was a pressing need for a steadier and more continuous medium for articulating party policy. The total abolition of censorship, one of the first actions of the Provisional Government, had the welcome effect of lifting the ban on *Pravda*, which dated back to the early days of the war, and on March 2 the Russian Bureau assigned to Molotov the task of reestablishing the party newspaper. A printing press was soon found, and editorial offices were established in the same building. At its meeting on March 4 the Russian Bureau formally resolved to publish *Pravda* as the organ of the party Central Committee and jointly, pending other arrangements, of the Petersburg Committee. Reflecting this dual responsibility, the editorial board was to be composed of two representatives of the bureau and one of the Petersburg Committee. The first number of the new *Pravda* appeared on the following day, with free distribution, while the second issue, on March 6, sold one hundred thousand copies, according to Shlyapnikov, an indication of the eager response of the Petrograd workers to the Bolshevik line as defined in *Pravda*.

Under Molotov's editorial direction *Pravda* took a clear-cut stand of opposition to the Provisional Government as a bourgeois institution and continued to call for the election instead of a provisional revolutionary government, in accordance with the bureau's manifesto of February 27. It soon became apparent, however, that in this matter *Pravda* did not speak for all the Bolsheviks of Petrograd; in particular, the Petersburg Committee (PK) took a less hostile position toward the Provisional Government. At a meeting on March 3 the PK, after listening to Molotov's advocacy of the bureau's policy, voted instead "not to oppose the power of the Provisional Government insofar as its actions correspond to the interests of the proletariat and the broad democratic masses of the people," a conciliatory position indistinguishable from that of the Menshevik-SR leadership in the Executive Committee of the Petrograd Soviet. Thus on this crucial point an influential group of Bolsheviks in the capital occupied a position close to that of the other socialist parties.

The Family

For many young people in tsarist Russia one of the most potent lures of the revolutionary movement was the opportunity it provided for association with an extended social grouping of friends, collaborators, and like-minded individuals. The time-honored greeting within the revolutionary movement, *tovarishch*, "comrade," had not yet lost its warmth. Especially for "illegals" like Stalin, revolutionaries who had run afoul of the law and who were forced to live in hiding, the knowledge that in virtually any town or city throughout the Russian Empire they could be sure of finding a friendly welcome, food and lodging, and the technical facilities to continue their revolutionary activities went far to mitigate the loneliness, danger, and insecurity of their lives.

Stalin was nearly thirty before he had the opportunity to see at first hand the splendors of St. Petersburg. It was in July 1909 that he made his first fleeting visit to the capital, and another two years before he returned. Once again, ironically, it was the tsarist authorities who helped shape the course of Stalin's future destiny. By forbidding him to live in the Caucasus, including his native province, Georgia, some nameless tsarist official in June 1911 contributed to Stalin's emergence from the provincial backwater where he had spent the first ten years of his revolutionary career. True, the same administrative order banned him from residing in the capital cities, St. Petersburg and Moscow, as well as other major industrial centers, but it was easy for an experienced "illegal" to slip through the police surveillance network. In September 1911 Stalin enjoyed a three-day visit to St. Petersburg before the police caught up with him, and in April 1912 he managed to live there illegally for three weeks before being arrested. In the autumn of that year he was back for what would prove to be his longest prerevolutionary sojourn in the capital, from September 12, 1912, to February 23, 1913, with time out for two short trips abroad.

When Stalin arrived in Petrograd in March 1917, therefore, he was coming back to a city where he already knew his way around. Losing no time he headed for the apartment of an old friend, Sergei Alliluev, a skilled engineer who lived with his family in the working-class Vyborg district north of the main channel of the Neva River.

The Alliluevs, a close-knit family of father, mother, and three lively daughters, provided Stalin with an adoptive family that offered him the warmth, concern, and affection of which his life had hitherto known all too little. Stalin's first marriage had ended in 1908 with the death of his young wife, Yekaterina Svanidze; his son by that marriage, Yakov, took his father's legal surname, Dzhugashvili, but was never close to his father, and his death in a German prisoner-of-war camp during World War II left Stalin apparently unmoved.

Stalin's own father was a cobbler by trade and a heavy drinker by reputation, with a foul temper which he was prone to take out in beating his wife and infant son, the future dictator. It was Stalin's mother, a devout and pious woman, who implanted in the frail and sickly boy the conviction that he had the potential for greatness, and it was his mother who set him on the path to advancement by arranging for his entry, after elementary school, into the Tiflis Theological Seminary where he could receive the training qualifying him for membership in the upper clergy of the Georgian Orthodox Church. But there is no evidence that Stalin was ever emotionally close to his mother; not a single letter from him to her has been published.

Stalin had, it seems, a second son, whose name and identity have been lost to history. During his last, longest, and most rigorous exile, from 1913 to 1916, he lived for stretches of time in complete isolation, and in a moment of uncharacteristic frankness he later told one of the Alliluev girls that he had taken as mistress a peasant woman who bore him a son. Both mother and son, if they really existed—and the evidence is far from conclusive—seem to have been brusquely abandoned when Stalin returned to European Russia at the end of 1916; except for Stalin's indiscreet revelation, they were never heard of again.

Thus it was to none of his closest relations—parents, wife, mistress, or sons—that Stalin could look for family affection. All the more important in his private life, then, were the Alliluevs. The close family ties between Stalin and the Alliluevs were cemented by marriage: two years after the revolution one of the Alliluev girls, Nadya, became Stalin's wife. (Thirteen years later, in despair over what he had become and his harsh policy toward the peasants, she committed suicide.)

Sergei Alliluev, the father, was employed in the Tiflis railway shop as a skilled mechanic when he first observed young Dzhugashvili, a fledgling revolutionary, in 1900; within a few years Alliluev made the young man's personal acquaintance and a friendly relationship grew up between the older Russian worker, who had been deported to the Transcaucasus because of his political radicalism, and the young Georgian who was just embarking on a revolutionary career.

Sergei's wife, Ol'ga Yevgen'evna, took little part in the men's political activities but devoted her energies to maintaining the home and raising her children. A woman of warmth and sympathetic temperament, she found room in her maternal affections for the rough but susceptible young Georgian whom her husband had befriended. It was to Ol'ga Yevgen'evna that Stalin wrote the only personal letter of his which has survived from the prerevolutionary years, a note in which Stalin thanks Mrs. Allilueva for her "kind and good sentiments" toward him as well as for a parcel she had sent him. Evidently something of the Alliluev family warmth transmitted itself to the normally unresponsive Stalin, for in the same letter he urged Ol'ga Yevgen'evna not to spend money on him which the Alliluevs needed themselves.[2]

It is to the reminiscences of Sergei Alliluev and his daughter Anna that we are indebted for a number of glimpses, fleeting but revealing, into the personal and emotional life of Stalin in 1917. With the Alliluevs Stalin felt at home; in the warmth of their family circle he could relax and show a side of his nature—fun-loving, even playful—of which the world would otherwise have no inkling.

A Sour Welcome

Having touched base with the Alliluevs and arranged for a temporary lodging elsewhere (the Alliluevs were in the process of moving to a larger apartment, and Stalin asked them to include a room for him), Stalin, together with his Krasnoyarsk colleagues, made his way to Bolshevik headquarters. It was symptomatic of the topsy-turvy world of revolution that party headquarters were now established, not, as would have been customary under tsarism, in some obscure, out-of-the-way worker's rooms, carefully hidden from the snooping of the

Okhrana, but in the center of the most fashionable district of the capital, in a mansion that had been commandeered from its previous owner, Matilda Kshesinskaya, whose talents as a prima ballerina in the Imperial Ballet had done less to earn her this valuable property than her brief but well-publicized liaison with the heir to the throne, the future Tsar Nicholas II.

Party headquarters in early March 1917, pending Lenin's return, meant the Russian Bureau of the Central Committee, comprising at first the three young men whom we have already met—Shlyapnikov, Zalutsky, and Molotov. One of the three, Molotov, was already acquainted with Stalin, having worked with him on *Pravda* in the period 1912–13.

During the first days of March, as party life quickly revived in an atmosphere of unbounded political freedom, additional party figures were added to the bureau, so that by the time of Stalin's return it numbered more than a dozen members. It was this body that met on the afternoon of March 12 to consider how best to employ the services of the recruits who had just come back from Siberia.

With regard to Muranov, the members of the bureau had no hesitation: by unanimous vote he was invited to join with full privileges. The vote showed that the bureau was not insisting that its members follow a strict party line, for it was generally known that Muranov, as a deputy to the State Duma, had been less than firm in his support of Lenin's antiwar stance. But Muranov's record in exile was unblemished, and it was no doubt this fact that earned him the bureau's cordial welcome.

Stalin's candidacy proved more difficult. In the words of the protocol of the bureau's session, first published in 1962,

> It was reported that he [Stalin] had been an agent of the Central Committee in 1912 and therefore it would be advisable to have him as a member. . . . However, in view of certain personal characteristics, the Bureau decided to give him only a consultative vote.[3]

Thus at the very outset of the revolution a group of Stalin's party comrades voted to deny him the prerogatives to which his party rank entitled him because of certain unspecified "personal characteristics." In so doing they struck a note that was to resound ominously throughout Stalin's entire career, reaching its definitive formulation in the words of Lenin's *Testament*, "Stalin is too rude."

Regrettably, the protocols of the March 12 session are silent as to the specific nature of Stalin's "personal characteristics"; either the members prudently avoided spelling them out in the discussion of his candidacy, or the secretary who wrote up the protocols, a young woman named Yelena Stasova, considered it wise not to record them. The result is that we are left to speculate on the exact nature of the charge, with the further result that a number of differing guesses have been offered by recent biographers of Stalin. For Adam Ulam, the reference is "undoubtedly" to Stalin's work on the editorial board of *Pravda* in 1912–13, and the source of the negative report would thus logically be Molotov. If true, this would be, as Ulam says, "piquant," in view of the fact that Molotov was later one of Stalin's most faithful supporters. Elsewhere Ulam recognizes that "unflattering rumors about Stalin's behavior in exile must have reached some Petrograd comrades," but he fails to connect this insight with the March 12 vote of the Russian Bureau.[4]

Robert C. Tucker, on the other hand, believes that "undoubtedly . . . the allusion was to his [Stalin's] arrogance, aloofness, and uncomradely behavior during the Turukhansk exile."[5] Despite the confidence with which these explanations are advanced, complete certainty in the matter is unobtainable by the very nature of the laconic wording of the protocol, but the weight of available evidence points to Tucker's hypothesis as the more probable one. It is supported by the unpublished memoirs of an Old Bolshevik, Boris I. Ivanov, in which Stalin is described as being " 'as proud as ever, as locked up in himself, in his own thoughts and plans' " and as keeping " 'aloof from all other political exiles' " as Ivanov saw him toward the end of 1916.[6] With new arrivals from Siberia pouring into the capital daily, gossipy reports on the exiles' behavior were bound to become common knowledge, and Stalin's record in exile provided ample grounds for the kind of hostile criticism which lay behind the March 12 verdict.

Ivanov's description of Stalin shows a keen insight into the latter's psychology. "Proud," "locked up in himself and his own plans"—these words go far beyond the surface observation of Stalin's "uncomradely" behavior and indicate on Ivanov's part a recognition in Stalin of an inner motivation different from that of the other Siberian exiles. Ivanov's testimony enables us to postulate that as early as December 1916 Stalin was thinking of himself as not merely one of the leading group of the Bolshevik party but potentially as something greater, possibly not yet clearly formulated in his own mind. Thus the "uncomradely" behavior that lay behind the Russian Bureau's unfavorable vote on March 12 concealed something much more startling: nothing less than Stalin's image of himself as party leader, a concept significantly different from that of collective leadership held by virtually all other Bolsheviks.

Stalin and Kamenev

Like Stalin, Kamenev was dealt a stinging rebuff by the Russian Bureau at its meeting on March 12. According to the protocol, the bureau

> decided to add him [Kamenev] to the staff of *Pravda* if he offers his services. . . . His articles are to be accepted for *Pravda*, but he is not to get a by-line.[7]

Nothing was said about membership in the bureau. In Kamenev's case, however, the motive behind the bureau's adverse vote was made clear. Its reasons, as set forth in the protocol, centered around a trial in a tsarist court in February 1915 at which Kamenev had appeared as one of the defendants, along with the five Bolshevik deputies to the State Duma. The charge was that of treason, based on Lenin's policy of "turning the imperialist war into a civil war." As editor of *Pravda* and as adviser to the Bolshevik fraction in the Duma, Kamenev was held accountable for the policies that Lenin, in emigration, was enunciating. Partly because he sincerely disagreed with Lenin on the nature of the war—Kamenev saw Russia as fighting a defensive war against Germany and her allies—and partly from considerations of prudence—he was a man who deplored violence and who tried to avoid unnecessary controversy—Kamenev at the trial dissociated himself from Lenin's position.

Despite this apostasy, which amounted to a violation of the Bolshevik principle of democratic centralism under which party members were bound to support policies adopted by the leadership even when they disagreed with them, Kamenev was found guilty, but the punishment imposed was a comparatively mild one: exile to the Yenisei district of Siberia, a far less rigorous area than the one to which Stalin had been banished. There, at the settlement of Monastyrskoe in the summer of 1915, Kamenev was forced to face a second "trial," this time before a group of his revolutionary comrades. As it happened, Stalin was present, having been allowed to make the trip downriver from Kureika for the purpose.

During the period of Stalin's dictatorship the record of his participation in the 1915 trial was falsified to make it appear that "he stigmatized the cowardly and treacherous behavior of Kamenev at the trial of the five Bolshevik members of the Fourth Duma."[8] There was, in fact, a group among the exiles which took this line, but it was led not by Stalin, who maintained a noncommittal silence, but by Yakov Sverdlov and Suren Spandaryan, two Central Committee members in exile. Years later Spandaryan's widow, Vera Shveitser, in Trotsky's stinging words, "was forced to ascribe to Stalin what had actually been done by her husband," that is, to portray Stalin as the leader in condemning Kamenev's disavowal of Lenin's policy on the war.[9] Thanks in part to Stalin's refusal to join Sverdlov and Spandaryan, the Monastyrskoe trial ended with a resolution approving the behavior of the Duma Bolshevik fraction at the earlier trial. The verdict constituted a vindication for Kamenev, and Stalin, by his refusal to support the party militants, had made a significant contribution to this outcome.

In part, no doubt, Stalin's reluctance to become embroiled in the controversy reflected his lack of interest in the time-honored Russian practice of heatedly debating politically urgent but abstract questions. As Isaac Deutscher puts it,

> Thrashing out principles for their own sake, without the faintest chance for their immediate application, was not his [Stalin's] pet occupation.[10]

In its effect on his relations with Kamenev, however, Stalin's restraint at the 1915 trial had a more positive aspect: it helped shield Kamenev from a reproof that the militants were intent on inflicting on him, and that could have had serious consequences for his future standing in the party. The March 12 censure of Kamenev by the Russian Bureau, at a time when Sverdlov was still thousands of miles from Petrograd and Spandaryan's body was rotting in a Siberian grave, showed the depth of feeling among party members on the war issue. Stalin's restraint in 1915 had certainly earned him some credit in Kamenev's eyes as a possible ally, if not a friend. Years later, when Kamenev had been exposed as an "enemy of the people," Stalin's official biographers were at pains to dissociate him completely from any indication of approval of Kamenev's position on the war in 1915; hence the need to dragoon Vera Shveitser into substituting Stalin's name for that of her husband, Spandaryan, in her memoirs.

Behind the cordial relationship between Stalin and Kamenev established by the 1915 episode lay a long record of contacts which stretched back as far as 1904, when Kamenev first met the youthful Dzhugashvili on a trip to Tiflis where he was carrying out an assignment by Lenin to organize a conference of Caucasian Bolsheviks. Dzhugashvili, though three years older than Kamenev, was by comparison a raw, provincial party worker, too obscure and powerless to play any part in Kamenev's activities, too insignificant and unknown to attend the conference when it met in November 1904.

After that first, inconclusive contact the two men lost touch with each other for more than ten years. Though they both served on the editorial board of *Pravda*, they missed each other there, since it was only after Stalin's arrest in February 1913 that Kamenev was directed by Lenin to take over the editorship of the party journal. By 1915 both men had climbed high in the party hierarchy, Stalin as a member of the Central Committee, Kamenev as its most prominent journalist.

Stalin's prudent restraint vis-à-vis Kamenev at the Monastyrskoe trial in July 1915 can therefore be seen not simply as the result of a lack of interest in debating abstract principles but as the prudent avoidance of censuring a party functionary whose record and standing in the party made him a figure to be reckoned with, someone whose friendship it would be worth Stalin's time to cultivate.

In terms of self-assurance and a well-defined position in the party, Kamenev was far superior to Stalin. The 1915 episode represents a turning point in their relationship, when Stalin for the first time ranked in a position of approximately equal authority with Kamenev, the first time when he was in a position to extend a helping hand to the younger man.

We catch a revealing glimpse of the two men on the eve of the revolution through the eyes of Anatoly Baikalov, a member of the Yenisei Union of Cooperatives who happened to be in Achinsk in February 1917 and who later wrote several accounts of what he remembered of that occasion. Despite the lapse of many years between the actual observations and the publication of Baikalov's recollections in 1940 and 1950, his account carries conviction in its portrayal of a taciturn, pipe-smoking Stalin yielding to the more articulate Kamenev in conversation and nodding his agreement with Kamenev's forecast that the war would end with a German victory, to be followed by a bourgeois-democratic revolution in Russia.[11]

Muranov Lends a Hand

Stalin was not forced to submit to the indignity of conditional membership in the Russian Bureau for long. On the very next day, March 13, the bureau reversed itself and accepted him as a full member, at the same time naming him a member of the editorial board of *Pravda*. At the same session Molotov, pleading inexperience, asked to be relieved from his duties on the editorial board.

If the people with whom Stalin came into contact in 1917 are grouped into categories in accordance with the degree to which they were attracted to or repelled by him, Molotov must be ranked in the category of clients and disciples. He was to be one of the first who accepted at face value Stalin's own vision of his future greatness and who helped contribute to the realization of that vision by selfless devotion to Stalin. Conclusive evidence is lacking as to just when

Molotov saw the light and recognized in Stalin someone greater than himself, service to whom would be his life work. The March 13 session of the Russian Bureau was evidently not yet that moment, but it represented the first recognition by Molotov that contesting Stalin's ambition was not the path he wanted to follow.

Stalin, we can be sure, was present at the March 13 session and must have made a strong case for himself. The decisive effort on his behalf, however, is likely to have been made by Muranov, who, it will be recalled, had been accorded voting privileges on the preceding day. The events of the next few days show that the three exiles who returned from Siberia on March 12 worked closely together for the promotion of their common interests, with Muranov providing the initial push.

The results of this campaign were announced by *Pravda* on March 15. To facilitate the conduct of current business in the rapidly expanding Russian Bureau a new five-person presidium was established, in which two of the newcomers, Stalin and Muranov, confronted an equal number of "old" members, Shlyapnikov and Zalutsky. To provide balance and help avoid a tie vote a fifth member was added, the faithful party stalwart Yelena D. Stasova, who also brought needed secretarial skills to the position. (It is to her well-kept protocols, amazingly preserved during the years of the Stalinist tyranny, that we are indebted for our knowledge of the work of the Russian Bureau at this period.)

Also announced by *Pravda* on the fifteenth was a radical shakeup in the newspaper's editorial board. Muranov, claiming rank as one of the Bolshevik deputies in the State Duma, assumed overall responsibility for *Pravda's* editorial policies, on the ill-founded but convenient pretext that the newspaper was the organ of the Bolshevik fraction in the Duma. (In fact and in theory, *Pravda* was the organ of the party Central Committee or its authorized representative, the Russian Bureau, but during the tsarist period, to ease its troubled relations with the censors, it had made use of the legal subterfuge that it was simply the organ of the Bolshevik fraction in the Duma.)

Serving with Muranov were his Krasnoyarsk comrades, Stalin and Kamenev. Kamenev had, in fact, already jumped the gun by publishing a signed article in *Pravda* on the thirteenth, thereby violating the Russian Bureau's order denying him a by-line.

Finally, on March 15 *Pravda* reported the designation of Muranov, Kamenev, and Stalin as Bolshevik representatives to the Executive Committee of the Petrograd Soviet. Thus in the short space of three days Stalin overcame his lame start and earned a triple promotion: to full membership in the Russian Bureau, to the editorial board of

Pravda, and to the Executive Committee of the Petrograd Soviet. His mandate as a member of the party Central Committee, dating back to 1912, was still valid, giving him a position of potential strength which enabled him to outface any rivals. (Shlyapnikov, too, was a member of the Central Committee, but he lacked Stalin's talent for self-assertion.) It was an impressive start, made all the more dramatic against the background of the unflattering reception accorded him by the Russian Bureau on March 12.

Gratitude for services rendered is a motive that Stalin's biographer is seldom called on to attribute to him. Yet a long view of the relationship between Stalin and Muranov provides grounds for suspecting the existence of this, for Stalin, rare emotion. The strongest evidence is the fact that Muranov was one of the handful of Old Bolsheviks who had served alongside Stalin in 1917 who survived the Great Purge (1936–38), and who died as an honored state pensioner in 1959. Muranov's discreet silence over the years is, without doubt, an essential part of the explanation for his unusual good fortune; unlike Shlyapnikov and others, Muranov never incurred Stalin's wrath by publishing the memoirs of 1917 which his experiences richly qualified him to write.

Muranov, however, had other, more positive services to Stalin to his credit. For example, in 1931 he served as a member of the judicial board in one of the early show trials mounted by the secret police, the trial of the so-called Menshevik Center. There were many Old Bolsheviks, of course, who could point to a record of service to Stalin no less meritorious but who nevertheless fell victim to the Great Purge. The speculation therefore arises that Stalin must have recognized some special bond linking him with Muranov, must have felt some lingering warmth, which earned Muranov one of the rare winners' tickets in the macabre lottery known as the Great Purge.

This consideration serves to strengthen the suggestion that it was Muranov, more than anyone else, who gave Stalin his first boost up the ladder of political advancement in 1917. It might be argued that Kamenev, too, had helped Stalin over the first obstacles in his path in 1917, yet earned no such gratitude later. We shall, in fact, find Stalin defending Kamenev against Lenin's wrath in the days just before the Bolshevik seizure of power in October, and to that extent, a feeling of obligation or gratitude might be postulated in Stalin. As to the difference between Muranov's and Kamenev's fate in the Great Purge, it is enough to point to the fact that Kamenev, after Lenin's death, proved to be one of the staunchest and most effective critics of Stalin's claim to supreme power. Furthermore, unlike Muranov, who never aspired to a position in the top leadership, Kamenev was a close confidant and ally of Lenin and possible successor to his power. For all these reasons Stalin could feel no lasting sense of indebtedness to Kamenev. Muranov, by a combination of positive and negative factors—helpful actions and equally helpful silences—may therefore have given Stalin the opportunity to display one of his rarest and least often employed traits, gratitude for services rendered.

Did Stalin Pull Rank?

The association of the names of Muranov, Kamenev, and Stalin in the reorganizations and appointments announced by *Pravda* on March 15 strongly suggests the existence of a working agreement amongst the three. Within this troika—the first in Stalin's revolutionary career—the predominant role at the outset appears to have been played by Muranov, with Kamenev supplying the theoretical basis and Stalin playing the role of junior partner. Muranov, it will be remembered, was the only one of the three who was accepted into full membership by the Russian Bureau at its March 12 meeting, the only one against whom no objections were raised.

Once granted full membership in the bureau, Muranov was in a position to affect its future course of action, and he presumably used this power to help bring in Stalin as a full member and ally on the thirteenth. Together the two collaborators were then able to solidify their position by taking over *Pravda*, in company with Kamenev, moving into the newly formed Presidium of the Russian Bureau, and, for good measure, establishing a beachhead in the Petrograd Soviet. Altogether the three-day operation represented a triumph of organizational skill in manipulating party politics.

Several biographers of Stalin, impressed by the seeming ease with which he established a strong position in the Bolshevik organization in Petrograd, have assumed that he was the real instigator of the organizational changes announced by *Pravda* on March 15. The lead in establishing this view was taken by Trotsky, writing at a time when the evidence was less extensive than it now is. For Trotsky, there could be no doubt that the central role in the takeover of *Pravda* was played by Stalin:

> As soon as he reached Petrograd . . . Stalin went directly to Bolshevik headquarters. . . . Letting others crack their voices addressing workers' and soldiers' meetings, Stalin entrenched himself at headquarters. More than four years ago, after the Prague conference, he had been co-opted to the Central committee. Since then much water had run over the dam. But

the exile from Kureika [Stalin] had the knack of keeping his hold on the Party machine; he still regarded his old mandate as valid. Aided by Kamenev and Muranov, he first of all removed from leadership the "Leftist" Central Committee Bureau and the *Pravda* editorial board. He went about it rather rudely, the more so since he had no fear of resistance and was in a hurry to show that he was boss.[12]

Trotsky was followed in this interpretation by Deutscher, who writes:

On the grounds of his formal seniority as a member of the Central Committee of 1912, he [Stalin] "deposed" the Petersburg trio [Shlyapnikov, Zalutsky, and Molotov] and, together with Kamenev, took over the editorship of *Pravda*.[13]

Ulam puts essentially the same view more colorfully:

Stalin had won his first open political contest. He could not have had too much assistance from the mild and indecisive Kamenev. [Ulam does not even mention Muranov.] But he had his self-assurance and his domineering manner, distasteful to his comrades and yet impressive at a bewildering time. He was far from being the polished intriguer that he would become in a few years, but he towered over his opponents. . . . Stalin was indisputably the senior Bolshevik on the spot.[14]

Edward E. Smith also sees Stalin as the ringleader in the changes effected between March 12 and 15:

He [Stalin] hurried off to the offices of *Pravda* where, using his credentials as a Central Committee member co-opted in 1912 by Lenin himself, he began to clean house. . . . He brought into the *Pravda* offices a new staff, which was, of course, subservient to his direction.[15]

The same point of view is espoused by Boris Souvarine:

[Stalin] brusquely evict[ed] the management of the paper [*Pravda*], without taking any notice of the organization or of the cadres, solely on the strength of his membership in the Central Committee by simple co-optation.[16]

Robert V. Daniels agrees:

At this juncture the leaders from Siberia arrived. Kamenev and Stalin, ranking as Central Committee members [Kamenev was not, in fact, a member of the CC], quite naturally took over the party organization and the editorial control of *Pravda*.[17]

W. H. Chamberlin echoes the general line but confines himself to the change in editorship of *Pravda*:

Stalin, Kamenev and Muranov returned to Petrograd on March 25 [New Style] and, resting on their superior status in the Party organization, carried out a sort of coup d'état in the editorial office of *Pravda*.[18]

Robert C. Tucker adopts a more cautious tone but takes basically the same position:

After his [Stalin's] chilly initial reception, he successfully asserted his authority.[19]

In a balanced account, E. H. Carr writes:

Kamenev was an experienced writer and had been appointed editor of the central party organ—at that time the *Rabochaya gazeta* [a cover name of *Pravda*], by the Prague conference of 1912; Stalin, having been a member of the central committee of the party since 1912, replaced Shlyapnikov as senior party organizer in Petrograd; Muranov was one of the Bolshevik deputies of the fourth Duma. . . . They at once took over the reins of authority from Shlyapnikov and his young colleagues.[20]

But even Carr sees Stalin's membership in the Central Committee as the decisive lever. Following Trotsky's lead, all these writers in varying degrees draw a picture that reflects their knowledge of Stalin's later career. If we confine ourselves to the evidence for March 1917, however, a picture less flattering to Stalin emerges. The first point to be noted is that Bolshevik principles did not provide any basis for the assertion of seniority by a member of the Central Committee, certainly not the overriding of a valid vote taken by a duly constituted party organization such as the Russian Bureau. Even if Bolshevik policy had sanctioned such an action, however, the situation in Petrograd ruled it out, for one of the local Petrograd Bolsheviks whom Muranov, Kamenev, and Stalin pushed aside, Shlyapnikov, was no less a member of the Central Committee than Stalin, and had been in much more recent touch with the party leader than Stalin in his remote Siberian exile. To suppose, with Trotsky and others, that Stalin in March 1917 could have used "his old Party mandate" to "show them who was boss" is to misread the events of 1917 in the light of party practice at a much later time when Stalin had in fact made himself "boss." It is also to misjudge Stalin's still precarious and uncertain position in March 1917, and, in consequence, to underestimate the difficulties he faced before he emerged into a position of recognized authority. He had shown he knew how to use power, in alliance with his Siberian comrades, but he was still far from "towering over his opponents." Now he would have to consolidate the position he had won by showing he could produce ideas capable of generating an enthusiastic following in the party and among the workers. The pages of *Pravda* during the next few weeks throw a searching light on the question of how well he rose to that challenge. As that evidence shows, Stalin's appetite for power had far outstripped his capacity to generate ideas and policies keyed to the demands of the revolutionary situation.

Stalin as a Member of the Editorial Board of *Pravda*

Between March 14, when Stalin's first signed article appeared in *Pravda*, and March 28, the date of his last contribution before Lenin's return, Stalin published six short articles and one editorial in *Pravda*, all but one of which he signed "K. [for Koba, his old revolutionary pseudonym] Stalin." Chronologically the articles fall into two distinct groups: four were published almost daily between the fourteenth and eighteenth, skipping only issue number nine on March 15 (the date of *Pravda's* announcement of the triple promotion affecting Stalin), then a week's hiatus, followed by a group of three on March 25, 26, and 28. (If Stalin took a day of rest on Sunday the twenty-sixth, that would account for his absence from the columns of the newspaper on the twenty-seventh.)

In terms of content, too, there is a distinct break between the two groups of articles. The first four deal with some of the basic issues confronting the party—the Soviets of Workers' Deputies, the war, the Provisional Government—while the second group is concerned primarily with the national question and its implications for the future state form of Russia, an important topic, to be sure, but one peripheral to the party's central concerns at the time.

In searching for an explanation of this pattern, one notes that the week-long silence on Stalin's part coincides with an event of cardinal importance for the party, for the editorial board of *Pravda*, and for Stalin personally. This was the receipt by the board of the first of a series of letters from Lenin in Zurich analyzing the progress and prospects of the revolution on the basis of the scanty reports available to him in the Western press. It was on March 19 that Aleksandra Kollontai brought the first two of these "Letters from Afar" into the *Pravda* editorial office where Kamenev and Stalin were ensconced. Two days later *Pravda* published Lenin's first letter, but not in full: nearly one-fifth of the text had been cut by the editors to bring it more nearly into line with the policies they considered it proper for *Pravda* to pursue and to obscure the fact that Lenin's position differed radically from their own. The remaining three "Letters from Afar" seem to have drifted into the *Pravda* office at irregular intervals. (Lenin wrote the first four in a burst of activity from March 7 to 12, then, preoccupied by the concerns attendant on his return to Russia, let two weeks elapse before starting the fifth, on March 26, just before the final arrangements for the sealed train were completed.) The editorial board of *Pravda* (read: Kamenev and Stalin) dealt even more cavalierly with Lenin's second letter than they had with the first: they simply consigned it to the archives, where it remained unpublished until after Lenin's death. It appears that the remaining three letters failed to reach Petrograd. By the time Lenin arrived in person, on April 3, they had been overtaken by events.

According to the Soviet historian I. I. Mints, the first two "Letters from Afar" were delivered to the *Pravda* office by A. M. Kollontai on March 19. At the time of the first publication of letters 2–5 in 1924, Kamenev asserted that letters 2–4 (and presumably the later, unfinished letter number 5) were not received at the *Pravda* office in 1917. According to Mints, it has been established that letters 3–5 were sent by Lenin to Ya. S. Ganetski (Hanecki) in Stockholm on March 12. Mints does not, however, assert that these letters reached the editors of *Pravda* at the time.[21]

The seven-day break in Stalin's writing for *Pravda*, taken in conjunction with his turn away from topics of major importance, provides ground for the surmise that it was his reading of Lenin's first "Letter from Afar" that drove him into temporary silence, and then into an avoidance of high-risk subjects. Thus for Stalin the encounter with Lenin's ideas and personality, which was to be decisive for his behavior in the revolution, began not on April 3, when Lenin made his physical entrance into Petrograd, but on March 19 when his uncompromising, insistent, and deeply disquieting (for Stalin) voice reached the *Pravda* office in the form of the first two "Letters from Afar." Still strongly under the influence of Kamenev and his friends in the Executive Committee of the Soviet, Stalin seems to have had difficulty at first in grasping the outlines of Lenin's radical vision of the future course of the revolution and Bolshevik prospects in it. For Stalin, the period of rethinking which began on March 19 eventually led him to accept Lenin's vision. It would take him almost exactly a month to complete the process of mental conversion, a month during which we can observe Stalin cautiously feeling his way, clinging to the familiar Kamenev-Menshevik policies, then gradually realizing the greater opportunities opened to him personally, as well as to the party, by Lenin's radical vision.

Stalin on the Soviets

Stalin's first contribution to *Pravda*, an article entitled "The Soviets of Workers' and Soldiers' Deputies," appeared in the March 14 issue and was therefore probably written on the thirteenth, the day after his return.[22] Considering the short time that this gave him to orient himself, the article can be judged a creditable effort, lacking neither in originality nor in a bold if confused vision of the future prospects of the revolution. In the article Stalin showed that he had already grasped the fact that Petrograd, where the revolution broke out, had forged far ahead of the rest of Russia:

> Now, as always, Petrograd is in the forefront. Behind it, stumbling at times, trail the immense provinces.

Stalin also recognized that the victory of the revolution had not yet been fully consolidated and that it faced the danger of counterrevolution:

> The forces of the old power are crumbling, but they are not yet destroyed. They are only lying low, waiting for a favorable moment to raise their head and fling themselves on free Russia.

Destruction of the old forces, an alliance between the revolutionary capital and the awakening provinces, and the "further advance" of the revolution were defined by Stalin as "the next immediate task of the proletariat in the capital." Using his favorite device of posing rhetorical questions, Stalin asked, "But how is this to be done? What is needed to achieve this?" His answer was to strengthen the temporary "alliance between the workers and the peasants clad in soldiers' uniform."

> For it is clear to all [another of Stalin's favorite rhetorical devices] that the guarantee of the final victory of the Russian revolution lies in consolidating the alliance between the revolutionary workers and the revolutionary soldiers.

Fortunately for the revolution, the "organs of this alliance," Stalin asserted, were already present in the form of the Soviets of Workers' and Soldiers' Deputies. Now it was necessary to "weld" the soviets more closely together and "organize" them. "Revolutionary Social-Democrats," Stalin urged,

> must work to consolidate these Soviets, form them everywhere, and link them together under a Central Soviet of Workers' and Soldiers' Deputies as the organ of revolutionary power of the people.

> Workers, close your ranks and rally around the Russian Social-Democratic Labor Party!
>
> Peasants, organize in peasant unions and rally around the revolutionary proletariat, the leader of the Russian revolution!
>
> Soldiers, organize in unions of your own and gather around the Russian people, the only true ally of the Russian revolutionary army!

To close his article on a ringing note, Stalin resorted to a stripped-down version of the minimum demands of the socialist parties, which he called "the fundamental demands of the Russian people":

> land for the peasants, protection of labor for the workers, and a democratic republic for all the citizens of Russia!

As a first effort, the article has some merits. It recognized that the revolution was not completed, that it faced the danger of counterrevolution, and that the soviets had already emerged as essential organs for its continuation and completion. One can also give Stalin a good mark for his adherence to the Bolshevik line in defining the proletariat as the leading force in the revolution. But the weaknesses and omissions of the article far outweigh its modest strengths; as Carr says, it "was less remarkable for what was said than for what was omitted."[23] Among its principal omissions Carr lists the Provisional Government and the war, but it can be urged in Stalin's defense that the article's subject was, after all, the soviets; that it was brief; and that Stalin would shortly turn his attention to exactly those subjects whose omission Carr criticizes.

Much more astonishing than the omissions to which Carr calls attention, however, are other omissions and blunders in the article. First and most surprisingly, Stalin seemed to have forgotten that a single Russian Social-Democratic party no longer existed; that the party had split as far back as 1903; and that he, Stalin, had committed himself to the Bolshevik fraction, since 1912 a self-proclaimed independent organization. The article repeatedly refers to a Social-Democratic party around which the workers are urged to rally. The author seems ignorant not only of the Bolshevik party's separate existence but of its claim to speak on behalf of the poor and landless peasants. The article calls on an undifferentiated peasantry to "rally around the revolutionary proletariat," just as though the Bolsheviks had made no effort to speak directly to and on behalf of the poor peasants. As to the soldiers, their rallying point, in the author's view, should be "the Russian people" (*narod*), an appeal not only strikingly un-Marxist in its failure to distinguish between various socioeconomic categories but also a grotesque distortion of the ethnic complexities of the Russian Empire, a blunder especially surprising in a writer whose chief claim to attention in the party's literary activities up to that point had been his essay on "Marxism and the National Question."

Given the fact that the subject of the article is the Soviet of Workers' and Soldiers' Deputies, it is astonishing that the author nowhere mentions the existing Petrograd Soviet nor makes any attempt to define the relationship he envisages between that already flourishing body and the hypothetical "Central Soviet of Workers' and Soldiers' Deputies," which he evokes as "the organ of revolutionary power of the people."

Finally, the article defines the goal of all this revolutionary activity in singularly mild and nonsocialist terms: "protection of labor" is all the workers can look forward to (protection against whom? The implication is that the capitalist system will still be flourishing when the "fundamental demands of the Russian people" have been met). The Constituent Assembly is another of the article's striking omissions; somehow, in a manner the author never explains, a "democratic republic" will be established "for all the citizens of Russia." Although the terms are vague, the implication is clear: as Deutscher points out, these words show that in Stalin's mind

> the revolution was still to be anti-feudal, but not anti-capitalist; it was to be "bourgeois democratic," not socialist.[24]

Along with its modest strengths and startling weaknesses, Stalin's first published article in 1917 is noteworthy for its brief but suggestive anticipation of a much later war, when Stalin would appear not as an inexperienced and confused journalist but as the mighty and unchallenged leader of a Russia fighting for its survival. In the appeal to the soldiers to "gather around the Russian people, the only true ally of the Russian revolutionary army," one catches an uncanny prefiguration of Stalin's victory toast "to the Russian people" in May 1945 as the basic source of support for the army and the true guarantor of Russia's survival in World War II.

Stalin was a slow learner, and this first article shows how much he still had to learn in mid-March 1917, but he had a tenacious memory, and the echoes of his 1917 experience can be detected in his writings and speeches of World War II.

Stalin Tackles the Question of the War

For his second signed contribution to *Pravda*, an article entitled "The War," Stalin turned to a subject that had already proved highly divisive within the socialist movement and that was to constitute one of the chief points of conflict between the Petrograd Soviet and the Provisional Government. The Soviet had just heard a report from General Lavr Kornilov, commander of troops of the Petrograd Military District, to the effect that the Germans were planning an offensive against Russia. In response, two prominent bourgeois political figures, Alexander Rodzyanko and Mikhail Guchkov, had appealed to the army and the people to fight the war to the end.

It was this appeal that formed the subject of Stalin's article.[25] His principal argument was that revolutionary Russia in 1917, unlike revolutionary France in 1792, was not endangered by a coalition of enemy powers. "The present war is an imperialist war," Stalin maintained, whose principal aim is "the seizure (annexation) of foreign, chiefly agrarian territories by capitalistically developed states." Given that definition of the character and war aims of the belligerent powers, Stalin argued,

> The present war is not, and cannot lead necessarily to interference in the internal affairs of the territories annexed, in the sense of restoring their old regimes.

Thus,

> the present situation of Russia provides no warrant for sounding the alarm and proclaiming: "Liberty is in danger! Long live the war!"

The real aims of the "Russian imperialists," Stalin asserted, are "the Straits and Persia." He cited with approval the "anti-war resolutions of the Zimmerwald and Kienthal Socialist Congresses of 1915–1916," neglecting, however, to mention that both these left-wing socialist gatherings had failed to endorse Lenin's uncompromising rejection of *any* justification for support of the war whatsoever, along with his demand for "turning the imperialist war into a civil war." Support of the Zimmerwald and Kienthal congresses' position was the furthest Stalin was prepared to go, a fact that conclusively demolishes any claim that he had supported Lenin's stand on the war while in Siberian exile.

In answer to his customary rhetorical questions, "What should be our attitude, as a party, to the present war? What are the practical ways and means capable of leading to the speediest termination of the war?" Stalin brusquely rejected Lenin's antiwar stand, as well as that of the Vyborg *Raion* Committee, and asserted that it is "unquestionable"

> that the stark slogan, "Down with the war!" is absolutely unsuitable as a practical means, because . . . it does not and cannot provide anything

capable of exerting practical influence on the belligerent forces to compel them to stop the war.

Faced with the challenge from Kornilov, the Petrograd Soviet at its March 14 session had adopted an appeal to all the peoples of the world urging them to force their governments to end the war. One "cannot but welcome this appeal," Stalin wrote, but he felt it alone would "not lead directly to the goal," especially since, in his view, it was far from certain that the German people could overthrow their "semi-absolutist regime."

Stalin's solution—identical to that of the Menshevik-SR leadership in the Soviet, as Trotsky later pointed out[26]—was

> to bring pressure on the Provisional Government to make it declare its consent to start peace negotiations immediately. The workers, soldiers and peasants must arrange meetings and demonstrations and demand that the Provisional Government shall *come out openly and publicly* in an effort to induce all the warring powers to start peace negotiations immediately, on the basis of the recognition of the right of nations to self-determination.

When this article was later reprinted, Stalin, faced with the embarrassing need to justify his divergence from Lenin on the question of the war, admitted that in "The War" he had adopted "a profoundly mistaken position,"

> since it sowed pacifist illusions, contributed to the position of defencism and impeded the revolutionary education of the masses.[27]

What he failed to mention, however, was that the 1917 article showed no awareness of the fact that Lenin had drawn a sharp line between his position and that of all other socialist parties and groups. Also unmentioned was the fact that the February 27 manifesto issued by the Russian Bureau had staked out a position much more sharply opposed to the war and much closer to that of Lenin. Again, as in his first article, one is struck by the extent to which Stalin, in "The War," showed himself ignorant of Bolshevik policy on a key issue, as defined by Lenin.

A short, unsigned article, "Bidding for Ministerial Portfolios," which Stalin contributed to *Pravda* on March 17, amounts to little more than an extended footnote to "The War."[28] It takes the form of a commentary on several resolutions passed a few days earlier by a group calling itself "Yedinstvo" (unity), organized and led by the veteran Russian Marxist G. V. Plekhanov. In its resolutions the Yedinstvo group called for "*participation* of the working class democracy in the Provisional Government" and continuation of the war by the proletariat, among other reasons, in order "to deliver Europe from the menace of Austro-German reaction."

Again Stalin identified his stand on the war as that of the Social Democratic party as defined by the Zimmerwald and Kienthal resolutions, against defensism and against participation in the Provisional Government. On that basis Stalin rejected the Yedinstvo group's appeal for unity among the different groups and parties of socialists. But he implicitly accepted the idea of an alliance or merger between the Bolsheviks and other socialists on the basis of the Zimmerwald-Kienthal position.

"The War" and "Bidding for Ministerial Portfolios" provide a valuable clue to Stalin's associations and the source of his ideas in the first week after his return to Petrograd. Both articles reflect the gossip and intellectual interchange characteristic of the Executive Committee of the Soviet, to which Stalin had been appointed on the fourteenth. The articles give no indication, on the other hand, that Stalin had been absorbing or sharing a Bolshevik outlook. The whole thrust of the Muranov-Kamenev-Stalin party coup had been to elbow aside the previously dominant Bolshevik leadership and discredit its line on the problems facing the party. Caught up in the bureaucratic talk-shop that the Executive Committee was rapidly becoming, Stalin unconsciously parroted the ideas characteristic of that milieu. It would be pointless to search for the source of Stalin's ideas as of mid-March 1917 in his earlier writings; the bitter years of exile in Siberia had in effect wiped his mind clean of the accumulated intellectual baggage of the preceding decade and a half of revolutionary activity and had made him susceptible to the nearest intellectual guidepost, provided it seemed to point in the direction of power. And to Stalin in March 1917 the Executive Committee of the Soviet appeared to offer a much more direct path to power than the small, faction-ridden, and contentious Russian Bureau of the Bolshevik party. With his position on the editorial board of *Pravda* secure and his foot in the door of the Executive Committee, Stalin obviously felt this was not the moment to stress the irreconcilability of the Bolshevik position.

Member of the Executive Committee

Stalin's reception by his fellow Bolsheviks in the Russian Bureau had been cool in the extreme, and the brusque manner in which, with Muranov's and Kamenev's help, he had overcome that setback caused a feeling of bitterness among those he had pushed aside which still rankled years later. In the Executive Committee of the Soviet, in contrast, Stalin encountered a warm welcome from his fellow Georgians, including the Mensheviks Nikolai Chkheidze, president of the Soviet, and Iraklii Tseretelli, its leading theorist.[29]

It might be supposed that Stalin would have used the opportunity of his appointment to the Executive Committee of the Soviet to raise a staunchly Bolshevik voice in that forum dominated by the Mensheviks and the SR's. The reality, however, was quite different. For Stalin the Executive Committee proved a welcome haven where he could rub elbows with the rising politicians of the new phase of the revolution and absorb their point of view. Trotsky gives a hostile but essentially accurate characterization of Stalin's role in the Executive Committee:

> There has not remained in the minutes or in the press a single proposal, declaration or protest in which Stalin in any distinguishable manner counterposed the Bolshevik point of view to the flunkeyism of the "revolutionary democracy" toward the bourgeoisie.[30]

Trotsky then quotes what is arguably the single most famous image of Stalin in the revolution:

> Among the Bolsheviks, besides Kamenev, there appeared in the Executive Committee of the Soviet in these days Stalin. During his modest activity in the Executive Committee [he] gave us the impression—and not only us—of a grey blur which would sometimes emit a dim and inconsequential light. There is really nothing more to be said about him.[31]

The "grey blur" passage has been widely quoted, sometimes as a kind of blanket characterization of Stalin's participation not merely in the Executive Committee but in the revolution in general. Of course, it was not meant to be read in this sweeping way and should not be used for this purpose.[32]

Stalin on the Prospects of the Revolution

By the time Stalin's fourth article, "Conditions for the Victory of the Russian Revolution," appeared in *Pravda*, he had had time to form a coherent general picture of the future prospects of the revolution, the dangers it faced, and the steps that, in his opinion, it must take to head off those dangers.[33] It was a picture identical in all important aspects to that of the "revolutionary democracy" as represented in the Executive Committee of the Soviet. There was nothing specifically Bolshevik about it, and much in it with which Lenin was bound to disagree violently.

Again, as in "The War," Stalin asserted the existence of a split between revolutionary Petrograd and the "inertia" of the provinces, a split that he believed found its expression in the "dual power,"

> that actual division of power between the Provisional Government and the Petrograd Soviet of Workers' and Soldiers' Deputies.

The former he called "an organ of the moderate bourgeoisie," the latter "an organ of revolutionary struggle of the workers and soldiers." Ignoring the fact that Moscow had already gone over to the side of the revolution, Stalin asserted that the split he saw between Petrograd and the rest of Russia ("the provinces") represented both a danger to the revolution, insofar as it was a source of weakness, and an opportunity, since the provinces, following Petrograd's lead, were shaking off their inertia and "are being revolutionized." What was needed, Stalin declared, was

> an all-Russian organ of revolutionary struggle of the democracy of all Russia, one authoritative enough to weld together the democracy of the capital and the provinces and to transform itself at the required moment from an organ of revolutionary *struggle* of the people into an organ of revolutionary *power*, which will mobilize all the vital forces of the people against counter-revolution. Only an all-Russian Soviet of Workers', Soldiers' and Peasants' Deputies can be such an organ.

Here, as in his first article, Stalin advocated an idea that had no visible support in the population and formed part of no party's platform. Like the alleged problem it was designed to solve, the "all-Russian Soviet" was a figment of Stalin's imagination and simply showed the enormous distance that still separated him from both political realism and Bolshevik orthodoxy. Yet one must not be too harsh in judging this work. Stalin's all-Russian soviet never got off the ground, but it bears a recognizable kinship to the All-Russian Congress of Soviets in whose name the Bolsheviks did in fact take power eight months later. Stalin rightly saw that soviets of workers' deputies were being formed in what he called the provinces, together with peasants' and soldiers' "unions," but he had not yet grasped the possibility of a nationwide network of soviets drawn together and crowned by an all-Russian congress. The idea of a network of soviets had been formulated in the late months of 1905 during the revolution of that year, but in the swift pace of events, which saw the revolution crushed along with the December Armed Uprising in Moscow, the idea failed to reach the stage of embodiment. Even had someone recalled the 1905 experience, no one in March 1917 could have foreseen the way in which the establishment of an all-Russian congress of soviets would be dovetailed with the uprising that carried the Bolsheviks to power in October.

Stalin's second condition for the victory of the revolution was the establishment of a workers' guard, "the immediate arming of the workers." His reasoning here was that the regular army had already acquired "the character of a people's army," a fact that explained "the comparative ease with which the revolution broke out and triumphed in our country." Stalin was greatly exaggerating the degree to which the army had been radicalized, just as he appeared ignorant of the difference between the troops of the Petrograd garrison, whose support for the insurgent workers had made possible the victory of the February Revolution, and the soldiers in the field army, the great majority of whom still respected military discipline and were prepared to honor their commitment to the legally established government, tsarist or provisional. As an essay in the weighing of military capabilities, "Conditions for the Victory of the Russian Revolution" reflects scant credit on its author, the future generalissimo.

Equally weak was the logic behind Stalin's third condition, the early convocation of a constituent assembly. Here Stalin simply adopted one of the stock proposals in the arsenal of "revolutionary democracy," one to which even the Bolsheviks still paid lip service. Generations of Russian revolutionaries had regarded the convocation of a constituent assembly as the crowning achievement that would ultimately reward their efforts, giving the Russian people the opportunity to define the future form of their state and society once and for all. But Stalin apparently forgot that he had just called for the establishment of an all-Russian soviet of workers', soldiers', and peasants' deputies and its transformation into an organ of revolutionary power as the first condition for the victory of the revolution. What was to be the relationship between this super-soviet and the Constituent Assembly, described by Stalin as "the only institution which will enjoy authority in the eyes of all sections of society"? He offered no explanation, nor could he have, for there was an unbridgeable gulf between his first and third conditions.

Almost as an afterthought Stalin added a "general condition for all these necessary measures":

> the opening of peace negotiations as soon as possible and the termination of this inhuman war.

Again betraying complete disregard for Lenin's writings on the war, Stalin called continuation of the war "that submerged reef on which the ship of revolution may be wrecked." In actual fact, however, it was the Provisional Government, not the revolution, that was to be wrecked on the continuation of the war: for the Bolsheviks, as Lenin was quick to perceive, continuation of the war provided the party with its best opportunity for a bid for power, by exhausting its opponents and discrediting its rivals.

Pravda Edits Lenin

Between the first group of Stalin's contributions to *Pravda* and the second, as we have seen, there was a week's silence, during which we are deprived of the opportunity to observe at first hand the evolution of his thinking. It was in that week, however, that the editors of *Pravda*, particularly Kamenev and Stalin, were confronted with a formidable challenge in the form of at least one, possibly two letters from Lenin, written on March 7 and 9, which Kollontai brought to the *Pravda* office on March 19.

Reading the first "Letter from Afar" in the context of Stalin's contributions to the March 1917 *Pravda*, one cannot fail to be impressed with the broad sweep of Lenin's ideas, the vigor of their expression, and the boldness of his perspective.[34] At a time when Stalin, already on the scene in Petrograd, was feeling his way cautiously and awkwardly, Lenin, still far from Russia, showed the ability to grasp the essential elements of the situation; to locate the February Revolution in a coherent framework of time, dating back to the Revolution of 1905–7, and of place, ranging over the entire array of belligerent and war-weary powers; and to lay down the main points of the strategy the Bolshevik party would follow to victory eight months later. With slashing strokes Lenin drew a devastating picture of the Provisional Government, at a time when Kamenev and Stalin were urging its conditional support. The Provisional Government, Lenin wrote,

> cannot give peace because it is a government for war, a government for the continuation of the imperialist slaughter, a government of conquest. . . . It cannot give bread because it is a bourgeois government. . . . It cannot give freedom, since it is a government of landowners and capitalists, who are afraid of the people.

Lenin defined the current situation as "a period of transition from the first stage of the revolution to the second" and identified the allies of the revolution as, first, "the broad masses of the semi-proletarian and, partly, the petty peasant population of Russia," and second, "the proletariat of the warring countries and of all countries in general." With the aid of these allies, he confidently predicted, the proletariat of Russia can and will proceed on to win, first, a democratic republic and the victory of the peasantry over the landlords, then Socialism, which alone can give peace, bread, and freedom to the peoples exhausted by the war.

Faced with this blast of molten intellectual power, Kamenev and Stalin temporized. To shut out the letter altogether would be too direct a repudiation of Lenin's leadership, yet to print it in full would jeopardize the comfortable working relationship they had established with other members of the "revolutionary democracy" by their redirection of Bolshevik policy since March 12. The solution they found was a makeshift one: they printed roughly four-fifths of Lenin's text, but cut out his more scathing references to the Provisional Government and the Menshevik leaders in the Soviet, leaders whose good opinion they valued and with whom they had reached a general understanding of the needs of the moment.

With regard to Lenin's second "Letter"—assuming that it actually was delivered by Kollontai on March 19 and that Kamenev's 1924 denial of that event was the result either of a lapse of memory or, more probably, of embarrassment—the editors took the more drastic step of suppressing it entirely, consigning it to the files from which it emerged only after Lenin's death some seven years later.

As for Stalin, he showed his awareness of the arrival of Lenin's "Letters" by his characteristic response of silent withdrawal in the face of a new challenge: for a week he wrote nothing for *Pravda*, and when his contributions were resumed, on March 25, his subject was the comparatively safe one of the national problem and the future state form of Russia. The outcome of this first encounter between Lenin and Stalin in 1917 was thus one that provides little useful copy to the future manufacturers of the legend of Stalin as Lenin's closest collaborator and most faithful supporter in 1917. Always uneasy in the presence of intellectual power, and none too sure of his own position, Stalin preferred to give his cautious support to the nearby and reasonable Kamenev rather than to the still distant and incalculable Lenin.

Stalin on the National Problem

While he was in Siberian exile—or so he later claimed—Stalin wrote an article on the question of national minorities in a multinational state such as Russia. The article, entitled "Cultural-National Autonomy," was allegedly completed by February 1916. In the chronology of Stalin's life included in volume 2 of his *Works* it is stated that on February 5, 1916, he wrote a letter to "the Party centre abroad" concerning the article, and on February 25 he sent a second letter to the same address, to be transmitted by Inessa Armand, in which he inquired about the article "which he has sent abroad."[35]

In her memoirs published in 1946 Anna Allilueva stated that her father, Sergei Alliluev, forwarded the manuscript at Stalin's request to Lenin, but there is no evidence that it reached him, nor has it been published. A Soviet scholar, M. A. Moskalev, writing in 1947, claimed that the manuscript was intercepted by the tsarist censor and confiscated and that it was still preserved in the Okhrana file in the Krasnoyarsk district.[36] That would explain why it never reached Lenin, but raises the more serious question why it was not included in Stalin's *Works*, the second volume of which ends with an article written in early 1913 and the third volume of which opens with Stalin's *Pravda* article on the soviets written shortly after his return to Petrograd in March 1917. There is thus an awkward four-year gap in the official record of Stalin's writings, which a carefully thought out and well-prepared essay on the national question would do a great deal to fill.

The conflicting evidence provides a basis for various hypotheses. First, the article may simply never have been written. In that case, the entries referring to it in the chronology of volume 2 of Stalin's *Works* must have been falsified, along with the memoir of Anna Allilueva and the book by Moskalev. Even though such a broad-scale effort at falsification is by no means inconceivable, it seems unlikely, since the witnesses agree that there was in fact an article while disagreeing on the details of its transmission. This lack of coordination sounds more like the normal discrepancies among sources than a well-orchestrated exercise in falsification. It is noteworthy that the evidence tends to cluster around the years 1946–47, when the editing of Stalin's *Works* was in progress and the question of his activity in exile from 1913 to 1916 urgently demanded an answer. It seems inherently probable that Stalin, during the long and tedious years of exile, would have made an effort to continue his work on the national question, both because the subject was of genuine concern to him and because his first essay in that field had been favorably received by Lenin. On balance, therefore, it seems unlikely that the reports of the manuscript's existence were falsified. Stalin did write something on the national question. What did it say, and what happened to it?

Some writers think it possible that the article did reach Lenin, and explain its nonpublication by its poor quality. Deutscher, for example, writes:

It [the article] was never published; either it was lost on the way or it was not up to the standards of his [Stalin's] previous work and did not please Lenin.[37]

It would have been most uncharacteristic of Lenin, however, to destroy even an unsatisfactory article from a party member without recording its arrival or making some effort to get in touch with the author to elicit from him a better piece of work. Reasoning along these lines, Tucker has suggested a link between the missing article and two inquiries that Lenin made in 1915 in an effort to learn Stalin's last name (Dzhugashvili), which he had forgotten.[38] The first letter, written to Zinoviev, is undated but was written not later than July 23, 1915, according to the editors of the fifth edition of Lenin's *Works*.[39] In it Lenin inquires, "Do you remember the last name of Koba?"— Koba being the pseudonym by which Stalin was best known in the party before 1917.

In Lenin's second request, in a letter to V. A. Karpinsky which the editors date "earlier than November 8 [1915]," the tone is more urgent:

A big request: find out (from Stepko or Mikha et al.) the last name of "Koba" (Iosif Dzh. . . . ?) We have forgotten. Very important.[40]

(The two names Lenin gives as possible informants are party pseudonyms of Georgians living in emigration, N. D. Kinkadze and M. G. Tskhakaia, who could be expected to know the real name of their fellow Georgian.)

Tucker's suggested link between these letters and the missing manuscript appears unlikely, however, since on the evidence of the chronology in volume 2 of Stalin's *Works*, he did not send off the manuscript until February 1916, three months after Lenin's second inquiry.

During the period when Lenin was trying to learn Stalin's real name, he was engaged in an attempt to reestablish the Russian Bureau of the Central Committee, of which Stalin had been named a member in 1912. The last reference to a message from Stalin which occurs in Lenin's pre-1917 correspondence is in a letter to Karpinsky dated August 1915, in which Lenin writes, "Koba sent greetings and the news that he is well."[41] Two days later Lenin wrote to Shlyapnikov that he considered it "extremely important" that the Russian Bureau should be reestablished.[42] It was toward the middle of September (the editors date the letter "earlier than September 13") that Lenin wrote to Shlyapnikov informing him that he had been co-opted to the Central Committee,[43] the same action that had been taken in regard to Stalin in 1912, and for almost exactly the same reason—to organize (as of 1912) or reorganize (as of 1916) the Russian Bureau of the CC.

Shlyapnikov was unable to carry out this mission until his return to Russia in November 1915.[44] It was apparently at just about this time that Lenin wrote the letter to Karpinsky in which he made his urgent request for Stalin's last name.

This evidence suggests that it was some problem in connection with the reestablishment of the Russian Bureau, not Stalin's manuscript on the national question, that prompted Lenin's attempt to learn Stalin's name. If his inquiries on that subject in summer and autumn 1915 cannot be linked with the missing article, it appears that there is no record in Lenin's correspondence of any trace of the manuscript or the correspondence concerning it.

There is an unbridgeable gap between Moskalev's testimony as to the manuscript's continuing existence in Krasnoyarsk as of 1947 and Anna Allilueva's assertion, in 1946, that her father sent it to Lenin. The negative evidence from Lenin's secretariat (maintained by the faithful Krupskaya) casts a strong shadow on Anna Allilueva's account. We are left with Moskalev, who believed that the manuscript was still extant. Why, then, did the editors of Stalin's *Works* pass up this golden opportunity to include an article by Stalin which would support his claim to having continued his party researches in exile? Possibly, one suspects, because its publication in 1946 would have done nothing to strengthen Stalin's claim as a theorist on the national question. That this may be the correct explanation is strongly suggested by two articles on the national question which Stalin contributed to *Pravda* in March 1917 and which presumably represent his mature thinking on the subject. The first article, "Abolition of National Disabilities," appeared on March 25; the second, "Against Federalism," followed three days later.[45]

"Abolition of National Disabilities" opens with the confident assertion that the source of the oppression of national minorities is "the obsolescent landed aristocracy." In a rapid survey of world conditions, Stalin reveals his ignorance of social arrangements in a number of countries, beginning with "old Russia." There, says Stalin, at a time "when the old feudal landed aristocracy was in power" (when would that be? one wonders), "national oppression operated to the limit, not infrequently taking the form of pogroms (of Jews) and massacres (Armenian-Tatar)." Passing rapidly over England, where he sees a rule shared between the landed aristocracy and the bourgeoisie with a correspondingly mild form of national oppression, Stalin moves on to Switzerland and what he calls "North America" (evidently meaning the United States), where idyllic conditions prevail: since "landlordism has never existed" in those countries and "the bourgeoisie enjoys undivided power," the nationalities develop more or less freely, and, generally speaking, there is practically no ground for national oppression.

For Stalin, evidently, the Negroes and Indians of "North America" simply do not exist.

On this naive and ill-informed basis Stalin proceeds to erect an equally unsound general principle:

Thus the way to put an end to national oppression and to create the *actual* conditions necessary for political liberty is to drive the feudal aristocracy from the political stage, to wrest the power from its hands.

Returning to Russia, Stalin takes as his premise the full victory of the revolution:

Inasmuch as the Russian revolution has triumphed [!], it has already created these actual conditions, having overthrown the power of the feudal serfowners [NB: serfdom was in fact abolished in 1861] and established liberty.

All that remains, in Stalin's view, is to safeguard these newly won rights by "(1) defin[ing] the rights of the nationalities emancipated from oppression," and "(2) confirm[ing] them by legislation." This brings him to the Provisional Government's decree, just enacted, abolishing legal and social inequalities on the basis of nationality, the terms of which he summarizes and to which he extends a guarded approval: "This is all very good."

But there are several steps that must still be taken, Stalin warns, "to guarantee national liberty." First, the government's decree fails to specify that national minorities may use their own language rather than Russian in schools and public institutions such as parliaments; second—and here at last, one feels, Stalin shows some awareness of the real issues underlying the national problem—it is necessary to adopt "a positive program which will guarantee the elimination of national oppression." Two principles must be proclaimed: (1) political autonomy (Stalin stresses that he does *not* mean federation)

for regions representing integral economic territories, possessing a specific way of life and populations of a specific national composition . . .

and

. . . (2) the right of self-determination for such nations as cannot, for one reason or another, remain within the framework of the integral state.

Only in the final sentence does Stalin remember something of his training as a Marxist:

This is the way towards the real abolition of national oppression and towards guaranteeing the nationalities the maximum liberty possible under capitalism.

One is reminded of Trotsky's caustic characterization of the article—"this hopelessly provincial analysis"—and his fully justified condemnation of Stalin as a theorist:

In theory he [Stalin] had not moved forward since the beginning of the century; more than that, he seemed to have entirely forgotten his own work on the national question, written early in 1913 under Lenin's fescue.[46]

When Stalin returned to the national question a few days later, he took as his point of departure an article by one Jos. Okulich in the SR newspaper, *Delo naroda*, entitled "Russia—a Union of Regions." In line with SR thinking on the problem, Okulich proposed the conversion of Russia into a federal state in which the Ukraine, Georgia, Turkestan, and so forth would each enjoy "internal sovereignty" in a federal union analogous to what the author believed the American colonies had created in 1776. The central government in this proposal would retain control of the army, the currency, foreign policy, and the supreme court, but otherwise

the various regions of the single state [would] be free to build their new life independently.[47]

Granting that the article was "interesting, . . . original [and] intriguing," Stalin dismissed it as "a peculiar piece of muddleheadedness," due to "its more than frivolous history of the United States of America (as well as of Switzerland and Canada)." Stalin then proceeded to set Okulich straight on his U.S. history, which he depicted as a transition from the "confederation of what until then were independent colonies, or states," in 1776, to the "federation" that was established as the result of the victory of the northern states in the Civil War. This governmental structure, Stalin asserted, proved "intolerable," and

in the course of its further evolution the United States was transformed from a federation into a *unitary* (integral) state, with uniform constitutional provisions and the limited autonomy (not governmental, but political-administrative) permitted to the states by these provisions.

Only in name could the present-day United States be described as a federal union of states, in Stalin's view:

The name "federation" as applied to the United States became an empty word, a relic of the past which had long since ceased to correspond to the actual state of affairs.

The evolution of state form took a similar course in Canada and Switzerland, according to Stalin:

> The development was *from* independent regions, *through* their federation, to a unitary state.

It followed that

> the trend of development is not in favor of federation, but *against* it. Federation is a transitional form, [the reason being that] . . . the development of capitalism in its higher forms, with the concomitant expansion of the economic territory, and its trend towards centralization, demands not a federal but a unitary form of state.

Since this was the clear trend of history, Stalin argued,

> it follows from this that in Russia it would be unwise to work for a federation, which is doomed by the very realities of life to disappear.

Following a recapitulation of his reasons for rejecting Okulich's analogy between Russia in 1917 and the United States in 1776, Stalin offered his own "solution to the national problem," which he called "as practicable as it is radical and final." It combined two principles (and here Stalin did, *pace* Trotsky, show that he had not entirely forgotten his 1913 essay):

> (1) The right of secession for the nations inhabiting certain regions of Russia who cannot remain, or who do not desire to remain, within the integral framework; (2) Political autonomy within the framework of the single (integral) state, with uniform constitutional provisions, for regions which have a specific national composition and which remain within the national framework.

In December 1924, less than a year after Lenin's death, when plans were launched for reprinting this essay in a collection of documents on the 1917 revolution, Stalin felt it advisable to add an explanatory note.[48] In general the reason for Stalin's later embarrassment in regard to his 1917 writings was that he had failed to align himself with Lenin's position on various issues. Here, on the contrary, Stalin for once could show that in early 1917 his rejection of a federal solution for Russia's future state form was good Leninism *at that time*. He was able to cite a letter from Lenin to Shaumian in November 1913 in which Lenin categorically asserted,

> We stand for democratic centralism unreservedly. . . . We are opposed to

federation in principle—it weakens economic ties, and is unsuitable for what is one state.[49]

Only with Lenin's August 1917 work, "State and Revolution," said Stalin, did

> the Party, in the person of Lenin, [make] the first serious step towards recognition of the permissibility of federation, as a transitional form "to a centralized republic."[50]

Thus, for once Stalin was in the happy position of being able to explain away his "mistakes" of March 1917 on the ground that he had simply been following Lenin's position as then defined. (Wisely, Stalin made no attempt to foist onto Lenin the faulty historical data on the basis of which he, Stalin, had tried to justify his opposition to federalism.)

More was involved, however, than a mere matter of correcting a position taken at the outset of the revolution and long since modified. Underlying Stalin's discomfort in 1924 may well have been his still fresh memories of the bruising and bitter struggle he had waged against Lenin over exactly this question, and the sharp reprimand he had received from Lenin for his harsh centralizing policies, as commissar of nationalities, in curbing the autonomy of national minority regions, including Georgia. If the March 1917 article had been reprinted without explanation in 1924, it would have reminded knowledgeable party members all too forcibly that the centralizing tendencies expressed in "Against Federalism" had reflected Stalin's real convictions, which motivated his later policies, policies that had earned Lenin's condemnation. Thus the author's note of December 1924 is really an act of self-justification, not of self-criticism, as it would appear to be on the surface; in it Stalin is really saying, "The position I took in March 1917 may have been mistaken, but if so the mistake was Lenin's, not mine."

Stalin Calls for Milyukov's Resignation

Perhaps the most effective article contributed by Stalin to *Pravda* in March 1917 was a brief commentary, "Either—Or," published on March 23, which dealt with an interview given by Paul Milyukov, foreign minister in the Provisional Government and leader of the Constitutional Democrat (KD, Cadet) party.[51] Although it was unsigned, the article is included in Stalin's *Works* and has apparently not aroused any suspicion among scholars as to its authenticity. If the attribution to Stalin is valid, the article helps strengthen his reputation as a perceptive and alert political observer.

In the interview Milyukov had defined Russia's war aims as embracing a number of traditional tsarist territorial goals: Constantinople and Turkish Armenia from Turkey, Galicia from Austria-Hungary, and northern Persia. In view of the flagrant discrepancy between these imperialist aims and the Petrograd Soviet's manifesto calling for an immediate end to the war "without annexations or indemnities," Alexander Kerensky, minister of justice in the Provisional Government, thought it wise to issue an announcement to the effect that Milyukov's statement represented his personal opinion, not that of the Provisional Government.

Shrewdly, the author of "Either—Or" impaled Milyukov on the horns of an awkward constitutional dilemma. As a liberal political figure in the State Duma, Milyukov had repeatedly demanded that ministers in the tsar's government must be held accountable to the Duma. (Under the Fundamental Laws of 1906, the tsar alone had the power to appoint or dismiss ministers, and while the Duma might discuss their conduct and criticize their policies, it could not demand their resignation.) Now, as the writer pointed out, Milyukov, having himself become a minister in the Provisional Government, had been disavowed by a spokesman for that government. Either Milyukov must resign in accordance with his own principles, or Kerensky's statement of disavowal was untrue,

> in which case the revolutionary people must call the Provisional Government to order and compel it to recognize its will.

Milyukov's rash interview had thus caused a flareup that cast a revealing light on the real power relationships of Russian politics: in the Provisional Government Kerensky, though only one of several ministers, was already assuming responsibility for defining the policy of the entire government. Meanwhile, the Provisional Government itself enjoyed power only "insofar as" it continued to earn the grudging approval of the Petrograd Soviet, a fact of which Kerensky, as his announcement showed, was well aware.

To have perceived all this promptly and to have formulated it concisely reflects credit on Stalin, assuming he was the author of the unsigned article. If he was in fact the author, one wonders why he did not sign the article, or at least append his initials. *Either* (as Stalin would have said) the other members of *Pravda's* editorial board (Kamenev especially) disliked the sharp tone of the article and its shrewd thrusts at Kerensky and the Provisional Government, and insisted that the article must appear anonymously, *or* (and this appears less probable) the position taken in the article represented the consensus of the editorial board, including Kamenev, and its appearance without identification was thus meant to signify that it spoke for the editorial board as a whole. *Either* Stalin was by now developing his own independent and penetrating political insights, *or* he had integrated himself so well with his colleagues that he could speak on their behalf.

One other possibility merits consideration: that the article was based on a general view prevailing in the Executive Committee of the Soviet, where the original interview, Kerensky's disavowal, and the Soviet's recently passed manifesto on the war were all bound to arouse the most intense interest. If that was the case, the author's anonymity might be a prudent calculation that would conform to some known attributes of Stalin's personality: the bolder the stroke, the more desirable to avoid personal identification, in case the sally proved too risky.

Whatever the correct explanation may be, and whoever the author was (let us assume it was Stalin), the article correctly identified a source of conflict which would shortly cause the first major crisis in the Provisional Government.

The author of "Either—Or" shared with other Bolsheviks the belief that the question of war aims was of fundamental importance, but his position was much more moderate than that of the Russian Bureau of the CC (of which Stalin was a member), as set forth in a resolution adopted by the bureau on March 22 and published in the same issue of *Pravda* which included "Either—Or." The resolution took a position closely resembling that of Lenin and may, in fact, have been influenced by the first two "Letters from Afar," which were received in Petrograd on March 19. The resolution, as David Longley has pointed out, states

> (1) that the Provisional Government cannot solve the tasks of the revolution; (2) that the soviets are the embryo of the new power which at a given moment in the development of revolution will implement the demand of the people in revolt; (3) in the meantime the Petrograd Soviet should keep a careful check on the government's action and (4) consolidate the soviets and deepen the revolution by arming the whole people and creating a Red Guard.[52]

As Deutscher notes there is historical irony in the fact that Stalin in March 1917 sharply criticized Milyukov for expansionist war aims when "nearly thirty years later he himself would rehash some of Milyukov's war aims."[53] Here, as in other instances, the biographer of Stalin receives the impression that for Stalin the two world wars formed parts of a single continuous experience, so that he often acted, during his years as Soviet war leader in 1941–45, along lines foreshadowed in 1917–18. Similarly, a connection could be drawn between the rather oversimplified views on the nature of the war set forth by Stalin in his article "The War," where he rules out the possibility of a war of national defense à la revolutionary France in 1792 on the ground that the war is, by definition, imperialist, and thus does not endanger the political gains of the revolution (since Germany and her allies were supposedly interested only in acquiring territory), and Stalin's comment to Milovan Djilas in 1945, "This war is not like others."[54]

Stalin at the All-Russian Bolshevik Conference

The Russian Bureau's resolutions of March 22 were drawn up in preparation for the first big Bolshevik gathering of the revolutionary era, an all-Russian conference held in Petrograd from March 27 to April 4. The conference, which opened at party headquarters in the Kshesinskaya mansion and then shifted to the Tauride Palace, former meeting place of the State Duma, overlapped with an all-Russian conference of soviets called on the initiative of the Petrograd Soviet, which opened on March 29 and closed on April 3.

Stalin's growing stature as one of the top-ranking Bolsheviks in Petrograd was attested to by his assignment to deliver one of the principal reports, "On the Provisional Government," at the March 29 session of the conference.[55] The report showed the influences of Lenin's first "Letter from Afar" in its analysis of the complex class-economic factors that had produced the February Revolution, with its characteristic creation of "two governments, two forces"—the Provisional Government and the Petrograd Soviet. But Stalin was unwilling to endorse Lenin's unequivocal demand for rejection of the Provisional Government; for Stalin, the Provisional Government had its positive sides, at least for the present:

> The Provisional Government has in fact taken the role of fortifying the conquests of the revolutionary people.

But this situation was only temporary:

> The bourgeois layers will in the future inevitably withdraw from us.

Meanwhile, it was to the party's advantage to stall for time:

> It is necessary for us to gain time by putting a brake on the splitting away of the middle bourgeois layers so that we may prepare ourselves for the struggle against the Provisional Government.

Eventually, political questions would give place to social questions, and "the middle bourgeois layers [will] split away"; at that time the Provisional Government will become transformed from an organ for fortifying the conquests of the revolution into an organ for organizing the counter-revolution.

Stalin claimed to see the beginnings of this process already, in the form of agitation in the army against the Petrograd Soviet, coupled with support for the slogan "War to a victorious conclusion!" Thus for Stalin the question of whether or not to support the Provisional Government was not, as it was for Lenin, a simple one to be answered solely on the basis of the government's class composition but a tactical one in which the question of timing was of paramount importance:

> Insofar as the Provisional Government fortifies the steps of the revolution, to that extent we must support it; but insofar as it is counterrevolutionary, support to the Provisional Government is not permissible.

Stalin cautioned against too rash a test of strength:

> Many comrades who have arrived from the provinces ask whether we shouldn't immediately pose the question of the seizure of power. But it is untimely to pose the question now. The Provisional Government is not so weak. The strength of the Provisional Government lies in the support of Anglo-French capitalism, in the inertia of the provinces, and in the sympathy for it. . . . We must bide our time until the Provisional Government exhausts itself, until the time when in the process of fulfilling the revolutionary program it discredits itself.

When that time comes, Stalin argued,

> The only organ capable of taking power is the Soviet of Workers' and Soldiers' Deputies on an all-Russian scale.

Here Stalin reverted to the idea advanced in his *Pravda* article of March 14; the possibility of an all-Russian congress of soviets had not yet occurred to him, even though the first steps toward the organization of such a congress were actively going ahead at the very moment he was speaking.

Stalin's final recommendation was for cautious preparation for an eventual test of strength:

> We . . . must bide our time until the moment when the events will reveal the hollowness of the Provisional Government; we must be prepared, when the time comes, when the events have matured, and until then we must organize the center, the Soviet of Workers' and Soldiers' Deputies, and strengthen it. Therein lies the task of the moment.

Stalin then read the resolution on the Provisional Government adopted by the Russian Bureau on March 22, rejecting that body as "incapable of solving the tasks posed by the revolution" and calling for

the consolidation of all forces around the Soviet of Worker's and Soldiers' Deputies as the embryo of revolutionary power.

Stalin made it clear, however, that he favored the more moderate position adopted by the Krasnoyarsk Soviet, which employed the "insofar as" formula:

To support the Provisional Government in its activities only insofar as it follows a course of satisfying the demands of the working class and the revolutionary peasantry in the revolution that is taking place.

In his summing up, however, Stalin swung over to a more critical attitude:

Up to now the revolutionary initiative has come from the Soviet. The Soviet of Workers' Deputies has issued declarations, broached issues and made threats, while the Provisional Government has balked, struggled, only finally to agree. In such a situation can one speak of supporting such a Government? One can rather speak of the Government supporting us. It is not logical to speak of the support of the Provisional Government, on the contrary, it is more proper to speak of the Government not hindering us from putting our program into effect.

Stalin then proposed that a resolution that did not support the Provisional Government be accepted as a basis. In the end, however, the conference voted unanimously in favor of a resolution presented by the Executive Committee which explicitly supported the Provisional Government.[56]

For the session of March 29 the protocols record a motion introduced by Yakov M. Sverdlov, who had just completed his arduous journey from exile back to civilization. Characteristically, Sverdlov's motion concerned procedure rather than substance and was designed to move forward the business of the conference. His motion, "to close the discussion, elect a committee, and give the floor to the reporters for summary," was carried.

It must have been shortly after this brief appearance that Sverdlov was sent off on his travels again, this time to Yekaterinburg in the Urals, to organize the local party body there. Soviet biographers of Sverdlov state that the assignment was made by the party Central Committee, and given the structure of Bolshevik politics in late March 1917, Ulam is probably correct in saying that this meant Stalin and Kamenev.[57] Stalin's part in the order, assuming that its aim was to remove Sverdlov from the scene of action, would be compatible with other evidence pointing to an antipathy between him and Sverdlov.

If that was the underlying purpose behind Sverdlov's new assignment, he neatly circumvented it and, within less than a month, was back in Petrograd, this time as a duly accredited delegate to the party's Seventh Conference. From that point on, Sverdlov never looked back. Until his untimely death in March 1919, he remained at the nerve center of the party machine, designing and carrying out policies that helped shape the destiny of the party, the revolution, and Stalin.

During the next two days, March 30 and 31, Stalin took little recorded part in the conference's proceedings, but he made a noteworthy appearance at the April 1 session, where the principal topic was the question of unification between the Bolsheviks and left-wing Mensheviks, following a proposal by Iraklii Tseretelli, one of the Menshevik leaders in the Executive Committee of the Soviet.

> Stalin expressed enthusiasm for holding exploratory talks: We ought to go [to a proposed meeting with the Mensheviks]. Unification is possible along the lines of Zimmerwald-Kienthal.[58]

Molotov differed sharply:

> Tseretelli wants to unite heterogeneous elements. Tseretelli calls himself a Zimmerwaldist and a Kienthalist, and for this reason unification along these lines is incorrect, both politically and organizationally.

Also at odds with Stalin was Pyotr Zalutsky, like Molotov one of the original members of the pre-March 12 Russian Bureau. In his view,

> It is impossible to unite [with the left-wing Mensheviks] on the basis of a superficial Zimmerwald-Kienthal token. . . . It is necessary to lead the masses behind us. It is necessary to advance a definite program.

Molotov and Zalutsky were defending a line that they shared with Lenin. But that fact did not deter Stalin. Assuming the role of mediator and conciliator he urged,

> There is no use running ahead and anticipating disagreements. There is no party life without disagreements. We will live down trivial disagreements within the party. But there is one question—it is impossible to unite what cannot be united. We will have a single party with those who agree on Zimmerwald and Kienthal, i.e., those who are against revolutionary defensism. That is the line of demarcation.

To quiet fears that the party might find itself committed to a merger as the result of the proposed talks, Stalin added,

We must inform the Mensheviks that our desire is only the desire of the group meeting here and that it is not binding upon all Bolsheviks. We ought to go to the meeting, but not advance any platforms. Within the framework of what we desire is the convocation of a conference on the basis of anti-defensism.

The delegates then voted on competing resolutions, one offered by Stalin, the other by Molotov. Stalin's called for unification with "those Mensheviks who held the standpoint of Zimmerwald and Kienthal, i.e., anti-defensism," Molotov's for preparation of a separate Bolshevik Platform. Both resolutions agreed that the proposed meeting with the Mensheviks should be "informative in character," nonbinding.

By a unanimous vote the delegates approved Stalin's proposal to go to the meeting. His initiative had won him his first victory. Discussion then moved on to the question of how best to carry out the talks. V. P. Milyutin (Lenin's first commissar of agriculture, later purged by Stalin) proposed that a bureau be elected "for contact with the centers," that is, the Menshevik and Bolshevik leaders. Stalin offered the counterproposal that negotiations should be channeled through the Executive Committee of the Petrograd Soviet, which could get in touch with "internationalist-Mensheviks on the question." This proposal, which was carried with only one negative vote (probably Milyutin's), serves as a useful indication of the easy familiarity that Stalin had by now acquired with the bureaucratic machinery of the Soviet Executive Committee.

In recognition of his leading role in the discussion, the conference concluded its April 1 session by electing Stalin to a four-member committee to negotiate with the Mensheviks and charged him with responsibility for making a report on the subject at a forthcoming joint session of the two parties.

Altogether, Stalin's achievements at the April 1 session constituted a modest but genuine triumph. He had displayed leadership in guiding the conference toward the goals he had formulated; he had made tactical concessions without sacrificing his major objectives; and he had carried the delegates with him in the voting.

In retrospect, however, Stalin's triumph was revealed as an April Fool's joke played on him by history. By obtaining approval of his policy, Stalin ensured that his activities during the next few days would be directed toward a goal that the party later disavowed. But it was not only in hindsight that Stalin's policies were exposed as a violation of Leninist principles. At the time of the March conference it was already known to many party members, including Stalin, that

Lenin had demanded that the party strictly avoid any compromise with other parties. A telegram of March 6 from Lenin to a group of Bolsheviks in Stockholm just about to leave for Russia included the stern admonition, "No rapprochement whatsoever with the other parties." The record shows that this telegram was read and discussed at the March 13 session of the Russian Bureau, with Stalin present.[59] It was Stalin's direct, open violation of Lenin's categorical instruction on this point which made the protocols of the March conference a seriously damaging piece of evidence undermining his later efforts to portray himself as Lenin's loyal follower and undeviating supporter. It was in part to reinforce that image that the memoirs of Sergei Alliluev, suitably doctored by party historians, were issued in 1946, at a time when the whole issue of Stalin's relations with Lenin was being reexamined in connection with the publication of Stalin's *Works*. Awkwardly inserted into Alliluev's modest and straightforward text is the obviously contrived statement (referring to 1904, but clearly meant to have general validity),

> In the numerous discussions and disputes Koba [Stalin] was the terror of the Mensheviks and of everyone who compromised with them. Lenin abroad, in emigration, Koba here in the Transcaucasus, carried out a common task—they laid the foundation of a new, Bolshevik Party.[60]

Furthermore, by pursuing the will-o'-the-wisp of unification, Stalin lost sight of a forthcoming event that was fundamentally to alter Bolshevik policy on the revolution and Stalin's position in the Bolshevik party. The long-awaited return to Russia of the party's leader, Lenin, was now only a few days away; preparations to make his reception a suitably impressive spectacle were already going ahead, and a greeting committee was being formed. All this eager preparation was going on without any participation by Stalin. Intent on achieving his goal of unification with the left-wing Mensheviks, he failed to realize the importance of Lenin's return for the party, for the revolution, and for himself.

2 // APRIL

The Return of Lenin

On the evening of Monday, April 3, another group of Bolsheviks arrived in Petrograd, this time not from Siberian exile but from emigration in the West. This was no routine group of party figures, however, since it included the party leader himself, Lenin, now returning to his native land for the first time in more than ten years. Life in the West had made him a more cosmopolitan figure than many of his party comrades—Stalin, for example—who had spent most of their lives in Russia, and he brought with him a point of view which placed events in Russia in an international context.

Before the train reached the Finland Station, the terminus of its run, it made a brief stop at Belo Ostrov on the Russo-Finnish border, and there a group of party officials, headed by Kamenev, climbed aboard to greet Lenin. Conveniently for the historian, one of the Bolsheviks present was a Kronstadt sailor named F. F. Raskol'nikov, who later published his recollections of the scene.[1] Raskol'nikov vividly remembered the first words uttered by Lenin, words not of greeting but of sharp reproof:

> "What's this you're writing in *Pravda?* We have seen several issues and really swore at you!"

As Raskol'nikov later recollected the scene, it was Kamenev who bore the brunt of Lenin's wrath; Stalin was not present, and no contemporary witness recalled his presence. Even though he first published his account in 1923, at a time when he was under no pressure to whitewash the record as far as Stalin was concerned, Raskol'nikov remembered that Lenin made no specific reference to Stalin, but Lenin's stinging rebuke obviously applied to him as well, for Stalin shared full responsibility with Kamenev for *Pravda*'s recent editorial line. (A footnote in the 1964 edition of Raskol'nikov's memoirs, added at a time of renewed debunking of the Stalin cult, explicitly identifies Stalin as one of the principal targets of Lenin's wrath.)[2]

Meanwhile, the main welcoming party for Lenin was getting ready at the Finland Station, with the faithful Shlyapnikov as master of ceremonies and the Soviet leader Chkheidze as the spokesman of "revolutionary democracy" to extend a formal welcome to the returning Bolshevik chief. For the Finland Station festivities we have an eyewitness account by that indispensable historian-diarist of the revolution, the Menshevik N. N. Sukhanov (Himmer).[3] His description of the scene has become a classic that should be read by everyone interested in Lenin's place in the Russian Revolution. For present purposes, however, Sukhanov's report is of interest chiefly for the fact that, like Raskol'nikov's recollections of the Belo Ostrov encounter, it makes no mention of Stalin as among those present. Other reliable observers lend confirmation by their silence: Stalin was not present at the Finland Station.

The point may seem of relatively slight importance. What significance could there be, one may ask, in the presence or absence of a given party figure at what was, after all, merely another arrival of a group of tired, bone-weary travelers, anxious to find their bearings in the confusing new Russia of the revolutionary era? (Lenin, uncertain of the temper of the authorities in revolutionary Petrograd, half expected to be carted off to jail on arrival.) Reasoning thus, some biographers of Stalin simply pass over the entire episode in silence, hurrying on to other, in their eyes more significant developments.

Stalin felt otherwise, for he subsequently went to enormous lengths to "correct" the historical record, either inserting himself into the Belo Ostrov greeting party or, more frequently, assigning himself the principal role in the welcoming ceremonies at the Finland Station. Anything less, he evidently felt, would have cast a shadow of doubt on his claim to being Lenin's closest, most faithful disciple. The unfortunate memoirists—Raskol'nikov, Sukhanov, and others who failed to remember and report Stalin's presence—were later made to pay a bitter price for their inconveniently accurate memories: Sukhanov was executed on trumped-up charges in one of the early Stalin-era show trials, while Raskol'nikov was rubbed out (the gangster term is fully justified) by Stalin's secret police thugs after refusing to return to Russia for virtually certain extermination during the Great Purge.

Eliminating inconvenient witnesses was a step toward establishing a more seemly version of the event, but something more positive was required. For this purpose Stalin's court painters, using all the illusionistic techniques of "socialist realism," were pressed into service, and imposing canvases were created depicting Stalin extending the hand of greeting to Lenin as he dismounted from the train. Photographs are stubborn things, and while an awkward and inconvenient figure can be blotted out with a little erasing fluid, it is not so easy to insert a new figure into an existing group. Luckily for Stalin, camera techniques in 1917 had not progressed far enough to permit the recording of such a tumultuous, rapidly shifting scene under artificial light as the one at the reception rooms of the Finland Station, so that there are no contemporary newsreel shots of the event. But there was nothing to hinder Soviet film makers from creating "historical reconstructions" of the event, under Stalin's orders.

As reconstructed, the Stalinist version of the April 3 ceremonies featured a historic meeting between the two titans of the revolution: the Great Lenin, who had guided the party from abroad, at last joins hands with the equally Great Stalin, who had faithfully supported him through all the difficult prerevolutionary years. Now finally united, the two are ready to lead the party step by step to victory in October.

This is exactly how the flexible Yaroslavsky, after suitable "instruction," described the "meeting" between Lenin and Stalin:

> On April 3, Stalin went to Belo Ostrov to meet Lenin. It was with great joy that the two leaders of the revolution, the two leaders of Bolshevism, met after their long separation. They were both about to launch into the struggle for the dictatorship of the working class, to lead the struggle of the revolutionary people of Russia. During the journey to Petrograd Stalin informed Lenin of the state of affairs in the party and of the progress of the revolution.[4]

So firmly established did the legend of Stalin's presence as head of the greeting party for Lenin become in Soviet writings that as late as 1960, seven years after Stalin's death and four years after Khrushchev's attack on his "cult of personality," the official party biography of Lenin still listed Stalin as among those present at the welcome for

Lenin.[5] It took the second wave of Khrushchev's anti-Stalin campaign, launched at the Twenty-second Party Congress in October 1961, to discredit for a time this persistent falsification. Yet party historians are a stubborn breed, and in volume 4 of the official chronology of Lenin's life issued in 1974 under the auspices of the Institute of Marxism-Leninism, the ghostly figure of Stalin has somehow reappeared in that long-distant welcoming ceremony for Lenin.[6]

Granted, then, that Stalin was not among those present to welcome Lenin, what explanation can be found for his absence? Various suggestions have been offered. Edward E. Smith, for example, argues that Stalin may have "anticipated Lenin's criticism and this was the reason he had absented himself from greeting him upon his arrival."[7] Whatever faults Stalin may have possessed, however, cowardice was not among them; caution, certainly, but not cowardice. And even if he had foreseen Lenin's rebuke, it was a mistake for him to pass up the opportunity to be present at a historical moment.

Trotsky, never loath to make a damaging point at Stalin's expense, draws an obvious moral from Stalin's absence:

> That little fact shows better than anything else that there was nothing even remotely resembling personal intimacy between him and Lenin.[8]

Trotsky's charge is valid, at least for the period before Lenin's return, but it tells only part of the story: Stalin's absence represented an error in judgment, a faulty scale of values. The real reason Stalin was absent was because he had, or thought he had, something better to do than hurry off to meet Lenin. Caught up in the party conference that he had been guiding, and sharing the political outlook of his associates in the Executive Committee of the Soviet, Stalin on April 3 was attending a preparatory conference looking to the eventual merger of the Bolsheviks with the left-wing Mensheviks. It was this concern, not cowardice or a lack of intimacy with Lenin, which best explains his absence from the welcoming ceremonies.

It was only because Stalin later made such enormous claims for himself and his role in the revolution that he came to feel so keenly the disgrace of his absence from the meeting with Lenin. His failure in April, though relatively small in scale, foreshadowed his far more serious failure in October, and the reasons that lay behind it— obtuseness, faulty judgment, preoccupation with secondary issues— were to recur in magnified form in October. Perhaps that is why Stalin came to assign such apparently excessive importance to the task of "correcting" the historical record with regard to the nonmeeting between him and Lenin in early April.

Lenin Presents the "April Theses"

Lenin's return marked the opening of a third phase in Bolshevik policy since the overthrow of tsarism. During the first phase, from February 18 to March 12, the party, represented primarily by the Russian Bureau and the Vyborg *Raion* Committee, tried to develop its own independent line: supportive of the Petrograd Soviet, distrustful of the Provisional Government, insistent on an immediate end to the war, hostile to other socialist and left-wing parties. The inexperienced young men who led the party in this phase tried to the best of their ability to steer the frail party vessel through the exhilarating but risky rapids of the revolutionary torrent, but they lacked the assurance or the authority to unite the party behind them.

The return of Muranov, Kamenev, and Stalin on March 12 brought the first phase of Bolshevik policy to an abrupt end and substituted in its place a more moderate line, characterized by the attempt to reach a *modus vivendi* with the new institutions that had emerged to take the place of the discredited autocracy. Though opposed by many militant workers and resented by the leaders of the first phase, the line adopted by the spokesmen of the second phase helped the Bolshevik party find a secure if limited place in the emerging world of pluralistic revolutionary politics.

Like the first phase, the second came to an abrupt end with the arrival of a new group of returning party figures. This time, however, the shift was fundamental, radical, and permanent. The new era inaugurated by Lenin is one that continues in an unbroken line from that time down to the present.

Briefly summarized, the "April Theses," which Lenin presented to a party gathering late on the evening of April 3 and then repeated before a mixed audience on the following day, represent a bold and imaginative amalgam of three diverse elements: first, an analysis of the existing situation not only in Russia but in the wider perspective of a world at war; second, a set of prescriptions for political action, designed to advance the revolution farther along the road to socialism; and third, a list of specific steps to be taken by the party to enable it to play the leading role in the revolution as thus conceived.[9]

Lenin began his "April Theses" with the war, which had been at the center of his thoughts ever since its outbreak and which to him represented the touchstone against which all other questions must be tested. In line with the analysis he had offered in his book, *Imperialism, The Highest Stage of Capitalism*, Lenin defined the war strictly in class terms. Capitalism, he argued, leads inevitably to to imperialism, while a capitalist nation in the era of imperialism is driven to wage war for profits, the annexation of territories, and the weakening or destruction of rival capitalist nations. Since the Provisional Government, headed by Prince Lvov and dominated by the middle-class Cadet and Octobrist parties, was by its nature capitalist (Lenin treated this proposition as a self-evident one not requiring proof), the war "unquestionably remains a predatory imperialist war."

Without mentioning *Pravda* or its editorial board, Lenin brusquely rejected the policy of conditional support for a defensive war, which the newspaper had advocated when Kamenev and Stalin were directing its policies. Only with the overthrow of capitalism in Russia, Lenin asserted, would a "truly democratic peace" be possible; it was the task of the party to explain this to the masses, "who are being deceived by the bourgeoisie." Lenin made a special point of calling for "the most widespread campaign for this view . . . in the army at the front" and for "fraternization" between Russian soldiers and those of the armies opposing them. (Within two weeks the Bolsheviks, using funds provided by the German General Staff, were able to begin publication of a special newspaper for the field army, *Okopnaia pravda*).

Having staked out his position on the war in his first thesis, Lenin turned for his second to the question of the nature of the revolution and the specific stage it had currently attained—matters of fundamental concern to any Marxist, since the agenda for the next round of actions would be determined by knowing exactly where one found oneself at the moment. The Menshevik leaders of the Soviet Executive Committee had their own answer to this question, based on their reading of Marxism: since the socioeconomic conditions in Russia were objectively suitable only for a bourgeois liberal-democratic revolution, the proper course of action for the workers' parties was to aid the bourgeoisie in carrying through its revolution in order to help create the conditions that would ultimately make possible a workers' revolution leading to the establishment of socialism. Though he was no Menshevik, Stalin, along with many other Bolsheviks, shared this perspective before Lenin's return.

To the indignation and shock of the Mensheviks in the audience that listened to Lenin's presentation of the "April Theses," and to the bewilderment of many of his own followers, Lenin now unceremoniously jettisoned this time-honored reading of the Marxist scriptures and asserted that the assumption of power by the bourgeoisie during the February Revolution was the result not of historical necessity but of a regrettable failure on the part of the proletariat, its "inadequate organization and insufficient class consciousness." Far from having achieved its goals, the revolution was in transition from its first phase, marked by the assumption of power by the bourgeoisie, to

> its second stage, which is to place power in the hands of the proletariat and the poorest strata of the peasantry.

Almost in passing, Lenin mentioned the genuine liberties the Russian people were currently enjoying:

> This transition is characterized, on the one hand, by a maximum of legality (Russia is now the freest of all the belligerent countries of the world); on the other, by the absence of oppression of the masses.

Lenin's view of the proletariat's failure in February dismissed Marx's assertion that the workers could make their own, socialist revolution only when the objective conditions for it were present.

In his Theory of Permanent Revolution, Leon Trotsky had devised an ingenious mechanism whereby backward Russia could escape from this apparently ironclad historical law: the workers of Russia, Trotsky argued, could initiate by their action a wave of revolutions which would quickly spread to the advanced capitalist nations of the West, and then the small but militant proletariat of Russia would find powerful allies in its worker-brothers of Western Europe. Without acknowledging his intellectual debt to Trotsky, Lenin developed a strikingly similar concept in his theory of the "uninterrupted revolution" and in his analysis of imperialism. Even though these premises are never set forth specifically in the "April Theses," they underlie Lenin's concept of "the present situation in Russia." No wonder that his audience, steeped in traditional Marxism, reacted in surprise, shock, or disbelief to Lenin's apparent disregard of the basic Marxist verities.

Having just paid tribute to the democratic internal policies of the Provisional Government, Lenin in his third thesis uncompromisingly condemned it as "a government of capitalists" and hence "imperialist" in its foreign policy, including its war aims. For Lenin there was no separation between foreign and internal policy: since, he asserted, the Provisional Government was capitalist, and hence, by definition, imperialistic, it *could not* renounce the goal of annexations and therefore *all* its promises were "utterly false." The Bolshevik party, Lenin insisted, must adopt a policy of *no* support toward it, not just the "insofar as" policy of the Menshevik-SR leadership in the Soviet Executive Committee (or of Kamenev and Stalin in *Pravda*).

In place of the Provisional Government, Lenin asserted in his fourth thesis, "the Soviet of Workers' Deputies is the only possible form of revolutionary government"—this, despite the fact that, as Lenin candidly admitted, the Bolshevik party "constitutes a minority, and a small one at that . . . in most of the Soviets of Workers' Deputies." It was the task of the party, Lenin urged,

> to present a patient, systematic, and persistent analysis of its [the Soviet's] errors and tactics, an analysis especially adapted to the practical needs of the masses.

Even the Constituent Assembly, in Lenin's view, must be brought within the scope of the Soviet as a government: in the impromptu speech with which he accompanied the "Theses" (which he had written out beforehand), Lenin asserted that "the Soviet is the only government that can convoke the Constituent Assembly," and, in any case, the work of the Constituent Assembly would be in effect determined for it in advance, since Russia needed (according to Lenin's fifth thesis),

> Not a parliamentary republic—a return to it from the Soviet of Workers' Deputies would be a step backward—but a republic of Soviets of Workers', Agricultural Labourers' and Peasants' Deputies throughout the land, from top to bottom.

For his concept of the Soviet as a revolutionary government Lenin drew heavily on Marx's analysis of the nature and policies of the Paris Commune of 1870-71:

> Abolition of the police, the army, the bureaucracy. All officers to be elected and to be subject to recall at any time, their salaries not to exceed the average wage of a competent worker's.

Turning to the agrarian question for his sixth thesis, Lenin revealed that even his boldness had limits. At a time when individual peasant seizures of gentry land were only beginning—a phenomenon that was to grow, with Bolshevik approval and encouragement, into a massive, fundamental peasant revolt by the late summer of 1917—Lenin still envisaged a fairly orderly process geared to an eventual socialization of the land:

> Nationalization of all lands in the country, and management of such lands by local Soviets of Agricultural Laborers' and Peasants' Deputies. . . . Creation of model agricultural establishments out of large estates . . . under the control of the Soviet of Agricultural Laborers' Deputies, and at public expense.

The basic point was emphasized in his accompanying commentary, "Agriculture on a Communal Basis." Only reluctantly over the next few months was Lenin to recognize that the peasants wanted to seize the land for themselves, not for socialism.

Centralization of the entire banking system of the nation, another point borrowed from Marx's analysis of the Paris Commune, constituted Lenin's seventh thesis, with the proviso that the "one general national bank" should be under the control of the Soviet of Workers' Deputies. The same body, in the eighth thesis, was to exercise "control of social production and distribution of goods," a task that Lenin was careful to distinguish from "the 'initiation' of Socialism as an immediate task."

As to the party, in his ninth thesis, Lenin demanded the "immediate calling of a party congress," changes in the party program to bring it into line with the theses on the war and the state, and—a symbolic step, but one to which Lenin attached great importance—the change of the party's name from "Social Democratic," a label now tarnished by the "betrayal of Socialism" by the majority of Social Democratic parties at the outbreak of the war, to "Communist."

In his tenth and final thesis Lenin reminded his listeners that for him the socialist revolutionary movement was an international phenomenon. Since, the Leninist argument ran, the parties of the Second International had "betrayed socialism" by voting national war credits in August 1914, the Bolsheviks had the obligation of

taking the initiative in the creation of a revolutionary International, an International against the social-chauvinists and the "center."

By the latter phrase, as applied to Russia, Lenin had in mind the left-internationalist group of Mensheviks represented by the Soviet leaders Chkheidze and Tseretelli—that group, in other words, with regard to whom Stalin, a few days earlier, had obtained approval from the March conference for exploratory talks looking to an eventual merger. It was with unmistakable reference to precisely this development that Lenin concluded his presentation of the "April Theses." "I hear," he said,

that in Russia there is a movement towards unity, unity with the defensists. This is a betrayal of Socialism. I think that it is better to stand alone, like Liebknecht, one against one hundred and ten.

There was no need for Lenin to identify the specific individual in the party against whom these fighting words were directed: by his signed articles in Pravda and his eloquent pleading at the March conference, Stalin had identified himself as the leader of the "movement" that Lenin now condemned as a "betrayal of Socialism." For Stalin the bitterness he must have felt at that moment was compounded by the fact that the reproof was delivered before the very audience, in the same meeting place, where he had expected to carry through to completion his plan for a merger of the Bolsheviks and the left-wing Mensheviks.

For Stalin, the third phase in revolutionary Bolshevik policy began even more inauspiciously than had the second. In March, with the help of a few comrades and his own forceful personality, he had emerged from the reproof of his party judges virtually unscathed. But on that occasion his opponents had been either junior and inexperienced functionaries whom he could easily thrust aside, or denouncers and gossip-mongers who sheltered themselves behind the cloak of anonymity (to this day we cannot be sure who told the Russian Bureau about Stalin's undesirable "personal characteristics"). Furthermore, the earlier setback had been administered in the privacy of a closed party meeting, and the record of it had been consigned to the archives, unknown to all but a few party members and to everyone outside the party. Stalin's quick recovery in March made it possible for him to treat the entire episode as something that had never taken place (only his complete forgetting of the March 12 reproof can explain the survival of the unretouched protocol of that session in the party archives during the decades of his unlimited power).

In contrast, the setback Stalin experienced at the start of the third phase took place in a public gathering, before a mixed party and nonparty audience; it was administered by the party's recognized leader, in terms that permitted no rejoinder and in a tone that left no apparent hope for recovery. The only aspect of the affair in which Stalin could take comfort was that Lenin had stopped just short of specifically identifying him as the figure personally responsible for the movement toward merger with the left-wing Mensheviks. And therein, as Stalin slowly came to perceive, lay the path by which he could find his way out of this new humiliation. Lenin, who never hesitated to employ the most violent and abusive language against those he regarded as enemies or rivals, could be extraordinarily patient and understanding in dealing with party members whom he saw as potential recruits for leading roles in the party. It was this pedagogical characteristic of Lenin, and the response it evoked in Stalin, which enabled the latter to emerge from his discomfiture at the outset of the third phase not merely with his old status in the party unimpaired but with an ascent to a position of which he had previously only dreamed.

Stalin and the "April Theses"

It took some time for Stalin fully to comprehend what had happened. The positions set forth in the "April Theses" were too radical, too little related to the questions he had been concerned with, for him to incorporate them immediately into his mental world. Nor was he disposed to accept automatically whatever Lenin advocated simply out of a sense of personal loyalty or party discipline.

When the "April Theses" were discussed at a meeting of the Russian Bureau on April 6, Stalin spoke against them. (The record of his brief remarks, stripped to their elements, was another of those "uncorrected" documents of 1917 which somehow survived in the archives, to be dug out and published as part of the anti-Stalin campaign under Khrushchev.) In the skeletal protocols, which are all that survives of the April 6 session, Stalin is quoted as saying,

> The picture of the bridge between the West and the East—destruction of the colonies. A sketch, but no facts, and therefore unsatisfactory. There are no answers about small nations.[10]

Brief though it is, this summary tells us a good deal about the stand Stalin took. It shows that he was still concentrating on his specialty, the national question (a question, incidentally, on which, as far as the record shows, Lenin said nothing in the "April Theses"). Stalin seems to have ignored entirely Lenin's central themes—the war, the Provisional Government, the Soviet. Furthermore, as Tucker has pointed out, Stalin's criticism fits in closely with the position taken by Kamenev at the same meeting, a position he was still defending at the April Conference, to the effect that "the general sociological scheme [in the "April Theses"] has not been filled in with concrete political content."[11]

For a description of what Stalin later wished he had done in the discussion of the "April Theses," we can turn to the ever-pliant Yaroslavsky, who writes,

> On April 4, Lenin addressed a conference and read his celebrated April Theses, in which he outlined the plan for the further development of the revolution, the plan for the capture of power by the Soviets. When Zinoviev and Kamenev, those traitors to the revolution, opposed this plan, they met with a severe rebuff at the hands of Stalin, who ardently defended Lenin's plan for the growth of the bourgeois democratic revolution into the socialist revolution.[12]

As of April 6, then, Stalin was still groping for a way to reject Lenin's new program, attacking it on a peripheral issue and relying for support on the familiar figure of Kamenev to provide him with a general critique. Thereafter, however, it was Kamenev, rather than Stalin, who carried the brunt of the fight against what he regarded as Lenin's unorthodox and dangerous proposals. When the "Theses" were published in *Pravda* on April 7 (the delay is in itself symptomatic of resistance), they were accompanied by an editorial note to the effect that they represented only Lenin's personal views, not those of the party. Since Stalin was still, at that point, one of the co-editors of *Pravda*, the note must have passed his scrutiny. As far as it goes, that fact indicates a wait-and-see attitude rather than one of outright condemnation and may be taken as the starting point of Stalin's reorientation toward a position closer to that of Lenin.

Kamenev's critique of the "April Theses" was developed more fully in an article he published in *Pravda* on April 8 under the title "Our Differences."[13] Again he emphasized that for him the "Theses" represented "the personal opinion" of Lenin, but he praised them as "concise" and "thorough." Defending the editorial line of *Pravda*, which he had helped establish, Kamenev pointed out that it had been supported by the Bolshevik delegates to the All-Russian Conference of Soviets in March, as formulated in the resolution on the Provisional Government and the soviets.

As his principal theoretical difference with Lenin, Kamenev named their divergent views on the character of the revolution. Lenin's general line, he said,

> appears to us unacceptable inasmuch as it proceeds from the assumption that the bourgeois-democratic revolution *has been completed* and it builds on the immediate transformation of this revolution into a Socialist revolution.

Kamenev called for a "broad discussion" of the issue in which he hoped to vindicate his point of view

> as the only possible one for revolutionary Social-Democracy in so far as it wishes to be and must remain to the end the one and only party of the revolutionary masses of the proletariat without turning into a group of Communist propagandists.

With the April 8 article Kamenev emerged as the most prominent Bolshevik critic of the "April Theses." As far as the record shows, Stalin, who had tacitly supported Kamenev as late as April 7, thereafter took no action and made no further statements, oral or written, which could be construed as a criticism of the "Theses." A basic shift in his allegiance from Kamenev to Lenin was under way. Once started, the process of rethinking by Stalin gathered momentum rapidly, and when he resumed publication of signed articles in *Pravda* on April 11 it was clear that he had executed a sharp change of position.

Stalin Swings Over to Support of Lenin

Between April 11 and the opening of the Seventh Party Conference on April 24, Stalin published three short articles in *Pravda*, two signed with his usual pseudonym, "K. Stalin," and one unsigned editorial. In addition he gave his first recorded speech of the revolution. Brief though they are, these materials are enough to enable us to chart the general flow of his reorientation.

In the first, a signed article published on April 11 under the title "Two Resolutions," Stalin showed how far he had already moved toward accepting Lenin's view of the war.[14] The Provisional Government had just announced the floating of a so-called Liberty Loan to raise funds for various purposes, principally continuation of the war. The Executive Committee of the Soviet, true to its policy of limited support of the Provisional Government, thereupon adopted a resolution calling on the population to support the loan. Defying both the government and the Soviet, a group of workers in the machine shops of the Russo-Baltic Railway Car Works came out against the loan, charging that it was

> being floated with the aim of continuing the fratricidal slaughter, which is advantageous only to the imperialist bourgeoisie.

The workers' resolution, in a clear indication of the Bolshevik influence that lay behind it, accused the Executive Committee of "betraying the International" by supporting the loan, a charge that Stalin in his article flatly endorsed. Thus he gave public notice that he now accepted Lenin's position on the war and had parted company with the supporters of a defensist position in the Soviet.

Three days later, on April 14, Stalin published a second article in *Pravda*, the message of which was conveyed in its title, "The Land to the Peasants."[15] In the sixth of his "April Theses," Lenin had called for "confiscation of all private lands" and their cultivation on a communal basis. Stalin now added his voice to this demand, spelling it out in detail:

> We therefore call upon the peasants, upon the peasant poor of all Russia, to take their cause into their own hands and push it forward. We call upon them to organize and form revolutionary peasant committees . . . , take over the landed estates through these committees, and cultivate the land in an organized manner without authorization.

Before Lenin's return, Stalin had written nothing as incendiary as this.

Along with his new militancy on the peasant question went a far more critical attitude toward the Executive Committee of the Soviet. There, the SR leaders, fearing to alienate the middle-class liberals by championing the peasant demand to take over privately owned estates, had counseled the peasants to be patient and await the convocation of the Constituent Assembly, which would settle the land question in a legal, orderly manner. In words that showed how far he had shifted from his earlier stance, Stalin brushed aside such scruples:

> We are told that immediate seizure of the landed estates would disrupt the "unity" of the revolution by splitting off the "progressive strata" of society from it.
>
> But it would be naive to think that it is possible to advance the revolution without quarreling with the manufacturers and landlords.
>
> . . . .
>
> Unauthorized cultivation of the landed estates and their seizure by the peasants will undoubtedly "split off" the landlords and their ilk from the revolution. But who would venture to assert that by rallying the millions of poor peasants around the revolution we shall be weakening the forces of the revolution?

Fully accepting Lenin's concept of the basic forces of the revolution and its future course, Stalin continued,

> The policy of waiting and procrastinating until the Constituent Assembly is convened, the policy recommended by the Narodniks [i.e., the SR's], Trudoviks, and Mensheviks of "temporarily" renouncing confiscation, the policy of zigzagging between the classes (so as not to offend anybody!) and of shamefully marking time, is not the policy of the revolutionary proletariat.

In his first two *Pravda* articles in April Stalin showed that a momentous shift had taken place not only in his ideas but in his intellectual allegiance. Where he had previously relied on the moderate Kamenev and the conciliatory Menshevik-SR leadership in the Soviet for guidance, Stalin was now deriving his ideas directly from Lenin. For the first time in his revolutionary career Stalin was sharing an office with Lenin and discussing with him the problems and opportunities that arose from day to day in the editing of the party newspaper. The close working relationship between the two men quickly led to a sharing of their editorial responsibilities. For example, the immediate point of departure for Stalin's article "The Land to the Peasants" was a telegram from Minister of Agriculture Shingaryov to the peasants of Ryazan' *guberniia* calling on them to abstain from illegal seizure of gentry lands. On April 15, the day after Stalin's article appeared, Lenin contributed a short follow-up to *Pravda*, reiterating the principal points Stalin had made and for good measure giving the full text of Shingaryov's telegram as printed in that morning's edition of the Cadet newspaper, *Rech'*.[16]

The third contribution by Stalin to *Pravda* in April, an unsigned editorial entitled "May Day," carried even clearer indications of the guiding role that Lenin had now assumed in shaping Stalin's thinking.[17] Previously (for example, in his March 16 article, "The War"), Stalin's vision had been confined to Russia. Now it widened to take in the whole of war-torn Europe:

> The world has begun to stifle in the grip of war . . . [leaders in the original]. The peoples of Europe can bear it no longer, and are already rising up against the bellicose bourgeoisie.

If an echo of Lenin's slogan "Convert the imperialist war into a civil war" could be detected in that statement, the Leninist inspiration of Stalin's next assertion was even more unmistakable:

> The Russian revolution is the first to be forcing a breach in the wall that divides the workers from one another. The Russian workers, at this time of universal "patriotic" frenzy, are the first to proclaim the forgotten slogan: "Workers of all countries, unite!"

For the first time in his career, Stalin now seemed to grasp the relationship between the Russian Revolution and the larger international socialist revolution about which Lenin and Trotsky had been talking and writing for years:

> Amidst the thunder of the Russian revolution, the workers of the West too are rising from their slumber. The strikes and demonstrations in Germany, the demonstrations in Austria and Bulgaria, the strikes and meetings in neutral countries, the growing unrest in Britain and France, the mass fraternization on the battle fronts—these are the first harbingers of the socialist revolution that is brewing.

The war, the land, the international socialist revolution—one by one, Stalin was directing his attention to the principal issues facing the Bolshevik party and showing the change in his outlook caused by Lenin's influence. A fourth major issue, policy toward the Provisional Government, was added in a speech Stalin delivered on April 18.[18] In March Stalin had favored the "insofar as" formula of conditional support of the Provisional Government. Now, under the influence of Lenin, he dropped all qualifications and called on the workers and soldiers to "support only the Soviet of Workers' and Soldiers' Deputies which they themselves elected."

The First All-Petrograd Conference of Bolsheviks

In preparation for the party congress for which Lenin had called in the "April Theses," the Bolsheviks of Petrograd met in an all-city conference between April 14 and 22.[19] Stalin's name occurs only once in the protocols of the conference, and then not as a speaker but simply as one of those elected to a seven-man committee, along with Lenin, Molotov, Zinoviev, and Kamenev, to draft a resolution on the Provisional Government and the war. (The other two members of the committee were S. Ya. Bagdatiev, using the party pseudonym "Sergei," and K. I. Shutko ["Mikhail"], both members of the Petersburg Committee. Neither Bagdatiev nor Shutko published any memoirs of their experiences in the revolution, a fact that may explain their survival through the Great Purge. Bagdatiev died in 1949, Shutko in 1941.)

It is possible that Stalin was not present at the conference. Trotsky asserts that

> Stalin did not even show up. Obviously, he sought to be forgotten for a while.[20]

For the rank-and-file delegates at the conference, Stalin's name was still not one to be reckoned with, and when they elected a presidium at their opening session, Stalin was not included. Lenin's stature was recognized by designating him "honorary chairman"; the actual work of the conference was assigned to his lieutenant, Zinoviev. Molotov, whom the party organization remembered as a leader in the February Revolution, was named a member of the presidium.

On April 14, the date of the conference's opening session, the delegates had only Stalin's April 11 article, "Two Resolutions," and "The Land to the Peasants" in *Pravda* for April 14 by which to evaluate his changing outlook. It took the party organization some time to realize that the moderate Stalin of the period before Lenin's return was now changing rapidly into a staunch Leninist. Stalin's virtual eclipse and lack of recognition at the Petrograd conference is a telling indication of his modest standing in the party as of mid-April.

Nevertheless it is difficult to accept Trotsky's explanation of Stalin's comparative obscurity at the Petrograd conference as the result of a withdrawal into protective silence. After all, at the very time the conference was in session Stalin was publicly proclaiming his new pro-Lenin stance in the pages of *Pravda*. A more cogent reason for Stalin's silence was that Lenin, at this point, simply felt no need to call on him for support.

There was, in fact, no special need for Stalin to speak at the Petrograd conference. The agenda, as announced by *Pravda* on April 12, included a report on the current situation, to be delivered by Lenin, and discussion of the party's attitude toward the Soviet, the structure of the party, the immediate arming of the workers, the municipal elections, and the attitude to be adopted toward other socialist parties, none of which called for any contribution on the part of Stalin.

For Stalin, the period between April 7, when *Pravda* published Lenin's "April Theses," and April 24, when the Seventh Party Conference opened, was a time of rapidly expanding horizons. Working side by side with Lenin in the *Pravda* office, Stalin readily absorbed the older man's point of view, the more so because his own outlook was only tentative and was based more on impulse than on firmly held principles.

During the first phase of his participation in the revolution Stalin had adopted the stance of Muranov and Kamenev; then, as his familiarity with the Executive Committee of the Soviet increased, he fell under the influence of Tsereteli, Chkheidze, and other left-wing Mensheviks in that milieu. He had little or nothing original to contribute by way of ideas, but he was eager, ambitious, and reasonably articulate and compensated for his intellectual shallowness by a doggedness that made him a valuable asset to any group.

What he did not have, except in his own fancy, were the attributes of leadership. He was still searching for a role that suited his talents and for an authority figure on whom he could model his own personality. In Lenin he seemed to have found what he was searching for, and the attempt to establish himself as a second Lenin was to dominate his later career, especially after the Leader's death in 1924. For Stalin, however, the Leninist path was to prove another of those false trails that he was to follow in his quest for power and glory, for it was not Lenin who ultimately provided Stalin with the key wherewith to unlock the gates of power but another party figure, Yakov Sverdlov. Or rather, it would be more accurate to say that Stalin's ultimately successful formula for total power represented a unique blend of attributes derived from two principal models: Lenin, the party leader, and Sverdlov, the party organizer. It was on his use of the legacy of Sverdlov that Stalin's real power came to be based.

The April Crisis

While the Petrograd all-city conference was in progress, a sudden political crisis broke out that shook the Provisional Government, troubled the Soviet Executive Committee, and galvanized the Bolshevik party into frenzied action. The root of the crisis was the still unresolved discrepancy between the war aims of the Provisional Government, as defined by its foreign minister, Milyukov, and the very different goals of the Petrograd Soviet, as set forth in its Appeal to the Peoples of the World of March 14.

With a political insight for which he is sometimes not given sufficient credit, Stalin had called attention to this conflict in his *Pravda* article of March 26, "Either—Or." In that article he demanded either that the Soviet apply pressure to the Provisional Government to bring its war aims into line with those of the Soviet or that Milyukov resign. It was by means of the former of these alternatives that the conflict was temporarily resolved. The Provisional Government on March 27 issued a statement signifying its acceptance of the formula "no annexations, no indemnities," and tension temporarily subsided. But the restored harmony was more apparent than real, for Milyukov had by no means accepted the Soviet's definition of war aims, not only because he did not share them, but because he was under intense pressure from the British ambassador to reaffirm in categorical terms Russia's loyalty to her allies and to the agreements she had reached with them.

Given this situation it was merely a question of time before the conflict would break out again, and on April 20 it did, with the publication of a note written by Milyukov on the eighteenth to the British and French ambassadors formally endorsing the government's redefinition of war aims of March 27 but actually undercutting it by assuring the Allies that Russia would carry the war "to a definite conclusion" with the aim of obtaining certain "sanctions and guarantees."

Publication of Milyukov's note touched off a series of angry demonstrations by workers and soldiers which soon raised the threat of an attempt at armed overthrow of the government. Some eager Bolsheviks in the Petersburg Committee and the Bolshevik Military Organization, notably Bagdatiev, were prominently associated with these actions, a fact that forced Lenin soberly to evaluate the party's prospects for success in the event of a test of strength between the Provisional Government and the Soviet.

Meetings of the Bolshevik Central Committee were held daily while the crisis raged (April 20–22), with Lenin drafting the resolutions that defined the party line. On the morning of the twentieth the committee resolved that the Milyukov note fully confirmed the party's condemnation of the Provisional Government as "imperialist through and through, tied hand and foot to Anglo-French and Russian capital."[21] The resolution called on the revolutionary proletariat, with the support of the revolutionary army, to take "the entire power of the state into its own hands . . . in the form of the Soviet of Workers' and Soldiers' Deputies," an injunction that could be, and in some quarters was, read as an open invitation to try to overthrow the Provisional Government by force.

On the twenty-first, with violence in the streets mounting rapidly and some militant Bolsheviks calling for a direct assault on the government, the Petrograd Soviet tried to calm the storm by issuing a two-day ban on all street meetings and demonstrations. On the same day the Provisional Government made public an "explanation" of Milyukov's note which amounted to a repudiation of it and of him. The effect of these moves was to put a damper on the demonstrations, cooling the ardor of the angry crowds besieging government headquarters in the Mariinsky Palace.

For Lenin and the Bolshevik Central Committee, the Soviet order was a danger signal, a warning to weigh the risks and opportunities that the mass demonstrations posed for the party. It was Lenin's reluctant judgment, expressed in a Central Committee resolution adopted late on the twenty-first, that the risks outweighed the opportunities and that further actions should be limited to *"peaceful* discussions and peaceful demonstrations."[22] To mollify the frustrated insurgents, the resolution called on the workers and soldiers to hold new elections to the Soviet as a means of forcing it to alter its policy of confidence in the Provisional Government. Finally, on April 22, the crisis subsided, and the Central Committee drew up a balance sheet on the whole episode in the form of yet another resolution, as usual drafted by Lenin.[23] The slogan "'Down with the Provisional Government,'" the resolution asserted,

> is an incorrect one *at present* [italics added] . . . because in the absence of a firm (i.e., a class-conscious and organized) majority of the people on the side of the revolutionary proletariat, such a slogan is either an empty phrase or, objectively, it leads to attempts of an adventurist nature.

In words that looked ahead to September the resolution continued,

> We will favor a transfer of power into the hands of the proletarians and semi-proletarians only when the Soviets of Workers' and Soldiers' Deputies adopt our policy and are willing to take the power into their own hands.

The protocols of the Central Committee sessions for April have not been published and apparently no longer exist. From the available evidence it seems that Lenin encountered no serious opposition to his views, and there is no record of any discussion of his draft resolutions.

As to Stalin, we know that he took part in one brief but significant action during the April Crisis, as a member of a committee set up by the Executive Committee of the Soviet to draft a telegram to the army headquarters in the Petrograd area "demanding that they not send military units to Petrograd without the explicit written invitation of the Petrograd Soviet of Workers' and Soldiers' Deputies."

Trotsky's comment on this action is characteristically barbed:

> From the official protocols we note, not without surprise, that the text of the telegram was composed by a commission that consisted of two Compromisers [i.e., Iu. M. Steklov and G. M. Erlikh, both Mensheviks] and one Bolshevik, and that this Bolshevik was Stalin. It is a minor episode (we find no important episodes pertaining to him throughout that period), but decidedly a typical one. The reassuring telegram was a classic little example of that "control" which was an indispensable element in the mechanics of dual power. . . . The Compromisers placed Stalin on the commission because the Bolsheviks alone enjoyed any authority in Kronstadt. That was all the more reason for declining the appointment. But Stalin did not refuse it.[24]

Thus during the height of the April Crisis Stalin was dividing his time between the Bolshevik Central Committee (assuming that he attended the sessions of April 20–22) and the Soviet Executive Committee. This policy of keeping a foot in both camps helps to explain the continued good standing he enjoyed among the Soviet leaders, even at a time when he was publicly identifying himself with Lenin's harsh criticism of them.

There is also evidence that Stalin, in his capacity as a member of the Executive Committee of the Soviet, attended a meeting between that body and the Provisional Government on April 22 at which an effort was made to patch together an agreement in order to overcome the crisis. Since Stalin's report on this meeting was delivered orally during the Seventh Conference and published a day later, it will be convenient to postpone discussion of it until we take up that party gathering.

Finland Raises the National Question

Just before the April Crisis broke, the Bolshevik Central Committee was turning its attention to one of the fundamental problems of the revolution, the national question. At a meeting on April 19 the committee heard and considered an appeal from the Social Democratic party of Finland concerning the growing movement for Finnish autonomy. In response Lenin advocated full support for the Finnish appeal, and he was even prepared to sanction the withdrawal of Finland from the Russian state and the establishment of an independent Finland. Lenin evidently failed to win majority support for this policy, however, for the resolution he drew up was not adopted.[25]

In view of Stalin's established reputation as the party's leading authority on the national question, it would be interesting to know what position he adopted at the April 19 session, if he attended it. Was he one of those whose opposition helped defeat Lenin's resolution, or did he speak in its support? Most likely neither: cautious silence when confronted by a new challenge was Stalin's favored tactic. If that is the line he took, it was a wise one, for the April 19 debate on the national question proved to be a springboard for an action by Lenin which completely transformed Stalin's position in the party and his relations with Lenin.

Lenin's failure to carry the Central Committee with him on the national question, to which he assigned cardinal importance in his overall strategy, must have made it clear to him that he faced an uphill fight over that subject at the forthcoming party conference. (The preliminary agenda for the conference, published in *Pravda* on April 13, listed the national question as the sixth and last substantive item for discussion, just before the elections to central party bodies.)

Lenin could expect opposition to his line on the national question not so much from ethnic Russians in the party as from representatives of the national minorities, for example, the Pole Felix Dzerzhinsky, who, despite his general endorsement of Lenin's line, refused to follow him in his policy on the national question. Clearly what Lenin needed most at this point was a non-Russian spokesman for his views who could effectively counter the attacks on them to be expected from other non-Russians in the party such as Dzerzhinsky. The solution to the problem was obvious: Stalin had all the necessary qualifications and had just been demonstrating, by his writings in *Pravda* since April 11, that he was amenable to Lenin's influence. What more natural than to ask Stalin to report on the national question at the conference whose opening was now just a week away? The fact that Stalin's most recent writings on the subject, his *Pravda* articles of the period before Lenin's return, were by no means to Lenin's liking, was of little importance: Stalin had shown a cavalier disregard for consistency once he had decided to shift his allegiance and ideas.

But Lenin had an even more potent inducement to offer Stalin. Made aware by the April Crisis of the need to strengthen the party's organization, Lenin was on the lookout for suitable recruits to the party's leadership. Stalin, he decided at some point, met his requirements. What Lenin had to offer Stalin, then, was an irresistible combination of power and policy. It was this offer, and Stalin's acceptance of it, which made the April Conference a major landmark in the latter's rise to power.

The Opening of the Seventh Conference

With his very first introductory statement to the Bolsheviks' Seventh Party Congress, on the morning of Monday, April 24, Lenin set the Russian Revolution within the framework of the world socialist revolution, which he foresaw as the inevitable outcome of the World War. "Comrades," he said,

> our conference is meeting . . . under conditions not only of the Russian revolution but of the growing international revolution. The time is approaching when the assertions of the founders of scientific socialism [i.e., Marx and Engels], and the unanimous forecast of the socialists who gathered at the Basle Congress [of the Second International in 1912], that world war would inevitably lead to revolution, are being everywhere proved correct.[26]

In the nineteenth century, Lenin asserted, Marx and Engels had prophesied that "the French worker will begin [the socialist revolution], the German will finish it." Instead,

> The great honor of beginning the revolution has fallen to the Russian proletariat. But the Russian proletariat must not forget that its movement and the revolution are only part of a world proletarian movement, which in Germany, for example, is gaining momentum with every passing day. *Only from this point of view can we define our tasks.*

With those wide-ranging words ringing in their ears, the delegates proceeded to the first formal action of the conference, the election of a five-man presidium. As at the Petrograd all-city conference a week earlier, the action served as a partial indication of the popularity and standing of the party leaders as viewed by the delegates. Of these there were a total of 151—133 with full voting privileges and 18 with consultative rights only. The delegates represented some 80,000 party members, in seventy-eight party organizations—still a minuscule figure in a state numbering over 125 million inhabitants, but up sharply from the January 1917 estimate of 40,000.[27]

Lenin, of course, easily won membership on the presidium, as did his close associate G. Ye. Zinoviev, one of those who had accompanied him on his "sealed train" return from Switzerland. The third member of the presidium, Ya. M. Sverdlov, was something of a surprise: had he not been sent off to the remote Urals at the end of March? But Sverdlov was not to be sidetracked by mere bureaucratic measures: himself a master at the art of political manipulation, he lost no time in reorganizing the party committee in Yekaterinburg to which he was assigned and was returned by that organization to Petrograd as its representative to the Seventh Conference. Henceforward, until his untimely death in March 1919, Sverdlov would never leave the center of power except for trips undertaken on behalf of the party leadership.

As the fourth member of the presidium the conference chose G. F. Fedorov, a member of both the Petersburg Committee and the Executive Committee of the Soviet. Something of the temper of the man can be gleaned from his later career: in 1927 he was ousted from the party as a Trotskyite; readmitted subsequently, he was again thrown out in 1934 and died, almost certainly in one of Stalin's labor camps, in 1940.

The fifth presidium member was our old friend M. K. Muranov, appearing at the conference as a delegate from the Kharkov party organization. Kharkov was his native city; evidently he had returned there shortly after the takeover of *Pravda* in mid-March. Was that move of his own choosing, or was he, like Sverdlov, given an assignment in the provinces by a party leadership consisting of Stalin and Kamenev—a move designed to remove him from the center? In any case his return to Kharkov left the field clear for Kamenev and Stalin to assume editorial responsibility for *Pravda*. Muranov was a less potent figure than Sverdlov, but he was nevertheless well enough regarded to be chosen to report on the entire southern region: in the interests of time, the conference voted to hear reports, not from delegates representing individual towns or cities, but about some ten to twelve broad regions of Russia. Neither Stalin nor Kamenev won a place on the presidium, an indication that the policies with which they were identified were not overly popular in the party.

The conference next chose a five-man mandate commission, the names of the members of which have not been preserved. (When the commission's report was presented on April 16, it was delivered by G. I. Bokii, a member of the Petersburg Committee.) It then established a twelve-point agenda. In comparison with the preliminary agenda published by *Pravda* on April 13, the new one was far more comprehensive, including, for example, discussion of the Constituent Assembly as well as the revision of the party program demanded by Lenin in the "April Theses." Like the April 13 draft, however, the new agenda still placed the election of party bodies at the end of the proceedings, following discussion of all substantive points on the agenda, including the report on the national question.

Lenin versus Kamenev (April 24)

The first day's work of the conference was dominated by a lengthy report by Lenin on "The Current Situation." In forceful terms Lenin reiterated and developed his by now familiar stand on the war, the Provisional Government, and the Soviets of Workers' Deputies. An element of conflict was added to the proceedings by the submission of a draft resolution from the Moscow regional party conference, the gist of which was to add the idea of "control" by the soviets over the Provisional Government and local governmental agencies. The Moscow draft resolution was presented by A. S. Bubnov, a delegate from the textile center of Ivanovo-Voznesensk. It defined "control" in broad terms and concluded with a forecast of the transformation of control *over* the existing governmental agencies into control *of* them:

> This control in the development of the victorious proletarian-peasant revolution will inevitably be transformed into control over all elements of state-administrative existence and will be a stage on the road to seizure of the entire governmental power by the organized masses of the proletariat and the poor peasants.[28]

Lenin seemed somewhat disconcerted by the Moscow proposal, which marred the appearance of unity behind his policies which he was striving to project. In his speech, he simply took note of the Moscow draft, refraining from comment on the ground that he had not previously had a chance to study it. Following Lenin's report the delegates took a three-hour break.

When the conference resumed its work, the first speaker was a gaunt, emaciated figure, the Pole Felix Dzerzhinsky, only recently freed from a tsarist jail in Moscow and not yet fully recovered from the effects of his prolonged imprisonment. Characteristically, however, Dzerzhinsky ignored his physical weakness and plunged directly into party controversy. "From private conversations," he said, "it has become clear that many [of the delegates] are not in agreement in principle with the theses of the reporter [Lenin]." Implying that Lenin's views were based on a faulty perspective in the eyes of those "who together with us lived through the revolution," Dzerzhinsky proposed that the conference hear a second, alternative report on the current situation.[29] If Lenin had hoped the conference would accept his report without debate, he misjudged the temper of the delegates, for by a majority they adopted Dzerzhinsky's proposal.

As their spokesman the Moscow delegation chose Kamenev, who had emerged before the conference as the party's most consistent and thoroughgoing critic of Lenin's tactics.[30] Kamenev opened his co-report with a brief summary of the stages through which the party had passed since February, then launched into a detailed critique of Lenin's report. His most serious charge, already familiar from his April 7 article, "Our Differences," was that Lenin was trying to push the party along at too rapid a pace. At a time when the gentry still owned the feudal lands, Kamenev asked, how was it possible to speak of the bourgeois-democratic revolution against feudalism as being already completed? Similarly, Kamenev argued, the situation in the soviets differed from the analysis offered by Lenin. Everyone recognized the soviets as the center of the workers' movement, yet there too the revolution had not yet reached the stage where the workers' party could successfully advance its own socialist program: in the soviets the parties of the petty bourgeoisie were in control, and the Bolsheviks were forced to work with them in a temporary bloc. Even Lenin, argued Kamenev, admitted that, as long as the Soviet placed its trust in the Provisional Government, it was impossible to talk of overthrowing the latter.

Eventually, Kamenev asserted, conflict was inevitable between the government and the petty bourgeois-proletarian bloc in the Soviet over the basic questions of the war, food, and democratic freedoms. It was not the task of the party, however, to try to speed up this process; let the revolution ripen at its own pace, thereby avoiding the kind of embarrassing zigzags that had characterized party policy during the April Crisis. With deliberate irony Kamenev agreed with Lenin that the slogan "Down with the Provisional Government" was unwise, but he said he would have welcomed a warning to that effect a little sooner—a sly dig at Lenin for having encouraged the hotheads in the party.

Speaking on the basis of his experience as the party's ranking representative in the Executive Committee of the Soviet, Kamenev complained that Lenin's policies provided no clear guidance to party members in the existing situation, whereas "control," in the sense of the Moscow resolution, had proved itself effective. As an example, Kamenev cited an order issued on April 21 by General Lavr Kornilov, commandant of the Petrograd Military Region, to deploy two artillery batteries on Palace Square to defend the government against the demonstrators. The order had been nullified, however, by a statement by the Soviet to the effect that the troops of the Petrograd garrison were answerable only to it. This action, said Kamenev, was "more than fine words"; in blocking Kornilov's order, the Soviet "had exercised a fair degree of governmental power." In Moscow and the provinces, he continued, the soviets were the real leaders of the revolution to an even greater extent than in Petrograd.

"Control" of this kind, Kamenev argued, would serve to hasten the transfer of power to the soviets, through a series of well-defined steps, a policy he contrasted with Lenin's tactics of awaiting the moment when the party had achieved a dominant position in the soviets, meanwhile patiently explaining party policies to the masses.

As to the war, Kamenev accepted Lenin's general analysis, which he called a "splendidly developed maximum program," but again he asked that the general outline be reinforced by specific measures toward which the party could work. As an example he cited the demand for publication of the secret treaties with the Allies, not because he thought Milyukov would agree to make the texts public but because his refusal would serve to enlighten the masses as to the government's real war aims.

Having heard both reports, the delegates plunged enthusiastically into a discussion that showed almost as many points of view as there were speakers. Six delegates mounted the speaker's rostrum one after another without significantly contributing to the clarification of the issues; what did emerge unmistakably was that none of them wholeheartedly supported Lenin, while several—Bubnov, for example, and Bagdatiev—sharply criticized Lenin's report and indicated their preference for Kamenev's stand.

With another thirty delegates requesting the right to speak, the prospect loomed of the transformation of the conference into a free-for-all. What had begun as a modest proposal by the Moscow delegation for a procedural addition to Lenin's report now threatened to develop into a widespread revolt against his leadership. (Kamenev, it should be noted, had been careful to avoid any direct challenge to Lenin, and made a noticeable effort to identify himself with as much of Lenin's position as he could.)

A series of procedural moves, undertaken on the initiative of delegates whose names are unfortunately not recorded, shut off this incipient mutiny and brought the conference back to a more disciplined mode of procedure. First, it was decided to close off the list of would-be speakers; then the delegates voted to conclude the debate by allowing two speakers to defend each of the principal positions which had emerged, Lenin's and Kamenev's.

During the discussion of these measures, Kamenev made the conciliatory gesture of reducing his disagreements with Lenin to a single issue, "control." The effect of this move was to bury the far more serious differences of principle which separated him from Lenin on the nature of the revolution and its future prospects, but it opened the way for a reconciliation—on Lenin's terms.

Stalin Comes Out in Support of Lenin

After a ten-minute break, the delegates reassembled to listen to the first champion of Lenin's cause. This turned out to be Stalin, perhaps to the surprise of some provincial delegates who had not kept up with his recent articles in *Pravda* but who remembered how far from Lenin's position he had been before Lenin's return.

Taking advantage of Kamenev's reduction of the disagreement to the single issue of "control," Stalin heaped heavy sarcasm on the whole proposal, arguing that the crisis over the Milyukov note showed that the Provisional Government was now in control of policy, while "the Soviet is following the government."

> The government attacks the Soviet. The Soviet retreats. To suggest after this that the Soviet controls the government is just idle talk. That is why I propose that Bubnov's amendment on control be not accepted.[31]

Stalin's speech was, of course, grossly unfair; it completely ignored Kamenev's serious criticisms of Lenin's position on the revolution, just as it misrepresented Kamenev's and Bubnov's patient explanation of how "control," as they envisaged it, would serve the needs of the party and advance the workers' cause. Stalin's ridicule of "control" was also premature: within a few weeks, Milyukov and his colleague Guchkov resigned, thereby providing a striking demonstration of exactly the kind of "control" which Kamenev and the Moscow delegation had in mind. In the long run it was the Provisional Government that had to retreat, not the Soviet. Nevertheless, Stalin's speech was undeniably effective, not merely because of its bluntness but also because in making it Stalin was serving public notice of his switch from the position he had shared with Kamenev to unqualified support of Lenin.

In contrast to Stalin's short speech, the statement by Zinoviev, who served as Lenin's second advocate, was wordy, involved, and unconvincing.[32] Clearly Stalin had come through with a solid hit for Lenin in a tight situation. And just as clearly he had not done so merely of his own volition: limited to two speakers, Lenin had deliberately chosen Stalin as his lead-off man in the concluding debate.

In the records of the Seventh Conference Stalin's statement of

April 24 stands out for its crudity: it is a startling prefiguration of the style, tone, and intellectual aridity of political discourse in the Stalin era. Whereas other delegates, no matter how impassioned their ideas, always clothed them in the texture of a closely reasoned intellectual analysis, Stalin reduced complex questions to a simple antithesis between his own (i.e., Lenin's) position, which he claimed made obvious good sense, and that of his opponents, which he derided as patent nonsense. Only fools, he implied, could support the position advocated by Kamenev, conveniently forgetting that only a few weeks earlier he himself had done just that.

The most important point about the statement, however, was not so much what it revealed about Stalin as what it implied about the relationship between him and Lenin. Lenin's obvious approval of the crudeness of Stalin's method indicates the concern he felt at the direction in which the conference appeared to be moving: here, at the opening session, his first major report was encountering not approbation but questioning and even opposition. Acting on Dzerzhinsky's suggestion, the conference had challenged Lenin by calling for a co-report on the current situation and had compounded the affront by selecting for that purpose Kamenev, the man who more than any other had voiced the hesitations, questions, and outright skepticism felt by many party members with regard to Lenin's policies. The debate on the two reports, before it was shut off by a procedural motion, showed all too clearly that the delegates were in no mood to accept Lenin's analysis docilely. In his report Kamenev had scored some damaging points. What Lenin needed now was not further intellectual hair-splitting but a sharp, brutal assault on the Kamenev position, and this Stalin effectively supplied.

Trotsky, alert as always to indications of Stalin's mental processes, contrasts Stalin's April 24 statement with Lenin's habitual method of analysis:

> Lenin's conception of the revolution was based on the interrelationship of classes, not on some isolated diplomatic note, which differed little from other acts of the government. But Stalin was not interested in general ideas. All he needed was some obvious pretext in order that he might make his shift with the least damage to his vanity. He was "doling out" his retreat.[33]

But Trotsky, as frequently happened when he was analyzing Stalin's tactical skills, missed the essential point. Stalin was not simply rising to make a statement as one among the many delegates who wished to join the debate; he was speaking on behalf of Lenin, as Lenin's number one chosen spokesman, ahead even of Zinoviev.

Trotsky was right in describing Stalin's statement as a characteristic sample of his mental processes, but he failed to recognize that the statement was made with Lenin's approval and was designed to achieve an important tactical goal: reassertion of Lenin's control over the party. Trotsky's handling of the episode thus casts a revealing light on *his* mental processes: acute in his judgment of Stalin, he was blind to the evidence of Lenin's use of Stalin to quell incipient opposition.

The spokesmen for the Kamenev-Moscow position were Viktor P. Nogin and Aleksei I. Rykov, an old associate of Lenin (he had been one of the *Iskra* agents in the period 1901–3), who was attending the conference as a representative of the Moscow organization. Nogin's report went over familiar ground, but Rykov introduced some new ideas.[34] Like Kamenev, Rykov questioned Lenin's view that the bourgeois-democratic revolution in Russia was already completed, adding the criticism that Russia, as "the most petty bourgeois country in Europe," could not be considered ripe for a proletarian revolution. That, said Rykov, must come from the advanced capitalist nations of the West. In Rykov's view, the party must realistically recognize the limitations it faced and adapt its program to existing conditions. For Rykov this included the continuation of the bloc between the party and other elements of "revolutionary democracy."

The conference concluded its first full day's work with an evening session at which the two co-reporters, Lenin and Kamenev, delivered their concluding statements. Kamenev's summing up amounted to a clarification and restatement of his principal points, especially the concept of "control."[35] Again he called for the addition of concrete directives to Lenin's general propositions, so that party workers would have clear guidance in their work; again he criticized the Central Committee—that is, Lenin—for its misleading slogans and sudden changes of front during the April Crisis. But on the essential questions of the war, the Provisional Government, and the international socialist revolution he took a stand not significantly different from that of Lenin.

Responding to Kamenev, Lenin frankly admitted that there had been a regrettable lack of coordination between the Central Committee and the "adventurists" of the Petersburg Committee during the April Crisis, and he added darkly,

> In the future we will take all measures so that we have the kind of organization in which there are no *Pekisty* [members of the Petersburg Committee] who do not listen to the Central Committee.[36]

Like Kamenev, Lenin reduced their differences to the single issue of "control," but he denied that this question was isolating the party from its former allies in the soviets: the real reason for the party's present isolation, Lenin said—and this was, for him, a significant concession—was that the peasants still supported the war (Lenin used the term "chauvinist" to define their position). Under these conditions, he frankly admitted, a worker-peasant alliance was out of the question. Logically, in a country of predominantly peasant population such as Russia, this should have led Lenin to see merit in Rykov's view that a Marxist-style socialist revolution could not succeed in Russia. Instead, Lenin simply denied the relevance of Rykov's objection:

> Comrade Rykov says that socialism must come from other countries, with a more developed industry. But this is not so. Nobody can say who will begin it and who will end it. That is not Marxism: it is a parody of Marxism.

This was as close as Lenin ever came to defending his view that Russia could make a socialist revolution notwithstanding the comparative weakness of her working class. A few months later, in July, we will find Stalin making essentially the same point in addressing a party congress, and defending it as an example of "creative Marxism."

Following Lenin's summing up, the conference elected a commission to draft the resolution on the current situation. The voting clearly reflected the mood of the delegates: Lenin and his supporters (Zinoviev and Stalin) were outnumbered by Kamenev, Bubnov, Milyutin, and Nogin. The remaining two members of the commission, I. G. Pravdin, representing a Urals district party organization, and I. A. Teodorovich, from Petrograd, had not joined the discussion but could hardly be classified as staunch Leninists.

Stalin Reports on Relations between the Soviet and the Provisional Government

While the April Conference was in session, *Pravda* on April 25 published a signed article by Stalin entitled, "The Conference in the Mariinsky Palace."[37] Although it was not included in the protocols of the April Conference, it seems that the article was first delivered as a report to the conference delegates, probably on the opening day, April 24. One delegate, S. I. Gopner, later recalled,

> During the discussion of Lenin's report on the current situation we were informed that a comrade would at once provide information about yesterday evening's session of the Provisional Government jointly with representatives of the Petrograd Soviet in the Mariinsky Palace.[38]

Gopner, who claimed to have heard Stalin speak, characterized his report as "clear and accurate" and even used the term "eloquent" to describe his account of the meeting. The published article is hardly eloquent, but it is undeniably effective in its crisp dissection of the motives of the Provisional Government spokesmen, Milyukov, Guchkov, and Shingaryov.

Surprisingly, in view of the brutal verbal assault on Kamenev, which Stalin delivered later on the twenty-fourth, his article concluded with an account of how Kamenev, as Bolshevik representative on the Soviet Executive Committee, had charged that the Provisional Government, because of its determination to fight the war to a victorious finish, was incapable of solving the nation's problems. The solution, Kamenev asserted,

> therefore lay in the transfer of power to another class, a class capable of leading the country out of the impasse . . . (Leaders in the original)

Perhaps inadvertently, Stalin's article provides valuable evidence of a noteworthy shift that had taken place in Kamenev's thinking on the war and the Provisional Government, one that brought him much closer to Lenin's position.

Was it Stalin's report on the meeting in the Mariinsky Palace which suggested to Lenin the idea of using Stalin as one of his two spokesmen in the debate during the second half of the April 24 session? It seems likely. Whether Lenin heard Stalin's report himself or simply learned of it from other delegates to the conference, he must have recognized that it provided a perfect basis for attacking Kamenev on the issue of "control." Choosing Stalin as his lead-off defender involved a certain element of risk: this would be the younger man's first appearance at a major party conference in defense of Lenin, and he might well fail. But the gains would be proportionately great if he succeeded: as late as April 6 Stalin had sided with Kamenev against Lenin; if he now publicly attacked Kamenev and supported Lenin, the switch might well help a number of hesitant party delegates to make up their minds in favor of Lenin.

Organizational Work (April 25–28)

After his uncharacteristic burst of activity on the opening day of the conference, Stalin sank back into the mass of delegates who listened in silence to the party leaders and who registered their views only through their votes. But Stalin was by no means idle during the next three days. He had been named a member of the commission to draft the resolution on the current situation, and even though Lenin supplied the driving force and the principal ideas, the other committee members were expected to take an active part in the work, since it was their collective responsibility to see that the finished resolution was framed with due regard to all relevant aspects of the problems facing the party in "the current situation."

No text of Stalin's April 24 report has survived, nor do we have any memoirs that might provide information on what contributions he made, if any, to the discussion of the report on the current situation. In any case, he was more concerned with absorbing Lenin's point of view and helping defend it than with expressing original ideas of his own. Far more challenging was the second task assigned to Stalin during these days: he had been chosen by Lenin to present the report on the national question, and he needed all the concentration he could muster to discharge that task worthily.

While Stalin was engaged in his editorial labors, the conference was proceeding with its organizational business. According to Lenin's original plan, most of the responsibility for this work was to be discharged by Zinoviev. It was Zinoviev who presided over all sessions of the conference for which the protocols indicate a chairman, and he may well have chaired some or all of the other sessions. Increasingly as the conference proceeded, however, the role of Lenin's troubleshooter and master organizer was taken over by the efficient and hardworking delegate from Yekaterinburg, Yakov Sverdlov. From the very outset of the conference, where, as we have seen, his stature in the eyes of the delegates was registered by election to the conference presidium, Sverdlov showed that he intended to take an active part in the proceedings. Even before the formal opening of the conference, he joined with Nogin in sponsoring an addition to the agenda, a report on the Social Democratic "peace conference" being organized in Stockholm.

It was Nogin who delivered the report on the Stockholm gathering, but the resourceful Sverdlov had his turn later in the April 25 session when he opened the series of reports from local areas. For his sphere of responsibility Sverdlov covered the Ural region, one of Russia's principal industrial areas and a Bolshevik stronghold only a little less powerful than Petrograd and Moscow.

At the fifth session of the conference, on the morning of April 26, Sverdlov made a key organizational move by proposing that the delegates split up into five sections in order to prepare the final reports. When Lenin rose to support the proposal, its adoption was assured. Under Sverdlov's watchful guidance the delegates settled down to the hard work of drafting reports, dutifully sacrificing the luxury of uninhibited debate which had marked the opening session.

By the seventh session on the morning of April 27, Sverdlov had established himself so firmly in Lenin's estimation that he was given the responsible task of reading the draft "Resolution on the War" paragraph by paragraph, and when the delegates assembled for the next to last time on the evening of April 29, it was Sverdlov who gave them instructions on how to turn in their secret ballots in the voting for the Central Committee.

The Election to the Central Committee (Evening, April 29)

Both the preliminary agenda of April 13 and the final agenda adopted at the outset of the April Conference placed the election of new party bodies at the very end of the proceedings, following debate on all the principal substantive issues. Instead, for reasons about which the protocols are silent, the election of a new central committee—the first in five years—was moved up to the first half of the ninth session, on the evening of April 29, ahead of the reports and discussion on the national question.

The mood of the delegates was tense: even from the laconic summary provided by the protocols, it is clear that they realized how much depended on the choices they would make. In the Bolshevik party, with its emphasis on central control and guidance, choosing able leaders was fully as important as formulating correct tactics.

By a number of procedural votes the delegates showed that they were in no mood to accept direction from Lenin or anyone else. At the outset Lenin proposed that the size of the Central Committee be increased from nine to thirteen members, including the core of the old CC dating back to 1912 but with new recruits to share the heavy burdens that the revolution was likely to place on the leadership of the party. Zinoviev seconded Lenin's proposal, arguing that experience showed that a nine-member CC was too small. Unimpressed, the delegates rejected Lenin's proposal, obviously clinging to the established forms of the party.[39]

A proposal by Zinoviev that the election be preceded by a discussion of candidates fared a little better: it squeaked by with a bare plurality, 35 to 33, with at least one-third of the delegates not voting. Although Lenin had prudently refrained from personally sponsoring this motion, he showed that he supported it by taking an active part in the discussion of candidates.

Probably the single most valuable document dug out of the long-sealed party archives and published for the first time as part of the 1958 edition of the Seventh Conference protocols was the record of the discussion of candidates for the Central Committee. It is a vital source of information on Lenin's tactics, as well as an indispensable clue to Stalin's emergence as one of the party's top leaders.

Even while they were relaxing their controls, however, the custodians of the party archives stopped short of full disclosure of the record. The protocols of the Central Committee for the period from early April through late July 1917 still remain unpublished, even though they were announced for publication in that same permissive year, 1958. A Soviet scholarly article published in 1977 purports to provide a summary of the missing protocols, but it is far from adequate as a substitute for the original texts.[40]

Twenty-six names were proposed for the Central Committee, ranging from the obvious and inevitable one of Lenin to relatively obscure figures of only local significance. Of the twenty-six, seven were not discussed at all—Lenin and Zinoviev because they were too well known, the others because no one felt the need to discuss their candidacies. Of those formally presented to the delegates, another eight attracted neither supporters nor opponents; these included Lenin's wife, Krupskaya, and his mistress, Inessa Armand.

Part of the drama of the election lay in the latent conflict between the two teams that had led the party before Lenin's return. Molotov, Shlyapnikov, and Zalutsky, all candidates for the CC, had provided leadership along Leninist lines in the initial period of the revolution; Stalin and Kamenev (Muranov was not a candidate) had veered sharply to the right.

Despite their fealty to Leninist principles, not a single member of the original team was elected to the CC, whereas both Kamenev and Stalin were, and by convincing votes: Stalin, with 97 votes, appeared to be the third most popular figure in the party, after Lenin (with 104 votes) and Zinoviev (with 101), while Kamenev lagged only a few votes behind, with 95 votes to his credit. There followed, at a considerable distance, Milyutin, with 82 votes, Nogin with 76, Sverdlov with 71, then (another sharp drop) Smilga with 53 and Fedorov with 48.[41]

The record of the discussion helps to explain these striking results. First, a fact of cardinal significance, Lenin himself spoke on behalf of only two candidates: not, as a naive delegate might have expected, Krupskaya and Inessa—their loyalty and services were assured Lenin in any case, and he had no need for them on the CC—but the two culprits of the second phase, Stalin and Kamenev.

Consideration of Kamenev's candidacy was the third item on the agenda, following those of Lenin and Zinoviev, both *hors concours*. A brash delegate named Soloviev (there were two with that surname at the conference, and the protocols do not make it clear which one spoke on this occasion) led off with a blistering attack on Kamenev's record, first, because of his behavior in the trial of the Bolshevik deputies to the Duma in 1915, and second, because of his March 1917 writings in *Pravda*, especially those in which he voiced his support of a defensist position on the war.[42]

The anti-Kamenev feeling among the delegates was evidently widespread, for in 1926–27 a number of party members who had been delegates to the Seventh Conference joined in a general attack on him (undoubtedly with Stalin's support), which took the form of recollections of how, at preliminary meetings of delegates before the formal session on the evening of April 29, Kamenev's candidacy had been rejected, both because of the 1915 trial and because of the telegram of congratulations to Michael Romanov, which he had co-signed in March 1917.[43] There was thus a groundswell of anti-Kamenev sentiment among the delegates as the voting for the CC got under way, and Soloviev was no doubt confident of speaking for a popular cause when he attacked Kamenev.

Lenin's method of meeting this challenge must have disconcerted many delegates.[44] He began by simply ignoring Soloviev's second point,

> in the first place, because I don't remember and, in the second place because after all many comrades wavered in the first phases of the revolution.

As for Kamenev's behavior at the 1915 trial, Lenin conceded that the point was a serious one, but asserted that it no longer counted against him:

> At the time the behavior of comrade Kamenev was condemned by the CC. In the central party organ abroad it was stated that the behavior of the deputies in the trial, and of Kamenev in particular, was inadmissible. With this the incident was closed. Some comrades felt that these measures were insufficiently harsh, but in my opinion they were sufficient. Therefore it is impossible to object to his candidacy on the grounds of a lapse for which comrade Kamenev has already been brought to trial and adequately evaluated and condemned. The incident is closed. There is no evidence of wavering.

Having thus drawn a veil over the past, and completely ignoring Soloviev's reference to Kamenev's recent misdeeds as one of the editors of *Pravda*, Lenin turned to the positive side of Kamenev's candidacy. "The activity of comrade Kamenev," he said,

> has extended over ten years and it is very valuable. He is a valuable worker, both in the Executive Committee [of the Soviet] and on the edito-

rial board [of *Pravda*]. There is no point in dwelling on the incident further. The fact that we disagree with comrade Kamenev yields only positive results. The presence of comrade Kamenev is very valuable. After convincing him, with difficulty, you will find that at the same time you have overcome those difficulties which arise among the masses.

Seeing which way the wind was blowing, and anxious to play down his differences with Lenin, Nogin jumped to Kamenev's defense, twisting the facts a little in the process. The Moscow *oblast* bureau of the party, Nogin said, had sharply censured Kamenev for his behavior at the Duma deputies' trial, but then, after impassioned debate, had selected him to report on the war (evidently at its conference on April 19–21). A footnote in the 1958 edition of the conference protocols points out that Nogin was in error: it was at the all-Russian conference on March 27–April 2, not at that of the Moscow *oblast* committee, that Kamenev delivered the report on the war.[45] More to the point, it was Kamenev who had been selected by the Moscow delegation to present their position in the debate on the current situation. In accordance with that decision, Nogin expressed "full confidence" in Kamenev.

By his endorsement of Lenin's favorable judgment on Kamenev, Nogin strengthened his own position: in the balloting he ranked second in the group just below the Big Four, despite an adverse verdict by Rosalia S. Zemliachka (Samoilova), one of the power brokers in the Moscow city committee. By contrast, the rash and impetuous Soloviev, who dared to speak against Kamenev before Lenin's position was disclosed, remains a cipher in party history; it is not even known which of the two Solovievs present at the conference opposed Kamenev.

Following the discussion of Kamenev's candidacy the delegates turned to that of I. A. Teodorovich, a member of the Petersburg Committee and a veteran of political struggle, including long years of imprisonment. Zinoviev spoke on his behalf, recalling his services in the socialist movement and praising him as "one of the model Marxists."[46] In contrast, F. I. Goloshchekin ("Filipp"), another member of the Petersburg Committee, spoke against Teodorovich with a complete lack of regard for any past services to the party. "Previously," said Goloshchekin,

he [Teodorovich] was a prominent figure, but ten years of hard labor and being cut off from the party life have left a distinct mark, and the man is not capable of work.[47]

For good measure, Goloshchekin added that newspaper reports from Krasnoyarsk indicated that Teodorovich had appeared there as a right-wing speaker. Not surprisingly, he failed to attract the necessary votes for inclusion in the CC, an indication that Zinoviev's recommendations carried no special weight with the delegates.

Overall, Zinoviev spoke on behalf of four candidates—Teodorovich, Nogin, Milyutin, and N. P. Glebov (Avilov), another Petersburg Committee member. Of these only two, Nogin and Milyutin, were elected to the CC, and their active participation in the conference would probably have ensured their election even without Zinoviev's support. Clearly the power wielded by Lenin had not rubbed off onto Zinoviev.

The fifth candidate presented to the delegates for consideration was Stalin, and only one speaker took the floor, Lenin. But Lenin's brief statement said it all, in words of authority which none of the delegates ventured to challenge. "Comrade Koba," Lenin said,

> has been known to us for a great many years. We saw him in Cracow, where our bureau was located. His activity in the Caucasus was important. A good worker in all responsible jobs.[48]

So much for Stalin's spotty record as a prominent party figure and as editor of *Pravda* in March! Clearly, Lenin had made up his mind to give Stalin his unqualified support and to overlook entirely all the false starts and faulty perceptions of which Stalin had been guilty over the years. It must have been a great moment for Stalin, a personal triumph equaled only by the results of the balloting, which showed Stalin with the third highest total—97, just behind Lenin with 104 and Zinoviev with 101, and a few votes ahead of Kamenev.

Writing in ignorance of the discussion of candidates first published in 1958, a number of authors have argued that the large number of votes cast for Stalin is proof that he had now achieved a strong position in the party on the basis of his record. Deutscher, for example, writes,

> This was the first time Stalin was confirmed in leadership by a large vote in a direct, open election. To the cadres of the party he was now a familiar figure, although to outsiders he was still a name only.[49]

Ulam concurs:

> His current stature in the Party was attested to by the fact that in the secret balloting he received ninety-seven of the hundred and nine delegate votes. . . . The barely known Caucasian of 1912, the man who five weeks

earlier it had been proposed should be kept out of the Party councils because of his bad temper and manners, was now freely acknowledged by his fellow Bolsheviks to be the leading "practitioner" in the Party.[50]

These opinions, however, and others like them, cannot be sustained in the light of the evidence provided by the discussion of candidates. The 1958 document shows unmistakably that it was Lenin's personal intercession on behalf of Stalin, far more than any personal merits of the latter, which earned him his high vote. After the sharp reproof implied to critics like Soloviev in Lenin's statement on behalf of Kamenev, none of the delegates cared to remind their comrades of the faulty guidance provided by Stalin before Lenin's return. If Lenin was willing to forget the mistakes of the recent past, the delegates were content to follow his lead. The high votes cast for Stalin and Kamenev reflect Lenin's popularity and power in the party, not theirs. Robert Payne is close to the mark when he writes,

> As usual, the Central Committee had been hand-picked by Lenin and the voting was a mere formality.[51]

If Trotsky is to be believed, Lenin later recalled that Sverdlov's name was not included in the original list of members to be elected to the CC.[52] "Fortunately," said Lenin, as reported by Trotsky, "we were corrected from below." In other words, the delegates voted for Sverdlov, even though he had not been included in the master list drawn up by Lenin and his closest aides.

Trotsky suggests that Lenin's failure to include Sverdlov was the result of Stalin's influence over Lenin (which Trotsky is otherwise inclined to minimize). Recalling the incidents at the *Pravda* office in 1912 and the period of exile in Siberia when relations between Stalin and Sverdlov had further worsened, Trotsky writes,

> He [Stalin] apparently tried to take his revenge at the conference and in one way or another, we can only guess how, managed to win Lenin's support, but his attempt did not succeed. If in 1912 Lenin met with the resistance of the delegates when he tried to get Stalin onto the Central Committee, he now met with no less resistance when he tried to keep Sverdlov off.[53]

Trotsky overstates his case: the published discussion of candidates indicates that Lenin did not actively oppose Sverdlov's candidacy. Only one speaker took part in the discussion of Sverdlov's candidacy, V. V. Kuibyshev from the Samara party organization, who said,

> Comrade Sverdlov is an old party worker, an irreplaceable organizer. His presence on the CC is essential.[54]

This concise but essentially accurate statement, representing as it undoubtedly did the viewpoint of a sizable group of delegates, was sufficient to earn Sverdlov inclusion on the CC, though with significantly fewer votes than the Big Four. Trotsky's recollection, based as it necessarily was on hearsay and later comments by Lenin, since he himself was not a delegate to the April Conference, implies the existence of a master list of candidates for the CC which Lenin drew up and which was circulated to the delegates before the voting began. It was this list, presumably, from which Sverdlov's name was omitted. Trotsky's anecdote also strongly implies that Stalin had a hand in helping Lenin prepare the list; in other words, that he was now effectively functioning as a member of the party's top leadership group. Confirmation of that deduction is provided by evidence from a variety of sources. First, however, it will be useful to consider Stalin's report on the national question.

Stalin and Makharadze Report on the National Question

Contrary to the procedure announced in the advance agenda, the conference took up its discussion of the national question *after* the elections to the Central Committee—but *before* the results of the balloting were announced.

What were the reasons for this procedural change? First, as we have seen, Lenin unmistakably wanted Stalin as one of the inner core of party leadership and may have felt it wise to take no chance of having an adverse reaction among the delegates as a result of the position Stalin would take on the hotly debated national question. Better to ensure his election first, Lenin may have reasoned, and then take his chances on the national question debate. The procedural change also had the advantage, from Lenin's point of view, that it gave him the opportunity to indicate his unconditional support of Stalin before the latter spoke on the national question. In this way the delegates would be aware that Stalin was speaking not merely in his own name but as the spokesman for Lenin's views.

The question may be asked, why did Lenin not deliver the report on the national question himself? It was an open secret at the conference that it was he who wrote the resolution on the subject which was finally adopted. Lenin had excellent reasons, however, for choosing Stalin as his spokesman on this particular question. Positions that Lenin, as a Russian, could hardly defend convincingly against the onslaughts of non-Russian party stalwarts such as the Pole Dzerzhinsky, the Ukrainian Pyatakov, or the Georgian Makharadze, would be less vulnerable when put forward by a non-Russian—for example, the "marvelous Georgian," Dzhugashvili-Stalin. Once again, as in 1913, Lenin was using Stalin to defend a position that was hotly disputed by some of the most articulate and outspoken representatives in the party of those same minority groups.

Just before the Seventh Conference opened, Lenin's attention had been forcibly drawn to the national question by an appeal from the Finnish Social Democrats for recognition of their support of the Finnish national independence movement. Early in the conference Lenin had been given a reminder that the question was certain to give rise to controversy and that his own position was going to come under attack. At the third session, on April 25, in the debate about the socialist "peace conference" in Stockholm, Dzerzhinsky raised the question of Poland's independence, which had been included as one of the party's demands in the draft resolution. "It is not appropriate for us," Dzerzhinsky argued,

> to raise the national question, for that delays the coming of the social[ist] revolution. I therefore propose that the question about Poland's independence be dropped from the resolution.[55]

Dzerzhinsky had a further opportunity to press his views as a member of the three-man commission that was set up to draft the conference resolution on the Stockholm conference, but he was evidently outvoted by the other two members of the commission, Lenin and Kamenev, for the resolution as finally adopted retained the paragraph on Polish independence.[56] The incident must have served as a reminder to Lenin of the explosive nature of the national question and the danger it represented of a challenge to his views in the debates of the full conference.

A further indication of the turbulent mood of the delegates with regard to the national question was provided by the conference's decision on procedure for discussion of the subject. According to S. I. Petrikovsky, a delegate from Petrograd whose notes constitute a valuable supplement to the official conference protocols, the delegates voted to hear thirty-minute reports from two rapporteurs on the national question and to follow the reports with ten-minute statements by two delegates for each report, for and against.[57]

Stalin's report, delivered at a late hour (midnight was already past when he took the floor), was comparatively brief.[58] Even so, he devoted approximately one-third of his time to a preamble in which he established "certain premises," in the process correcting some of the cruder mistakes he had perpetrated in his *Pravda* articles of March. There he had identified the landed aristocracy as the class mainly responsible for national oppression and had singled out Switzerland, the United States, and Great Britain as democratic states in which national oppression did not exist. Now he prudently restricted his examples of democracy to Great Britain, "where there is a certain degree of democracy and political freedom," and Switzerland, which "approximates to a democratic society," adding, for the benefit of Marxist scholars, "By democracy we mean that definite classes are in control of the state power."

This elementary Marxist premise provided an easy transition to an updating of Stalin's analysis of the class origin of national oppression. In his March articles he had identified the landed aristocracy as the class principally responsible for national oppression. Reluctantly abandoning an idea to which he was evidently attached (it was, after all, original with him), Stalin now added,

> It may be said from this point of view that the closer the old landed aristocracy is to power, as was the case in old Tsarist Russia, the more severe is the oppression and the more monstrous are its forms.

Having thus made an attempt to bring his ideas into line with Marxist principles, Stalin proceeded to the reading of the resolution, as drafted by Lenin. Its most controversial provision was that

> every nation forming a part of Russia must be recognized as having the right to secede freely and to form an independent state.[59]

As an example of the way that denial of this right leads to "a direct continuation of the policy of Tsarism," Stalin cited the conflict "which has recently broken out between Finland and the Russian Provisional Government." The resolution was careful to distinguish, however, between "the *right* of nations to free secession," and "the *expedience* of the secession of one nation or another at a given moment" (italics added). This was a question for the proletariat (i.e., the Bolshevik party, claiming to represent the proletariat) to decide "quite independently in each individual case, from the standpoint of the interests of overall social development and of the proletarian class struggle for socialism."

For nations not choosing the right of secession, the resolution continued, "the party demands broad regional autonomy," but it "resolutely rejects so-called 'national cultural autonomy.'" Furthermore, it

> demands inclusion in the constitution of a fundamental law prohibiting any special privileges whatsoever for one nation and any infringement whatsoever on the rights of a national minority.

But the whole carefully elaborated structure of ideas was fatally undermined by the final paragraph of the resolution, which ruled out any recognition of national minority rights in the party:

> The interests of the working class demand the merging of the workers of all nationalities of Russia into unified proletarian organizations—political, trade union, co-operative-educational, etc. Only such an amalgamation of the workers of different nationalities into single organizations enables the proletariat to wage a victorious struggle against international capital and bourgeois nationalism.

The remainder of Stalin's report consisted of a gloss on these propositions, presented with a fair show of conviction. Occasionally the strain of defending a position in which he did not really believe proved too much for him, however, and he let his real feelings show through. For example, in defending the Leninist principle of the right of minority nationalities to secession Stalin admitted,

> I personally would be opposed to the secession of Transcaucasia, bearing in mind the common development in Transcaucasia and Russia, certain conditions of the struggle of the proletariat, and so forth. But if, nevertheless, the peoples of Transcaucasia were to demand secession, they would, of course, secede without encountering opposition from us.

Stalin concluded his report by "reduc[ing] our views on the national question to the following propositions:"

(a) recognition of the right of nations to secession;
(b) regional autonomy for nations remaining within the given state;
(c) special legislation guaranteeing freedom of development for national minorities;
(d) a single indivisible proletarian collective, a single party, for the proletarians of all nationalities of the given state.[60]

In introducing his co-report Pyatakov announced that the nine-man section for preparation of the conference report on the national question had voted 7 to 2 in favor of a position that, in Pyatakov's words, "was taken by the revolutionary part of German Social-Democracy, Polish Social-Democracy, and others"—a position differing from that of Lenin, which Stalin had just presented. But Pyatakov recognized that there was general agreement at the conference on many aspects of the national question, and he therefore devoted his report to consideration of those aspects on which disagreement existed.[61]

Gently chiding Stalin, with his emphasis on the landed aristocracy as the chief source of national oppression, for dwelling on past history, Pyatakov drew the delegates' attention to existing world economic conditions. These conditions, he said, made national independence an "obsolete" principle, and the demand for national independence was "taken from another historical epoch, it is reactionary, for it tries to turn history backwards."

In contemporary society, Pyatakov asserted, the split between the bourgeoisie and the proletariat had deepened to such an extent that the "two camps" had virtually nothing in common. If the Polish bourgeoisie, representing a majority of the Polish population, wished to establish an independent Poland, while the Polish proletariat wished to have Poland included "in a general socialist organization," the Bolshevik party might well "carry on a struggle against the Polish bourgeoisie." Stalin's formulation of the question, Pyatakov charged, was "purely metaphysical."

Another distinguishing characteristic of the present epoch, according to Pyatakov, was the virtual merger between the economic system of capitalism and the state form of bourgeois democracy. Whereas the slogan of an independent state was a progressive demand in an earlier era, "now it is a reactionary factor, directed against socialism." The movements for national independence at present, Pyatakov argued, led as they are by the nationalistic bourgeoisie and directed "against the socialist revolution . . . have become obviously reactionary."

Pyatakov said he had nothing against the struggle to end the oppression of national minorities, but it was essential to keep that question separate from the struggle for a socialism "without national boundaries." Pyatakov noted Stalin's unguarded admission that he was not in favor of Transcaucasian independence but tactfully refrained from taking advantage of it.

Summing up, Pyatakov called for a concrete definition by the party of its goals on the national question, "not limiting itself to formulating the abstract 'right of self-determination,' a formulation which can play into the hands of petty bourgeois reaction."

In accordance with the ideas developed in his report, the resolution presented by Pyatakov asserted that

> the formation of national states under the conditions of the imperialist epoch, i.e., the epoch of the eve of the socialist revolution, is a harmful and reactionary utopia,

and it frankly proclaimed that

> the international party of the proletariat, in the event that there is a majority on its side on an all-European scale, cannot take into account the will of the majority of a nation if that will is in conflict with the will of its proletarian minority.[62]

The resolution accordingly affirmed that

> "the right of nations to self-determination" is merely a phrase lacking any specific content,

and it proposed corresponding changes in the party program. Echoing Lenin's draft resolution, the one presented by Pyatakov closed by demanding the "merger [*slianie*] of the workers of all nationalities of Russia into common proletarian organizations," on the grounds that such a merger

> will make it possible for the proletariat to wage a successful struggle against international capital and bourgeois nationalism.

Lenin himself spoke as the first defender of the resolution that Stalin had presented. The stenographic report of this speech is incomplete, but enough has been preserved to indicate the general trend of his argument. In attempting to respond to Pyatakov's demand for concrete guidance, Lenin virtually admitted that his national policy was a matter of tactics that varied from place to place.

> In Russia we must stress the right of separation for the subject nations, while in Poland we must stress the right of such nations to unite. The right to unite implies the right to separate. We Russians must emphasize the right to separate, while the Poles must emphasize the right to unite.[63]

Lenin spent most of his allotted ten minutes berating the Poles, especially Dzerzhinsky, for confusing the question of Poland's freedom with that of the socialist revolution. But no Pole, he charged, gave the party any guidance when it came to Finland, the Ukraine, and other national minority regions. Was the party to support national oppression in these regions? To do so, Lenin asserted, amounted to "chauvinism." Only the example of the revolution could provide effective propaganda for the oppressed masses.

Dzerzhinsky was not convinced by Lenin's arguments. Appearing as the first speaker in support of Pyatakov's draft resolution, he accused Lenin of sharing the position of the Polish, Ukrainian, and other national chauvinists.[64] As far back as the Second Party Congress in 1903, Dzerzhinsky reminded his listeners, the Polish Social Democrats had refused to join the party because of its stand on Polish independence. He castigated Lenin's two-track tactics:

> What kind of a social-democratic point of view is that? Our positions must be identical. After all, are not the interests of the Polish and Russian proletariat the same?

As to the "will of the nation," Dzerzhinsky asserted, it can manifest itself only under the conditions of socialism. For Poland the right of independence from Russia would mean, in effect, the right of the bourgeoisie to ensure its domination. The 1905 Revolution, in Dzerzhinsky's view, had ended any nationalist spirit among the Polish workers. As to Lenin's taunt that the Polish Social Democrats had no answer for the party on the national question, Dzerzhinsky categorically denied the charge:

> Our concrete answer: national oppression can be destroyed only under the complete democratization of the government, the struggle for socialism, whereas separatist efforts are efforts for the struggle against socialism. We concretely oppose the right of nations to self-determination.

As to Finland,

> The fact that Finland is a separate state is by no means evidence in favor of the separation of Finland from Russia. If the Provisional Government wants to take over those rights which the Tsar previously exercised in regard to Finland, our task, the only method for us, is to struggle against this Provisional Government, for the democratization of Russia, for the destruction of this shameful government which wants to coerce the will of the Finnish people.

Following Dzerzhinsky, Zinoviev spoke in support of Lenin's draft resolution.[65] He charged that, whatever his purposes, objectively Pyatakov was taking a nationalist stance. Extension of the socialist revolution to the colonial nations, Zinoviev maintained, demanded that the party adopt a consistently anti-imperialist position. As to Finland, let the Finnish people themselves decide their fate.

The final speaker was the Georgian Filipp Makharadze, representing the Tiflis party organization and speaking in support of Pyatakov's draft.[66] Makharadze made the significant, and for Lenin ominous, point that

> those comrades who are taking part in the conference, who are for the first time discussing the national question in common and who themselves are representatives of the oppressed nations, almost all unanimously reached the conclusion formulated here by comrade Pyatakov.

Speaking as a party member accustomed to working in the Transcaucasus, with its highly diversified national minority structure, Makharadze charged that adoption of Lenin's (Stalin's) resolution, with its "right to secession" clause, would harm the party's prospects in the minority regions. The national question will be solved,

Makharadze predicted, "only in a socialist order," and like Pyatakov he asserted that

the national state at the present time is related to the past, not to the future.

Pyatakov used his five-minute "concluding remarks" period to reply to Lenin and Zinoviev, making no substantially new points but pleading for further discussion of the national question in the party. The final statement was made by Stalin, who put the question in terms of tactics: the party must support the independence movement in Finland in order to show that it is opposed to the Provisional Government.

In his critique of Lenin's "April Theses" on April 6, Stalin had complained that Lenin's picture of the "bridge" between the socialist revolution in the West and the anti-imperialist movement in the East was a "sketch," lacking in facts and "therefore unsatisfactory." Since that time he had had an opportunity to work closely with Lenin and to absorb his outlook on revolutionary strategy and tactics. Now, in a statement that can fairly be described as pure Leninism, Stalin made amends for his April 6 strictures:

Either we consider that we must create a rear for the vanguard of the socialist revolution in the shape of the peoples which are rising against national oppression—and in that case we shall build a bridge between West and East and shall indeed be steering for a world socialist revolution, or we do not do this—and in that case we shall find ourselves isolated and shall be abandoning the tactics of using every revolutionary movement among the oppressed nationalities for the purpose of destroying imperialism.[67]

In a last-ditch effort to prevent the conference from adopting Stalin's resolution, Makharadze proposed withdrawing the entire national question and taking no resolution on the subject, but the delegates rejected this proposal by a vote of 42 against 21, with 15 abstentions. Stalin's resolution then won a substantial victory, 56 to 16, with 18 abstentions, while the vote on Pyatakov's draft was only a little less decisive—11 for, 48 against, with 19 abstentions. As these figures show, however, there remained a hard core of 30 delegates— more than a quarter of those present—who were unwilling to accept the Stalin/Lenin resolution with its "right of secession" formula. This was by far the largest bloc of votes opposing a policy sponsored by Lenin at the conference, a fact that provides graphic proof of Lenin's tactical shrewdness in bringing Stalin to his side in the debate. *Except for Stalin, not a single representative of the national minorities supported*

Lenin on this issue, and the most telling assaults on his position came from the Pole Dzerzhinsky, the Ukrainian Pyatakov, and the Georgian Makharadze.

Immediately following Stalin's concluding remarks the results of the election to the Central Committee were announced, and it became clear to everyone that Stalin had joined the top leadership group in the party—the only representative of a national minority to do so. (It should not be forgotten, of course, that the new CC included three Jews—Zinoviev, Kamenev, and Sverdlov. But their ethnic identity played no part—at this stage at least—in determining their party position, and one of them, Zinoviev, had come out strongly in support of Lenin on the national question.)

There remained only a few formalities to be completed. After a one-hour break, the weary delegates reassembled to listen to Zinoviev present the draft resolution on "The Situation in the International and the Tasks of the RSDLP(b)," which passed with a nearly unanimous vote, marred by one stubborn holdout in opposition and one abstention, following which Lenin brought the delegates back to their starting point with a presentation of the "Resolution on the Current Situation." Only Soloviev (was it the same brash Soloviev who had opposed Kamenev's candidacy to the CC?) ventured to offer a "correction" to Lenin's text, and he was quickly reduced to silence. The resolution passed with no nays but with eight abstentions. After a few more perfunctory votes, approving the resolutions on revision of the party program and on the Soviets of Workers' and Soldiers' Deputies, the weary delegates finally broke up. It was 4 o'clock in the morning, and they had earned the right to a few hours' slumber.

The Origins of the Politburo: Lenin's Deal with Stalin

It is customary for a new central committee to hold its first plenum immediately following the congress (or in this case the conference) at which it is elected, and there can be little doubt that the CC elected at the Seventh Conference duly observed this by now time-honored practice. Lacking as we do the protocols of the CC for this period, it is not possible, unfortunately, to cite direct documentary evidence for the organizational steps taken by the new post-conference CC, but a convergence of indirect clues enables us to establish one point of cardinal importance in the history of the party and the career of Joseph Stalin. The Central Committee that was elected at the Seventh Conference voted at its first post-conference plenum to establish a bureau or steering committee that was the original form of what later came to be called the Political Bureau, or Politburo. Further-more, we can be reasonably certain that this bureau, the exact name of which is unknown, was composed of four members: Lenin, Zino-viev, Stalin, and Kamenev, to name them in order of their vote totals in the balloting for the CC. Finally, there is good reason to believe that behind the action of the CC lay a *fait accompli* in which the CC merely endorsed a slate that Lenin had designated beforehand.

We have already noted part of the evidence which points to these conclusions, notably the pattern of voting for the CC, in which the four top candidates were marked off by a sizable interval from the next group of elected members of the CC. We have also noted the evidence pointing to the existence of a master list of candidates, drawn up by Lenin and made known to the delegates before the voting.

It is a striking fact that Stalin consistently claimed in later years that he had been elected to the Politburo *in May 1917, at the time of its establishment,* and had remained a member uninterruptedly thereafter. Perhaps the first time this claim appeared in print was in the autho-rized biography of Stalin written by I. P. Tovstukha, a Ukrainian party official who became the head of Stalin's Private Secretariat at some time in the mid-1920s. In Tovstukha's biography of Stalin, pub-lished in the *Granat Encyclopedia,* the following statements are made:

> At the all-Russian Conference of Bolsheviks in April [1917], at which two tendencies came to light in the Party, Stalin stubbornly defended Lenin's position. In May, the CC Politburo was set up. Stalin was elected to it and has retained his seat on it ever since.
>
> . . . .
>
> During the October days, the CC elected him [Stalin] a member of the *pyatyorka* (the group of five organizing the political leadership of the rising) and the *semyorka* (the group of seven entrusted with organizational control of it).[68]

Substantially identical statements appeared in the biographical sketches of Stalin included as part of the appendices of a number of volumes in the third edition of Lenin's *Works,* published between 1930 and 1935.[69]

Noteworthy is the fact that Tovstukha clearly distinguishes be-tween what he calls the Politburo, which he says was established in May 1917, and the committees of five and seven set up in October 1917. Especial interest attaches to the committee of five, since it was this body, although Tovstukha does not say so, which for the first time bore the designation of Political Bureau, or Politburo. This fact has led a number of scholars to conclude that this body constituted the original form of the Politburo, even though the October 1917

Politburo apparently never functioned as an entity and disappeared without a trace in the tumult of the Bolshevik uprising. Officially, the Politburo in the form in which it is best known—that is, the top policy-making institution in the party—was not established until the Eighth Party Congress in March 1919, and that date has generally been regarded as definitive, in part because it carried the endorsement of Merle Fainsod in his authoritative and influential text, *How Russia Is Ruled.*[70]

May 1917 has been given as the date of the Politburo's origin in a number of Soviet reference works published after Stalin's death.[71] Recently, however, Soviet reference works have dropped that date and have substituted for it October 1917, obviously having in mind the committee of five which Tovstukha specifically distinguished from the genuine Politburo.[72]

Light is cast on the problem by some entries in the published protocols of the Central Committee for the period October 1917– January 1918. From these we learn that at a meeting of the CC on November 29, 1917 (Old Style), it was decided to refer one knotty problem on the agenda—the renaming of the Ukrainian Social-Democratic party—to a "bureau of the CC" consisting of Lenin, Stalin, Trotsky, and Sverdlov.[73] "In view of the difficulty of assembling a [plenary] session of the CC," the protocols explain,

> it was decided that this foursome [*eto chetvero*] shall be given the right to decide all urgent matters, but that they are obliged to include all the CC members in the Smolny at the time of the decision.

This "bureau of the CC" is recognizable as a progenitor of the later Politburo, sharing with it such characteristics as its small size, its mandate to deal with urgent matters, and the obligation to include members of the CC present at the time a decision was taken.

The next reference to the "bureau of the CC" occurs in the protocol for January 8, 1918 (Old Style). In the sharply truncated notes written by the secretary, there is an agenda item, "Bureau of the CC," which reads,

(1) The CC [is to move] to Moscow.
(2) The Buro [is to function] in Moscow, *as in the April days.*[74]

Brief though they are, these entries provide the key to the problem. They tell us, first, that a special "bureau of the CC," performing tasks later assigned to the Politburo, was functioning by late November 1917 and was still operating early in January of the following year. Second, they tell us that the bureau included the four most powerful men in the party, as would be expected for a policy-making committee. Third, they tell us that the bureau was regarded as being in some way continuous with an earlier body that had functioned "in the April days." This can only mean April 1917. Bearing in mind that the CC protocols for the period before February 1918 were still using Old Style dates, whereas the biographies of Stalin cited earlier, as well as the reference works published in the period 1954–1963, employed New Style dates for the events of 1917, the "bureau of the CC" which harked back to "the April days" can be recognized as the Politburo referred to in Tovstukha's biography of Stalin and the Soviet publications that followed his lead in this matter.

The conclusion is virtually inescapable: a "bureau of the CC" was set up immediately after the April Conference, consisting of Lenin, Zinoviev, Stalin, and Kamenev, with the task of providing leadership for the party.

Yaroslavsky formulates the point concisely:

> In May 1917, after the April Conference, Stalin was elected a member of the Political Bureau of the Central Committee, and he has remained a member of that body ever since.[75]

For once, Yaroslavsky was telling the truth—a truth that Western scholars have generally ignored on the grounds that it was simply another of Yaroslavsky's shameless lies on behalf of the Stalin cult.

It would be interesting to know why the Soviet historical profession (read: the Communist party) has decided to suppress the facts about the date of origin of the Politburo and to adopt instead the erroneous version long current in the West. The decision may be in some way related to the parallel decision to withhold from publication the protocols of the CC from the period March–August 1917.

For our present purposes, the cardinal point is that Stalin was chosen by Lenin as a member of his "bureau of the CC" at the time it was set up in May 1917 (New Style). In making that choice Lenin had to overlook, not only Stalin's inept handling of his responsibilities as a member of the editorial board of *Pravda* in the period before Lenin's return in early April, but also the undesirable "personal characteristics" that had led the Russian Bureau on March 12 to exclude Stalin from full participation in its work. What were the positive features Stalin had to offer which, in Lenin's eyes, outweighed these shortcomings?

There seems little doubt that Stalin's major value to Lenin at this time was as spokesman for Lenin's views on the national question. No other prominent non-Russian party figures (except the Jews Zinoviev and Kamenev, who were unsuitable) were available to Lenin for that purpose, to which he attached cardinal importance. Given the stubbornness and the size of the non-Russian opposition to Lenin on this point at the Seventh Conference, it is entirely conceivable that if Stalin had not come out in support of Lenin and lent him his own authority as the party's recognized spokesman on the national question, a majority of the delegates would have defied Lenin and voted either to support Pyatakov's competing draft resolution or to follow Makharadze's proposal to defer consideration of the national question to a later date.

Stalin's value to Lenin in April 1917 transcended the national question, however. Since April 7 Stalin had shown a willingness to place himself entirely in Lenin's hands and accept without hesitation Lenin's views on the major problems facing the party. In pursuit of this purpose, Stalin had served effectively on the opening day of the conference in helping Lenin crush an incipient grass-roots mutiny. Stalin's intellectual crudeness, which led Trotsky and other party intellectuals to belittle his potential as a party leader, was exactly what Lenin needed at that point.

It was the combination of these traits and characteristics in Stalin which recommended him to Lenin. But there must have been something more to make Lenin offer Stalin a position on the policy-making "bureau of the CC." That something more may have been Lenin's recognition that Stalin had aspirations to leadership, that he was already, in his own eyes, one of the party's top figures. Seen in this light, Stalin's blunders in March acquire a different aspect from the one in which they are usually interpreted. What mattered to Lenin was not that Stalin made blunders—tactical errors were forgivable, if the wrongdoer was willing to correct them (and Lenin was happy to provide instruction). What mattered was the innate capacity for leadership, and by his actions in March Stalin had shown that he possessed that quality. He had overcome an initial setback, asserted his authority, redirected the party's course, and influenced the views of the party's membership. The fact that he did these things in pursuit of goals that Lenin regarded as misguided was less important than the fact that he had shown leadership qualities. It was for this above all that Lenin marked him out as one of the members of the ur-Politburo.

Is it possible to name the specific occasion on which Lenin decided to offer Stalin a position on the "bureau of the CC"? Indirect evidence provides some pointers.

Working with Stalin in the editorial office of *Pravda* in the period between April 7 and the opening of the April Conference on the twenty-fourth gave Lenin his first opportunity to evaluate the "marvelous Georgian" on a day-to-day basis. What he saw was an eager, ambitious young man, uncultured but not illiterate, lacking in original ideas and with only a shaky grasp of Marxist principles but willing to learn and able to formulate effectively what he had learned. For Stalin the opening session of the April Conference was a crucial test, and he passed it with flying colors. By choosing Stalin as one of his two defenders in the debate on the current situation at the session of April 24, Lenin indicated that he already regarded Stalin as one of his closest aides. In all probability the decision to invite Stalin to join the "bureau of the CC" had already been tentatively formulated at that point. If Stalin failed to rise to the challenge, Lenin could drop him and look elsewhere. Instead, Stalin made effective use of his opportunity, far surpassing the more experienced Zinoviev in the forcefulness of his defense of Lenin.

In all probability, therefore, the offer was made on or shortly after the first day of the conference and was linked with the invitation to Stalin to present the report on the national question, which was both a mark of confidence on Lenin's part and a responsible service to be performed. In that sense we can speak of a bargain between Lenin and Stalin: in return for supporting Lenin on the national question, Stalin was invited to join Lenin's inner circle. But we know that the offer was made and accepted before the report on the national question was delivered, since the voting on the CC preceded the report. As we have seen, that order of events represented a deviation from the agenda originally planned for the conference. The change must have had Lenin's approval, or rather, must have been initiated by him. The most obvious effect of the change, as far as Stalin was concerned, was to separate his report on the national question from the elections for the CC and consequently to force the delegates to decide on his candidacy entirely on the strength of Lenin's endorsement of him.

Did Lenin fear that Stalin might not handle himself well in presenting the report? Or did he want to make sure of Stalin's election to the CC before the debate on the national question, which was bound to be bitter and which might well damage Stalin's standing in the eyes of the non-Russian opponents of Lenin's national policy? If the vote had been taken *after* Stalin's report, the hard-core opponents of Lenin's national policy would scarcely have permitted Stalin to run up the third highest number of votes in the elections for the CC. The shift of items on the agenda can therefore best be explained as a tactical move by Lenin to protect Stalin's standing in the party from the potentially adverse effects of his participation in the debate on the national question.

What it cannot be used to explain is the alleged *helpful* effect of Stalin's report on his vote total in the CC election, since the delegates had to make their choice on the bare evidence of Lenin's endorsement, before Stalin had delivered his report. The high vote they cast for Stalin was therefore an indication of the strength of Lenin's authority in the party, not of Stalin's stature as party expert on the national question.

This analysis may serve to clear up one of the minor mysteries of the revolutionary period, namely why Molotov, who had been pushed aside by Stalin in March, later became one of Stalin's most faithful supporters. In terms of policy, the problem appears a difficult one: in March it was Molotov, not Stalin, who followed a line close to that of Lenin on all the major questions facing the party. If correctness of policy was to be the acid test for leadership roles in the party, it was therefore Molotov, not Stalin, who should have been rewarded by Lenin at the April Conference by elevation to a top position. Instead, Molotov's candidacy for the CC went unsupported by Lenin, and he failed to receive the necessary votes for inclusion.

By disregarding Stalin's blunders in March (and, by the same token, overlooking the correctness of the line pursued by Molotov, Shlyapnikov, and Zalutsky), Lenin provided a graphic demonstration of the relative importance in his eyes of policy and leadership potential. Stalin had the latter, as he had shown; his political blunders were venial, especially because he was eager to leave them behind under Lenin's tutelage. By conferring on Stalin the accolade of recognized leadership, Lenin indicated the prime value he assigned to power capability in his close associates. As to policy, he was fully capable of making that himself; all he required of his colleagues was a willingness to accept his views. It may well have been this demonstration that convinced the young Molotov that Stalin was, in very truth, the potential leader he believed himself to be. Whatever Molotov's reasons were, from the time of the April Conference he accepted Stalin as his personal leader.

3 / / MAY – JUNE

Stalin in the Doldrums

For Stalin the weeks following the April Conference marked a distinct letdown from the heady excitement provided by that event. Lenin had little immediate need for his services, and the issues facing the party were of minor significance. During the entire month of May and the first week of June Stalin published only three articles, two in *Pravda* and one in *Soldatskaia pravda*, the organ of the Bolshevik Military Organization. In addition, he contributed a signed "correction of a mistake" to *Pravda* on May 5 and volunteered a few comments at a meeting of the Petersburg Committee on May 10, neither of which was thought important enough to include in his *Works* in 1946. By any standards, this is a meager output for a man who had just been elevated to the top level of the party leadership. In contrast, Lenin, during these same five weeks, poured out a steady stream of articles, speeches, reviews, and drafts, enough to fill some two hundred pages in his *Collected Works*.[1]

Faced with this scanty record, Stalin's biographers have been hard-pressed to account for his deeds. Trotsky, as usual, set the tone:

> It is hard to trace Stalin's activities during the next two months. He was suddenly relegated to a third-rate position. Lenin himself was now directly

in charge of the *Pravda* editorial board day in and day out—not merely by remote control, as before the War—and *Pravda* piped the tune for the whole Party. Zinoviev was lord and master in the field of agitation. Stalin still did not address any public meetings. Kamenev, half-hearted about the new policy, represented the Party in the Soviet Central Executive Committee and on the floor of the Soviet. Stalin practically disappeared from that scene and was hardly ever seen even at Smolny. Sverdlov assumed paramount leadership of the most outstanding organizational activity, assigning tasks to Party workers, dealing with the provincials, adjusting conflicts. In addition to his routine duties on the *Pravda* and his presence at sessions of the Central Committee, Stalin was given occasional assignments of an administrative, technical or diplomatic nature. They are far from numerous. . . . For a while he felt acutely unwell. Everywhere he was superseded either by more important or more gifted men.[2]

After a brief look at Stalin's work on the Soviet Executive Committee in April, Trotsky then moves directly to early June, with the opening of the First All-Russian Congress of Soviets on June 3. Here, too, the record of Stalin's activities is skimpy, but Trotsky was able to quote from the 1928 memoirs of an émigré SR, Vereshchak, in a passage that helps bridge an awkward gap. "I tried in every way," Vereshchak wrote,

> to understand the role of Stalin and Sverdlov in the Bolshevik Party. While Kamenev, Zinoviev, Nogin, and Krylenko sat at the table of the congress praesidium, and Lenin, Zinoviev and Kamenev were the main speakers, Sverdlov and Stalin silently directed the Bolshevik Fraction. They were the tactical force. It was then for the first time that I realized the full significance of the man.[3]

In an uncharacteristic passage of grudging praise for Stalin, Trotsky comments:

> Vereshchak was not mistaken. Stalin was very valuable behind the scenes in preparing the [Bolshevik] Fraction for balloting. He did not always resort to arguments of principle. However, he did have the knack of convincing the average run of leaders, especially the provincials.

Even in praising Stalin, however, Trotsky could not resist the impulse to cut him down to size:

> But even on that job the pre-eminent place was Sverdlov's, who was permanent chairman of the Bolshevik Fraction at the Congress.

Trotsky's lead was followed by Deutscher. "In each Soviet," Deutscher explains, the Bolsheviks acted as a compact body; and as in the successive by-elections their numbers increased, their actual weight grew out of proportion to their numbers. Somebody had to keep in touch with them from day to day, convey to them the decisions of the Central Committee and instruct them how to vote in the Soviets and behave *vis-à-vis* the other parties. This arduous job was carried out by Stalin and Sverdlov. . . . While Lenin, Zinoviev, or Kamenev took the platform and engaged in battles of words and resolutions, Stalin and Sverdlov acted as the indefatigable and invisible conductors of the Bolshevik groups in the assemblies, making the rank and file behave in unison with the leaders.[4]

Though his account is unmistakably based in part on Vereshchak's testimony, Deutscher avoids direct use of that source, with the result that the picture he draws, though vivid, lacks any documentary foundation. By way of compensation, Deutscher pulls out all the stops in his praise of Stalin:

The tenacious and skillful organizer to whom Lenin had assigned so crucial a role in his scheme of the revolution now had to prove himself, not within the narrow confines of an underground but in the middle of an open and swelling popular movement.

If in fact Stalin had been carrying on a task involving such widespread and direct contact with rank-and-file party members, many of whom subsequently published their memoirs of 1917, surely, one would think, at least a few of them would have left written evidence confirming these colorful statements. Since none did so, however, Deutscher is forced to conclude, somewhat lamely,

By its nature, his [Stalin's] role remained as anonymous and modest as it had been. Not for him the popularity and fame which the revolution was generously and rapidly bestowing upon its great tribunes and master-orators.

Tucker essentially agrees, though in less effusive terms:

In the course of the developing revolutionary events, Stalin reverted to his old role of a special assistant to Lenin for delicate assignments. His astuteness, conspiratorial skills, and total reliability were now put to good use.[5]

Recognizing, perhaps, that the evidence for Stalin's behind-the-scenes activity during May and early June is tenuous, Ulam makes little attempt to account for his activities during this period but instead portrays a Stalin "enjoying his first real freedom since he was arrested that April day in Baku in 1901." Ulam attributes Stalin's "relatively benign temper" at this period to a "dramatic change in his personal life," namely, his quasi-familial existence with the Alliluevs, on which he cites Anna Allilueva's memoirs, with their picture of an "often smiling" Stalin. For Ulam, Stalin's existence at this time was that of "everyone in politics":

> always on the run—to hurried consultations with colleagues, committee meetings, visits to Party cells in suburbs, his work on *Pravda*, which at times kept him in its editorial offices overnight.[6]

Ulam offers no explanation as to why the slim total of Stalin's contributions to *Pravda* at this time made overnight work necessary.

For Smith, the period from April to July is simply a blank in Stalin's biography: Smith moves directly from mid-April, when Stalin "seems to have vanished into the most convenient place to nurse his political wounds and to wonder if his career had reached an ignominious conclusion," to early July.[7] Souvarine is equally dismissive: he ignores Stalin entirely for the period April–July, merely noting that

> it is still difficult to assign to him any considerable role without ignoring proportion. Whether calculated or not, this reticence is perhaps characteristic. He assumed administrative work at the headquarters of the Party and of its journals, and was careful to say and do nothing which would commit him irrevocably.[8]

One is left with the impression that for Stalin this was a period during which he neither was able to develop any initiative in political activity nor was assigned any major tasks by Lenin or the Central Committee. As far as it goes, the scanty evidence suggests that in addition to editorial work on *Pravda* he was serving as an assistant to Sverdlov in organizing and directing party delegates to conferences and meetings. For a man of Stalin's intensely ambitious nature, such a subordinate role could not be satisfying for very long.

Stalin's Account of the Party's Activities in May

A valuable source of information on the Bolshevik party's activities in May is a statement by Stalin which was included in his report for the Central Committee to the Sixth Party Congress on July 27.[9] These activities, Stalin declared, "were directed along three lines":

> First, it [the Central Committee] issued the call for new elections to the Soviet of Workers' and Soldiers' Deputies. . . . Our opponents accused us of trying to seize power. That was a calumny. We had no such intention. . . . New elections were therefore the keynote of our work in the month of May. In the end we won about half the seats in the workers' group of the

Soviet, and about one-quarter of the soldiers' group.

Second, agitation against the war. We took the occasion of the death sentence passed on Friedrich Adler to organize a number of protest meetings against capital punishment and against the war. That campaign was well received by the soldiers.

The third aspect of the CC's activities was the municipal elections in May. Jointly with the Petrograd [sic] Committee, the CC exerted every effort to give battle both to the Cadets, the main force of counterrevolution, and to the Mensheviks and Socialist Revolutionaries, who willingly or unwillingly followed the Cadets. We secured about 20 percent of the 200,000 votes cast in Petrograd. The Vyborg District Duma we won entirely.

Using Stalin's July statement as a yardstick against which to measure his party work in May, it becomes clear that as a member of the editorial board of *Pravda* he made only a minimal contribution to the three major campaigns that, by his own account, the party waged in May. For example, his sole published piece on the antiwar campaign was an article, "What Did We Expect from the Conference?" published in *Soldatskaia pravda* for May 5.[10] In an obvious effort to appeal to the supposedly illiterate soldiers, Stalin couched his article in the simplest terms, explaining, for example, what a conference is and reducing the complex problems of the war and the land to posterlike contrasts of black and white.

Since Stalin, we must assume, was deliberately simplifying his message, it would be unfair to conclude that the article's crudities are a valid indication of his own thinking. Nevertheless, the article conveys such a strong impression of a poorly educated mind grappling with problems too complex for its comprehension that one is virtually driven to the conclusion that something of Stalin's own helplessness in the face of current problems is reflected in it. Certainly Lenin could never have written so intellectually impoverished an article, nor could any of the party's other leading publicists.

As an indication of Stalin's long-term view of the political world, one notes the article's shrill insistence on total unanimity in the party:

> The struggle [for socialism] can be successful only if our party has unity and solidarity, if it has a single spirit and a single will, if it beats to a single stroke everywhere, to all the corners of Russia.

Also characteristic of Stalin is the article's unquestioning assumption that "the people" must be "led to victory" by a party so organized and so defined.

On the subject of new elections to the Soviet, Stalin published nothing in May, though that does not necessarily mean that he made no contribution in that area. The only substantial article he published concerned the party's efforts in the Petrograd municipal campaign, an article made to appear more important by being spread over three issues of *Pravda* from May 21 to 26.[11] In the cadenced rhythms that he had learned at the Tiflis Seminary, Stalin castigated the rivals of the Bolshevik party, from the Cadets to the "non-party" candidates, and called on the workers to vote only for the Bolsheviks. Judged as a rational analysis of the election campaign, the article was crude and oversimplified; viewed as a piece of party propaganda, it was no doubt effective.

Stalin's third article in May, "Lagging behind the Revolution," reverted to a theme he had explored in March, under very different conditions, the discrepancy in revolutionary tempo between the capital and the provinces.[12] Then, in March, he had portrayed a militant Petrograd leading the rest of the nation in revolutionary zeal. Now he found the opposite situation: the Executive Committee of the Petrograd Soviet, with its reluctance to sanction unauthorized land seizures, was lagging behind the provinces, where the peasants were increasingly taking the law into their own hands. It was not that the Executive Committee had reversed direction, merely that it had failed to keep pace with the peasants' rapidly developing land hunger.

In the article's final paragraph, Stalin tried his hand at the sociology of revolutions. "In a period of revolution," he wrote,

> it is impossible to halt, you have to move—either forward or backward. Therefore, whoever tries to halt in time of revolution must inevitably lag behind. And whoever lags receives no mercy: the revolution pushes him into the camp of counter-revolution.

This idea may well have been one that Stalin picked up from Lenin, since Lenin expressed essentially the same concept in his first speech to the First All-Russian Congress of Soviets on June 4.[13] Or the influence may have operated in the opposite way: sharing the *Pravda* office as they did, it was inevitable that Lenin and Stalin should experience a certain degree of intellectual interaction at this time. Interestingly enough, the May 4 article constitutes one of the rare instances in which one can plausibly infer an influence by Stalin on Lenin's thinking. A few days later, on May 6, *Pravda* published an article by Lenin applying the "lagging behind" concept to the newly formed coalition cabinet in the Provisional Government in relation to the delegates to the currently in session Peasant Congress.[14] Where Stalin framed the tension in geographical terms, however, thereby revealing his own sensitivity to capital-provincial differences, Lenin, with a surer grasp of Marxist theory, saw it as the expression of class conflict, the peasants versus the middle-class Provisional Government.

By a transparent journalistic device, Stalin managed to spread the short May 4 article over two issues of *Pravda*. On May 5 the newspaper republished the concluding paragraph, with minor editorial changes, under the heading "Correction of a Mistake." Since no point of principle was involved, the only tangible effect was to lend added weight, through repetition, to Stalin's criticism of the Executive Committee.

A major reason for Stalin's lack of journalistic productivity in May was that Lenin, as principal editor of *Pravda*, left him with little to do. Virtually every issue of *Pravda* carried one or more contributions by Lenin, ranging from short articles of a few paragraphs to more substantial pieces. All the burning questions of the day—the war, dual power, the land, workers' control, minority rights, party conflicts, the economic crisis—were subjected to Lenin's piercing scrutiny and illuminated by his trenchant phrases and biting wit. Working under Lenin as an editorial assistant must have contributed enormously to Stalin's training as a journalist, but it gave him little opportunity to practice his trade.

Lenin Woos Trotsky

For Stalin, the most important event that occurred in May 1917 was one in which he had no direct part but that was to affect his life profoundly. Ever on the lookout for fresh talent to strengthen the Bolshevik leadership, Lenin on May 10 took a bold step for which there was little support among his closest collaborators: he invited Leon Trotsky to join the Bolshevik party, not as a rank-and-file recruit but as one of the party's top leaders. To understand something of the significance of that action and its fateful effect on the Bolshevik party in general and Stalin in particular, it will be appropriate to look briefly at Trotsky's earlier career and his relationship with the Bolsheviks before 1917.

When the Russian Social-Democratic Labor Party (RSDLP), at its Second Congress in 1903, split into two wings, Bolshevik and Menshevik, the young Trotsky, already well known in party circles as an effective writer and original thinker, joined neither faction but, with the high sense of his own importance which was an essential part of his nature, kept aloof from the conflict, staking out for himself a position above the battle. In the period immediately following the split, Trotsky directed his polemics against both factions but concentrated his fire more frequently on Lenin and the Bolsheviks, whom he accused of trying to establish a tightly centralized party organization in which "the organization will replace the Party, the Central Committee will replace the Party organization, and finally, the dictator will replace the Central Committee."[15]

During the 1905 Revolution Trotsky showed a new side of his personality, emerging as an effective speaker and as the most prominent leader of the short-lived St. Petersburg Soviet of Workers' Deputies, which was dominated by the Mensheviks. In the period of reaction which set in after 1907, Trotsky tried to maintain an independent stance, holding aloof from both the Bolsheviks and the Mensheviks, but again it was Lenin and his Bolshevik group who were the target of Trotsky's sharpest barbs. In 1908 he acquired a journalistic base in the form of a small émigré newspaper, *Pravda*, published in Austria and smuggled into Russia. It was in this organ (known for convenience as the Viennese *Pravda*, to distinguish it from the Bolshevik paper of the same name which began publication in 1912) that Trotsky mounted some of his sharpest attacks on Lenin. For his part Lenin, never one to turn the other cheek, replied with equal spirit, not only in the Bolshevik press but in vituperative personal letters. Many years later, after Lenin's death, these polemical exchanges were exhumed from the party archives and used effectively by the party leadership, including Stalin, in their campaign to discredit Trotsky's claim to having been one of Lenin's closest colleagues and allies in 1917 and later.

Despite Lenin's attacks on Trotsky, he recognized the latter's brilliance as a writer and theorist. In particular, Lenin could not help but be impressed by Trotsky's original solution to the most serious dilemma confronting Russian Marxists: how were they to lead a proletarian revolution in a country where the working class, as a consequence of the backwardness of Russian capitalist industrialization, constituted not the overwhelming majority of the population—a prerequisite in classical Marxist theory for a successful proletarian revolution—but a mere 5 percent of the population in a nation predominantly peasant in social composition? Trotsky's solution to this dilemma (one that Stalin was too ignorant and unschooled to recognize) was to envisage the Russian Revolution in the framework of the world Marxist movement, so that the workers in the advanced industrialized nations, Germany above all, could be expected to come to the aid of a revolution in Russia initiated by the workers and carried forward by them in alliance with their class allies in a socialist Germany (the German workers having meanwhile been inspired by the Russian example to overthrow their own capitalist class).

It was this theory, labeled the Theory of Permanent Revolution, which constituted Trotsky's principal claim to fame as a Marxist theorist.

Although Lenin never explicitly recognized Trotsky's originality in developing the Theory of Permanent Revolution, he paid silent tribute to it by developing a closely similar concept (his label for it was "uninterrupted revolution," but in substance it was close to Trotsky's theory). It was this theory, as Menshevik critics of Lenin were quick to recognize, which underlay his "April Theses" and which was later to form part of the strategy on which he based the Bolshevik bid for power in October.

The February Revolution found Trotsky in the United States, editing a Russian-language newspaper and trying to organize a minuscule group of Russian-born factory workers. Dazzled by the vistas opened up by the overthrow of tsarism, Trotsky tried desperately to get back to Russia, but bureaucratic obstacles, coupled with political distrust of him on the part of U.S., Canadian, and British authorities, delayed his return to Petrograd. It was not until May 4—just after the Bolsheviks, at their April Conference, had rearmed themselves for the coming test of strength—that Trotsky finally reached the city where the fate of Russia was being decided. Like Lenin a month earlier, Trotsky was accorded a reception, though one considerably more modest than Lenin's at the Finland Station. According to Trotsky's later recollection, it was G. F. Fedorov, a moderate Bolshevik who had just been named a member of the party Central Committee, who welcomed him at the railroad station with a speech summarizing current Bolshevik policy as defined by Lenin's "April Theses." As later recalled by Trotsky, Fedorov

> in his speech of welcome posed sharply the question of the next stage of the revolution, the dictatorship of the proletariat and the socialist course of development.

Trotsky's response—again, in his own later recollection—

> was in full accord with Lenin's April Theses, which, for me, flowed unfailingly from the theory of permanent revolution.

It was this question, Trotsky believed, that "Lenin considered decisive with regard to the possibility of our collaboration."[16]

Trotsky lost little time in entering the political fray. Shortly before his return, the Provisional Government had undergone its first reorganization, the result of which was the entry of several Menshevik and SR leaders into a combined cabinet known as the First Coalition. On May 5 the new socialist ministers addressed the Soviet with an appeal for its support; it was this assembly that provided the opportunity for

Trotsky's first public speech after his return.[17] In it he called for the transfer of power from the Provisional Government to the soviets, the only bodies, in his view, which could "save Russia." Trotsky concluded his speech by hailing the Russian Revolution as the prelude to a world revolution, thereby placing local events in a universal context and echoing Lenin's similar ideas in the "April Theses." In content Trotsky's speech was close to Lenin's position; in the powerful effect it produced, for which we have the eyewitness account of Sukhanov, it marked the entry into the political arena of a new star of the first magnitude.[18]

Even before Trotsky's return, a group of his followers had come together in Petrograd. Known collectively as the *Mezhraionka* (literally the Interdistrict, a reference to their stance midway between the Bolsheviks and the Mensheviks), the group had been organized in 1913; now it was actively considering the possibility of merger with the Bolshevik party, whose current line, as defined by Lenin, held a strong appeal for the *Mezhraiontsy*. Trotsky's return served as a renewed stimulus to the merger proposal, and on May 10 Lenin, accompanied by Kamenev and Zinoviev, held a meeting with Trotsky and several of his followers to discuss it.

In preparation for the meeting Lenin had attempted to obtain the Central Committee's approval of an offer to Trotsky to take over the editorship of *Pravda*, but even Lenin's personal authority was insufficient to force that unpalatable suggestion down the CC's collective throat: the proposal was rejected, and Lenin had to scale down his offer, thereby lessening its appeal to Trotsky. The incentives he was able to offer Trotsky were relatively tame: the *Mezhraiontsy* were to be invited to name one of their representatives to the editorial boards of the two Bolshevik newspapers—*Pravda*, which was to be a mass-circulation paper, and a more restricted journal, yet to be established, which would serve as the official party organ.[19] In addition, the Bolshevik Central Committee was to be asked "to set up a special organizing committee to summon a party Congress (in six weeks' time)," to which the *Mezhraiontsy* would be invited to send delegates.

Even this watered-down offer failed to receive the support of the Central Committee, and Lenin was forced to present it "in his own name and in the name of several [unspecified] members of the Central Committee."[20] In reply Trotsky indicated his wholehearted approval of the proposal for unification, but only on condition that the Bolshevik party "internationalize" itself. To this end he suggested that representatives of several national minorities should be included in the organization bureau to prepare a party congress. Trotsky brushed aside as "less convincing" the offer of editorial collaboration on *Pravda*.

The real sticking point for Trotsky was retention of the party name, "Bolshevik." Trotsky insisted that before he and his followers could join it the party "must find a new name." "I cannot call myself a Bolshevik," he asserted, adding, "It is impossible to demand from us recognition of Bolshevism." The meeting therefore ended on an inconclusive note but went on record as being "decidedly and ardently in favor of unification."[21]

In the highly abbreviated notes that Lenin jotted down during Trotsky's reply there occur the cryptic words, "Bureau—(C[entral] C[ommittee] + . . .) acceptable." From this it would appear that Lenin had offered Trotsky a place on his "inner core" Bureau of the Central Committee and that Trotsky was prepared to accept the offer.[22]

Lenin's reasons for making such an offer have been well stated by Angelica Balabanoff, a Ukrainian-born Italian socialist who was close to Trotsky at this time. She writes,

> Aware of the serious difficulties Russia would have to overcome in order to survive and convinced that Trotsky would be able to compete with every obstacle, Lenin silenced all resentment, factional animosities, and his personal dislike of Trotsky's behavior to put at the service of the Bolshevik regime [sic] not only his [Trotsky's] unusual gifts but also his weaknesses, which Lenin knew how to exploit.[23]

Lenin was by no means willing to admit defeat, however, and for several weeks after the inconclusive meeting of May 10 he cherished the hope that Trotsky could be lured into the job of editing *Pravda*. As late as May 30 Lenin attended a meeting of the Petersburg Committee at which the question was discussed of authorizing the PK to publish its own newspaper. Concerned lest such an authorization weaken party discipline, Lenin strongly but unsuccessfully opposed the move, advancing as one of his reasons that "an agreement is about to be reached with the Inter-District Group [the *Mezhraionka*] for getting Comrade Trotsky to edit a popular organ." Lenin added that "the establishment of a popular newspaper is a difficult job that calls for considerable experience"—experience that, in Lenin's view, Trotsky had already acquired.[24]

Although opposition among his own followers and Trotsky's stiff-necked insistence on protocol defeated Lenin's plan for the time being, he already regarded Trotsky as a recruit to the Bolshevik party, as his use of the label "Comrade" demonstrated. For his part, Trotsky acted and spoke in full accord with the Bolshevik party line.

The formal entry of Trotsky and his followers into the party did not take place until the Sixth Party Congress in late July. Even then, Trotsky's assimilation into the party's inner leadership group was delayed, owing to his arrest by the Provisional Government, from which he was not freed until early September. Thus, during the four crucial months of late spring and summer Trotsky had no direct contact with the party decision-making apparatus in its day-to-day functioning.

This delay had important consequences for Trotsky, for the Bolshevik party, for the revolution, and for Stalin. Most immediately, it meant that Trotsky missed the opportunity to join the party's inner leadership group; instead, he remained, in Deutscher's words, a "free lance."[25] By the same token, Trotsky remained unaware of the group's membership and failed to realize that it included Stalin. Years later, when he came to write his biography of Stalin, he described him as "relegated to a third-rate position during the two months following the April conference,"[26] a misapprehension of Stalin's real status which has colored much subsequent writing. Only when one realizes the extent to which Lenin had advanced and flattered Stalin in April can one properly evaluate the resentment Stalin felt at Lenin's ardent courtship of Trotsky in May. Balabanoff provides a perceptive commentary:

> The Bolsheviks were not less hostile toward him [Trotsky] now than they had been before his conversion [to Bolshevism]. Some felt slighted by having to accept him as a leader; others suspected him of not having undergone a complete conversion, of being still heterodox. Still others, and they perhaps were the majority, asserted that Trotsky had joined the Bolsheviks and accepted Lenin's orders because the Bolsheviks had won.

As to Trotsky's motives for joining the Bolsheviks, Balabanoff is equally perceptive:

> He no longer had to deal with abstract entities and theories, but saw them transformed into living human beings, full of hope in a better future and sure that the goal was not only attainable but within reach. . . . The atmosphere of victory . . . gave him more élan, stimulated him to new strife, provided him with inner satisfaction as well as prestige, offered continually renewed outlets for his indomitable energy, and opened new areas for the application of his fertile mind. He no longer was, it seemed to him, the hated "counterrevolutionary" Menshevik—he now was the hero of the Revolution that was about to triumph, to immortalize his name in letters of gold in the book of history.[27]

With the entry of Trotsky into the party, another fateful figure was added to the small group that helped determine the course of Stalin's participation in the revolution. Unlike Kamenev, Lenin, and Sverdlov, however, who were role models, policy guides, and intellectual mentors, Trotsky represented something more challenging and more threatening for Stalin: a competitor for Lenin's confidence, a rival for the position of trusted colleague, and an aspirant for a top leadership position. The fact that Trotsky remained outside the party even while being welcomed by Lenin as a colleague at the highest level gave a unique, paradoxical character to Trotsky's position. Not fully accepted by the Old Bolsheviks, bitterly resented by most of them, Trotsky functioned not as a member of the party apparatus but as an independent tribune of the revolutionary masses. Avoiding submersion in the narrow confines of inner-party politics, he quickly blazed a trail into the larger world outside, the world of workers' meetings, soldiers' and sailors' assemblies, public gatherings of all kinds. Thus, at a time when Stalin was still cautiously groping toward the position of one of the party's leaders under Lenin's tutelage, Trotsky was building a solid position in the world outside the party, a world where the basic forces of the revolution were making themselves felt. Chamberlin notes that

> Trotsky, almost from the moment of his arrival, was a constant speech-maker and soon established himself as one of the outstanding personalities of the Soviet.[28]

Stalin, by contrast, seldom ventured onto the speaker's platform.

For Stalin, the immediate consequence of Lenin's failure to win over Trotsky was to postpone for several months the moment of his direct confrontation with Trotsky. Given Lenin's articulateness and his determination to define party policy on all important issues of the day, Stalin's editorial responsibilities were modest indeed, leaving him ample time for other activities. The surviving protocols of the Petersburg Committee preserve a record of one of Stalin's infrequent appearances before that body.

The May 10 Meeting of the Petersburg Committee

Stalin was not a member of the small group of Bolshevik leaders who attended the conference with Trotsky and his followers on May 10. Was this another instance of Stalin's faulty judgment, like his failure to greet Lenin at his arrival on April 3? That possibility can be ruled out, since the negotiations with Trotsky were the result of a personal initiative by Lenin. The inclusion of Kamenev and Zinoviev as members of the negotiating team was therefore Lenin's personal decision, as was the exclusion of Stalin. Stalin, in Lenin's eyes, was too recent a recruit to the party's "commanding heights," whereas Kamenev and

Zinoviev were seasoned veterans of the political struggle, known and trusted by Lenin for the kind of delicate maneuvering involved in the invitation to Trotsky.

It is unlikely, incidentally, that Lenin gave much weight to the hostility that had already developed between Stalin and Trotsky before 1917; after all, the contemptuous phrase, "a champion with fake muscles," which Stalin had twice applied to Trotsky in 1913, was mild by comparison with the vituperation uttered by Lenin himself, as well as by other party spokesmen.

But Stalin was not idle on the tenth of May; he attended an important meeting of the Petersburg Committee and made a number of noteworthy contributions to its deliberations.[29]

Three subjects constituted the agenda of the PK's May 10 meeting: the municipal elections, the structure of the PK itself, and the case of Sergei Bagdatiev, a member of the PK accused of violating party discipline by his impetuous actions in the demonstrations of April 20–21. It was Bagdatiev who, disregarding Lenin's and the CC's caution, had incited the workers by writing a leaflet calling for the immediate overthrow of the Provisional Government.[30] On all three subjects Stalin had something to say.

With regard to the municipal elections, Stalin proposed that the Executive Committee of the PK "take into its hands work on municipal questions, making use of all available forces." It was a sensible suggestion, in line with Bolshevik centralizing tendencies, and a recognition of the importance of the elections.

The question of the PK's internal structure was one of party bureaucracy—whether the PK should be divided into subcommittees along functional lines or should operate as a unit with diversified tasks. Foreshadowing something of the bureaucratic expertise that would later characterize his policies, Stalin offered a proposal whereby the Executive Committee would function as "a single, integral" body responsible to the PK but would be required to report at the PK's next meeting on the responsibilities it would assume. A division of the PK into political and economic sectors, Stalin argued, would be inadvisable, "since it is impossible to separate politics from economics."

The meeting found Stalin's logic persuasive, for it adopted his proposal in preference to those of Bagdatiev, who wanted a subdivision of the Executive Committee along functional lines, and N. I. Podvoisky, a member of the Military Organization, who advocated immediate election of functionally defined subcommittees. Both Bagdatiev's and Podvoisky's proposals would have led to a weakening of the PK's centralized authority, with a resulting increase in the autonomy of the functional subcommittees, including that for military affairs. Stalin, as usual, stood for centralized authority, albeit with functional diversification.

In the discussion of Bagdatiev's actions Stalin took a moderate line, asking whether the Executive Committee had the right to oust Bagdatiev from the party if he had "deliberately violated a [party] decision" and suggesting deferment of action until an investigation of the case could be completed. In the voting Bagdatiev escaped both ouster and censure, but the proceedings themselves constituted an unmistakable warning against further violations of party discipline. Given Lenin's direct personal interest in the case, it is a fair surmise that Stalin was speaking not only in his own name but on behalf of Lenin, and that it was to represent Lenin's interests in the Bagdatiev case that Stalin had been asked to attend the May 10 meeting of the PK. If the surmise is well founded, it constitutes one of those "special assignments" by Lenin which biographers of Stalin are prone to invoke to fill an otherwise scanty record.

At the end of the May 10 meeting a new nine-man executive committee was elected, including Molotov, representing the Vyborg District, and Podvoisky for the Military Organization. Given Stalin's active participation in the meetings and the fact that it adopted his proposal on the PK's internal structure, it seems a fair deduction that he deliberately refrained from standing as a candidate. With his editorial duties on *Pravda*, his work on the Executive Committee of the Soviet, and his responsibilities as a member of the party Central Committee and its policy-making bureau, he had ample calls on his time and energy. Occasional attendance at meetings of the PK when subjects of general significance were on the agenda would be sufficient to keep him in touch with its activities, and with Molotov as a member of the Executive Committee, Stalin could be sure of a faithful supporter and informant on the PK's affairs.

Preparations for the June Demonstrations

The relative calm of May was deceptive. Just below the surface, the problems and conflicts that had led to the overthrow of the tsarist regime were gaining in intensity, posing challenges that the Provisional Government was powerless to meet. Recognizing the government's weakness, strong-willed individuals inside and outside the Bolshevik party were working to provoke confrontations that would force the revolution along more radical paths. The demonstrations of April 20-21 had been only the opening skirmishes of what many hoped would be a struggle for power and the overthrow of the Provisional Government.

It was toward the middle of May that members of the Bolshevik Military Organization advanced the idea of a mass demonstration combining workers and soldiers in a display of revolutionary strength. Unwilling to let the initiative slip from its grasp and wary of premature boldness at a time when the Provisional Government still seemed well established and competent, the Bolshevik Central Committee turned a deaf ear to these promptings and reaffirmed its right to initiate all political actions.[31]

The hotheads in the Military Organization had little use for such caution. Disregarding the CC's ban on independent action, the Military Organization on May 23 held a meeting at which party representatives from various units of the Petrograd garrison reported on the mood of the soldiers. Encouraged by evidence of the troops' militancy, those present decided to get together with representatives from the Kronstadt naval base before making definite plans for a demonstration. This was a proposal that virtually guaranteed an affirmative decision, since the Kronstadt sailors had already established a reputation for untrammeled radicalism. Only a few days earlier the Kronstadt Soviet had passed a resolution denying the Provisional Government's authority in its area. The move, with its prophetic anticipation of the October Revolution, was soon formally rescinded, but it was a revealing index of the mood of the Kronstadt sailors.

For all his caution, Lenin himself at this point was thinking along lines closely parallel to those of the Kronstadters. In his article "Has Dual Power Disappeared?" which *Pravda* published on May 20, Lenin argued that

> the basic question of every revolution, that of state power, is still in an uncertain, unstable and obviously transitory state.

Lenin concluded that "this dual power cannot last long."[32] For the militants at Kronstadt, in the Military Organization, and on the Petersburg Committee, these words could be read as an invitation to speed up the process of revolution by a little direct action.

Mounting evidence of the government's preparations for a new offensive helped fan the flames of militancy among the troops of the Petrograd garrison. Alexander Kerensky, who had taken the post of minister of war in the coalition government established on May 5, was currently touring the front, attempting with scant success to arouse a fighting spirit in the war-weary troops. On May 26 Kerensky ordered the replacement of General Alekseev, a competent but pessimistic officer who had been serving as commander in chief, by General Brusilov, leader of the moderately successful offensive of 1916 and a man who was prepared to work with the Provisional Government.

Concrete evidence is lacking as to Stalin's activities during this period. *Pravda* carried his three-part article, "The Municipal Election Campaign," in its issues for May 21, 24, and 26, but it was to be several weeks before another article from his pen appeared in print. No statements by him have been recorded (or at least published) at any of the party or other gatherings that took place at this time. However, to judge by his attitudes and views when he does reemerge into the light of recorded history on June 6, the last weeks of May and the first week of June were another of those periods in Stalin's career when new associates brought new ideas and new perspectives into his life. This time it was the enthusiasts of the Military Organization who were to lead Stalin into untried and risky areas.

The First All-Russian Congress of Soviets

A new and potentially decisive factor was injected into the already complicated political balance on June 3 with the opening of the First All-Russian Congress of Soviets. The convening of this body, formed by delegates from the newly established soviets throughout Russia, gave the nation for the first time a kind of democratic forum in which the voice of the masses could make itself heard. Unlike the Petrograd Soviet, which could claim to speak only for the workers and soldiers of the capital, the All-Russian Congress possessed an authority based directly on the Russian masses. Recognizing this fact, the Bolshevik leaders made full use of the congress as a platform from which to advance their program.

In its political composition the congress was a faithful mirror of the still undecided but unmistakably socialist mood of the Russian workers and soldiers. The two moderate socialist parties had a clear majority of the delegates, the SR's holding a slight edge with 285 delegates to the Mensheviks' 248, each more than double the size of the Bolshevik fraction of 102 delegates.

Lenin gave his first major address to the congress on its second day, June 4, an address that Ulam justifiably characterizes as Lenin's "as yet most demagogic speech."[33] In it, among other things, he proposed to publish the profits of the capitalists arising out of the war and to arrest outright fifty to one hundred of the "largest millionaires." In Lenin's portrayal, the war was nothing but a capitalist plot to reap uncounted millions of rubles; by supporting it, even on a limited basis, the Provisional Government, in his view, was exposing itself as a tool of the capitalist bourgeoisie, while the Mensheviks and SR's who gave it limited support were little better.

It was in the course of the June 4 speech that Lenin, in response to a rhetorical question from the Menshevik leader Tseretelli, asserted that the Bolshevik party was "ready to take power in its entirety," a bold assertion that not unnaturally led Tseretelli to conclude that the Bolshevik party, small though it was, represented a direct threat to the existing revolutionary order.[34]

Stalin attended the congress as a member of the Bolshevik fraction but left no documentary record of his activities there. That he was gaining recognition as a prominent party figure is indicated, however, by the fact that on June 20, as the congress was nearing its end, he was elected to its Central Executive Committee, a body charged with maintaining continuity until a second all-Russian congress of soviets could be convened.[35]

The Abortive Demonstration of June 10 and Its Aftermath

Indications of the new direction in which Stalin was moving are provided by the records of two party gatherings held on June 6 to consider the by now well-developed plans for a mass demonstration. These plans, as we have seen, originated in the Military Organization during the second week of May. They were enthusiastically supported by the Kronstadt sailors and by some of the units of the Petrograd garrison, notably the First Machine Gun Regiment.

At a joint meeting of the party Central Committee, the Petersburg Committee, and the Military Organization on June 6, Lenin spoke in favor of organizing the demonstration and proposed meeting again on June 8 to work out the technical details. Stalin, in support, noted that the mood of the troops was "affected"—evidently by the government's increasingly obvious preparations for a new offensive—while the workers were in a "heightened" state. Under these circumstances, Stalin said,

> It would be wrong to force matters, but it would be [equally] wrong to let the opportunity slip.[36]

Stalin's characteristic balancing act could not entirely conceal the fact that he was speaking in favor of an armed demonstration of soldiers and workers. This was made clear by his contribution to a second meeting on the same day.

On the afternoon of June 6, Stalin attended a session of the Petersburg Committee at which the question of holding a demonstration was again debated. Here, without Lenin to restrain him, Stalin took a more militant stance. "It is our duty to organize this demonstration," he said, adding that it would serve as "a review of our forces." Displaying none of Lenin's sober realism and awareness of the residual strength still exercised by the conservative and moderate elements in Petrograd, Stalin added, "At sight of the armed workers the bourgeoisie will take cover."[37]

Implicit in the plans for a demonstration was the possibility of a clash with supporters of the Provisional Government, and some members of the Bolshevik party looked forward to that prospect with undisguised relish. Ivar Smilga, for example, one of the most radical members of the Central Committee, suggested at the June 6 meeting

> that if events should come to a clash, the demonstrators shouldn't abstain from seizing the post and telegraph offices and the arsenal.[38]

Other party members went even further; for example, Martin Latsis, a member of the Petersburg Committee, believed that

> in case of necessity we should seize the station, the arsenal, the banks, the post and telegraph offices, supported by the machine-gun regiment.[39]

Challenging the Provisional Government was one thing, but openly defying the All-Russian Congress of Soviets was something quite different. To do that would be to put the Bolshevik party on a collision course with the institution representing the popular masses, at a time when official Bolshevik policy, as formulated by Lenin, prominently featured the slogan "All Power to the Soviets." The congress, dominated as it was by the moderate socialist parties, had been moving closer to the Provisional Government ever since the reorganization of May 5 in which representatives of the Mensheviks and the SR's for the first time assumed ministerial responsibilities.

On June 8, just as the Bolsheviks were getting down to detailed planning for the proposed demonstration, the congress indicated its mood by adopting, by a large majority, a resolution pledging its full support to the Provisional Government. As yet the delegates to the congress, including many of the Bolshevik fraction, were unaware of the rapidly maturing plans for a massive demonstration—plans about which the party leaders had been careful to preserve a conspiratorial silence.

News of the preparations reached the congress only on the afternoon of June 9, by which time Bolshevik operations throughout the city were in full swing. Stalin's wholehearted participation in these actions is made clear by the fact that the principal document calling on the workers and soldiers to support the demonstration was a proclamation, "To All the Toilers, to All the Workers and Soldiers of

Petrograd," which was almost certainly written by Stalin, even though it appeared without his signature.[40] Internal textual evidence and the absence of any plausible alternative to Stalin's claim to authorship are among the strongest arguments in support of the official attribution of the proclamation to him. Not only does it manifest some of the characteristic fingerprints of his style, notably the cadenced rhetoric reminiscent of liturgical texts, but it also faithfully mirrors some of his known blind spots, notably his propensity to ignore revolutionary developments in the West.

As originally written the proclamation included no reference to revolutionary events outside Russia, a fact that conclusively rules out Lenin's authorship, or even his advance knowledge of the text. The proclamation was not, in fact, originally intended for publication in *Pravda* or one of the party's other newspapers; it was designed as a leaflet to be distributed throughout Petrograd in an effort to evoke the mass response needed for the success of the demonstration. It was one of these leaflets which a Menshevik, E. P. Gegechkori, read to the Congress of Soviets early on the morning of June 10, as confirmation of the widely circulating rumors of a Bolshevik-sponsored demonstration to be held that day.[41] Encouraged by the indignant response evoked from the delegates, Gegechkori thereupon introduced a resolution calling on the workers and soldiers to ignore the Bolsheviks' call and to remain quiet. Gegechkori's motion ended with a ringing appeal for inaction:

> Not a single company, not a single regiment, not a single group of workers should be on the street. Not a single demonstration should be held today.

With the Bolshevik and the *Mezhraionka* delegates abstaining, Gegechkori's motion passed unanimously—a striking testimony to the moderate socialists' fear of the Bolsheviks and their potential for arousing the restive masses.

By the afternoon of June 10, news of the impending demonstration had been relayed to the Petrograd Soviet and the Provisional Government, both of which reacted strongly, the Executive Committee of the Soviet by concerting antidemonstration plans with the presidium of the Congress of Soviets, the Provisional Government by calling on the population for order, with the added warning that "any use of force would be countered with all the force at the disposal of the government," and backing up this threat by sending out military patrols throughout the city.[42]

During the period when plans for the demonstration were being developed, communication within the Bolshevik leadership group was highly defective. Stalin's proclamation was evidently not submitted in advance to Lenin, since otherwise the omission of reference to events in Western Europe would have been rectified. Thus Lenin, in approving plans for the demonstration without fully grasping the dimensions of the planned action, was being pushed further in the direction of anti-government militancy than he might otherwise have deemed prudent.

Even more defective was the communication between the party Central Committee and the Bolshevik fraction in the Congress of Soviets. That group, headed by the moderates Kamenev and Nogin, learned of plans for the demonstration only along with other congress delegates on June 9. Thus, in addition to their instinctive rejection of the plans on political grounds, there were the hurt feelings of responsible party figures kept in ignorance of significant developments affecting the discharge of their responsibilities as delegates to the congress.

The man on whom the full weight of these faulty communications came to bear was Lenin's old comrade and close associate Grigory Zinoviev. It was Zinoviev, by temperament a worrier and a doubter, who had to attempt to mediate between the moderates at the Congress of Soviets and the risk-takers of the Military Organization.

At a hastily summoned informal meeting of several members of the Central Committee, the Petersburg Committee, and the Military Organization, which was held around 8 P.M. on June 9, Zinoviev voted with the majority in favor of the demonstration, even though he had already learned of the decision to oppose it taken that afternoon by the Congress of Soviets.

Following this session, Zinoviev hurried back to the Tauride Palace, where the congress was meeting, for a consultation with the Bolshevik fraction. By a unanimous vote these party members, headed by Kamenev and Nogin, opposed the demonstration, thereby lining up squarely alongside the congress itself. Shaken by this show of pro-congress solidarity, Zinoviev dashed back to Bolshevik headquarters in the Kshesinskaya mansion. By now it was past midnight, in the early hours of June 10, and most of the party figures who had taken part in the Joint CC-PK-MO meeting of a few hours earlier had gone to bed. Only five members of the Central Committee could be rounded up for a hastily summoned meeting with members of the Bolshevik fraction: Lenin, Sverdlov, Kamenev, Nogin, and Zinoviev. Under the enormous pressure being brought to bear on him, Zinoviev's earlier willingness to support the demonstration crumbled. Yielding to the impassioned antidemonstration arguments of Kamenev and Nogin, Zinoviev reversed his earlier stand and joined the opponents of the demonstration. This shift gave the antidemonstration group a one-vote majority, and the fact that Lenin and Sverdlov registered their distaste for the retreat by abstaining was, under the circumstances, irrelevant. According to one account, Lenin allowed himself to be half-persuaded by a technicality: a printer present at the meeting reportedly assured him that there would be no difficulty in withdrawing the proclamation from the not-yet-printed issue of the morning *Pravda*.[43]

Once the decision had been reached, effective steps were taken to carry it out. The morning edition of *Pravda* was hastily revamped; in the space originally allocated to Stalin's proclamation, there appeared an announcement canceling the demonstration. Over at the print shop where *Soldatskaia pravda* was being prepared, the shift was executed less smoothly: either through a misunderstanding or a willful refusal to comply promptly, someone from the Military Organization permitted a few copies of their newspaper to reach the streets with the officially withdrawn proclamation prominently featured on the first page.

News of the Bolshevik reversal was one of the most urgent items on the agenda when the delegates to the First Congress of Soviets reconvened at 8 A.M. on June 10. Their mood varied between elation over having, as it seemed, blunted the edge of a dangerous adversary and indignation over the threat that, in their eyes, the Bolshevik plans had represented to revolutionary law and order. Tseretelli spearheaded the movement to condemn the Bolsheviks and render them impotent. He failed, however, to gain the support of the delegates for the drastic measures he demanded. The most the majority of the congress was willing to sanction, after two days of impassioned debate, was a mild reproof that left the Bolsheviks virtually unscathed.

Confident that the Bolshevik menace had been subdued by this slap on the wrist, the congress then adopted, on the evening of June 12, a proposal by a trio of Mensheviks, Dan, Bogdanov, and Khinchuk, to capitalize on the supposed Bolshevik setback by staging a massive demonstration of workers and soldiers *in support* of the Congress of Soviets (and, by implication, of the Provisional Government).[44]

The Bolshevik leaders were quick to recognize in this action an opening through which they might recoup their losses, reestablish their influence among the workers and soldiers, and, in effect, reschedule their planned demonstration.

While the moderate socialists were thus helping the Bolsheviks outsmart them, the Bolsheviks were undergoing the turmoil of a radical party temporarily balked in its revolutionary drive. Party meetings held in the wake of the decision to cancel the demonstration showed just how seriously that decision had endangered party unity. Serious rifts became manifest between the Central Committee, which stood behind the decision to cancel, and the Military Organization and the

Petersburg Committee, both of which launched sharp criticism of the decision.

Even within the Central Committee there was bitter dissension. At a meeting of the committee on or about June 11, the two CC members most directly identified with the original plan, Stalin and Smilga, submitted their resignations, asserting that they considered the decision to cancel the demonstration an error.[45] The committee refused to accept the resignations and, by way of party discipline, ordered Smilga to "explain" the cancellation to a meeting of Kronstadt Bolsheviks, to be held later on June 11.[46]

The evidence of Stalin's proffered resignation from the CC, first disclosed by a Soviet historian in 1966, casts a sharp and revealing light on his conception of himself and his place in the party. At a time when he had not yet fully adjusted to his new eminence in the party leadership, he showed himself willing to throw it away over momentary pique. Furthermore, in criticizing the cancellation as an error, Stalin was, in effect, reprimanding Lenin, who had sanctioned the cancellation, albeit reluctantly, and who was now doing his best to defend it against angry and frustrated party militants. Retrospectively, Stalin's move to resign from the CC weakens his later boast that he had been a member of the Politburo from its inception. If he had had his way in June 1917, his tenure would have lasted just over one month.

Smilga's obstinacy in defense of the canceled demonstration earned him the implied reproof of having to defend the decision before what was certain to be an angry assembly of disgruntled Kronstadt Bolsheviks. There is no published evidence that Stalin was administered a similar reproof. Once again, as in April, he somehow escaped censure for his failure to follow the party line, and once again the evidence points to Lenin as the person who shielded him. The evidence is indirect but highly suggestive.

The Congress of Soviets' decision to hold its own demonstration was quickly recognized by Lenin as opening the door to a reversal of the Bolsheviks' setback. Under cover of the congress's sponsorship of the new demonstration, to be held on Sunday, June 18, the Bolsheviks could use their influence among the workers and soldiers to turn the demonstration into a pro-Bolshevik display. An indispensable prerequisite to carrying out this bold plan was the preparation of a suitable proclamation to the workers and soldiers. Conveniently, one was already in hand—Stalin's text for the canceled June 10 demonstration. With a little judicious editorial tinkering it could be made serviceable.

That this is what took place emerges clearly when one compares the text of Stalin's original proclamation, as printed "inadvertently" in the June 10 issue of *Soldatskaia pravda*, with the substantially revised text published in *Pravda* on June 17.[47] The fact that the proclamation appeared in *Pravda*, of which Lenin was the editor, conclusively establishes the fact that Lenin approved it. The generally Leninist tone of the editorial changes in the revised version provides confirmatory evidence.

The Two Proclamations: A Comparison

Among the editorial changes in the June 17 version of Stalin's proclamation are some that bring out or sharpen a class analysis of developments connected with the war. In the June 10 text Stalin wrote,

> The war, which is claiming millions of victims, is still continuing. It is being deliberately prolonged by the millionaire bankers.

In the June 17 version the bankers have become "the scoundrels, the blood-sucking bankers." In the June 10 text Stalin wrote, "High prices are strangling the population." This was changed to "High prices are strangling the urban poor."

A number of the changes brought out international aspects of the war, which Stalin's original text had omitted. Thus, where Stalin wrote,

> the Duma of June 3 [1907], which helped the Tsar to oppress the people, is now demanding an immediate offensive at the front. What for? In order to drown in blood the liberty we have now,

the June 17 text added, "in deference to the wishes of the Allied and Russian robbers." The same phrase was added to the following paragraph, which accused the State Council of "secretly splicing a treacherous noose . . . in order at a convenient moment to drop it around the neck of the people."

Several of the changes were designed to stress themes "overlooked" by Stalin in the June 10 text. The following two paragraphs, for example, unmistakably Leninist in inspiration, were added:

> Instead of the arming of the people, we have threats to disarm the workers and soldiers.
>
> Instead of liberation of the oppressed nationalities, we have a policy of pinpricks toward Finland and the Ukraine and a fear of granting them liberty.

A slight but significant shift toward a wider Leninist perspective occurred when Stalin's original text,

Let our call, the call of sons of the revolution, resound today through all of Russia, to the joy of all the oppressed and enslaved,

was changed into

Let your call, the call of the champions of the revolution, resound throughout the world, to the joy of all the oppressed and enslaved.

The global perspective implied in that change was made crystal clear in the following completely new paragraph in the June 17 text:

Over there, in the West, in the belligerent countries, the dawn of a new life, the dawn of the great workers' revolution is breaking. Let your brothers in the West know that you have inscribed for them on your banners not war but peace, not enslavement, but liberation!

Some of the editorial changes were designed to conceal the possibility of a split between the workers and the soldiers. In his June 10 text Stalin wrote,

Workers! Join the soldiers and support their just demands. After all, don't you remember how they supported you in the days of the revolution?

Evidently because this appeal disclosed too candidly a concern that the workers might not support the soldiers in a demonstration, the June 17 text was changed to

Workers, Soldiers, clasp hands in brotherhood and march forward under the banner of socialism.

Both versions ended with a series of "wishes," which the workers and soldiers were urged to express as they marched through the capital. Some significant changes were made in this section of the proclamation. Thus, where Stalin, repeating one of his now outmoded ideas of March, originally wrote,

All power to the All-Russian Soviet of Workers', Soldiers', and Peasants' Deputies!

the June 17 version substituted,

All power to the Soviet of Workers', Soldiers', and Peasants' Deputies!

In line with Lenin's emphasis on the need for an armed workers' militia, a new slogan was added:

Down with the disarming of the revolutionary workers! Long live a people's militia!

Stalin's slogan,

Hail control [i.e., workers' control] and organization of industry!

was fleshed out in Marxist categories for the revised version:

Long live control and organization of production and distribution!

A final difference between the two versions concerns the sponsoring organizations that affixed their signatures to the proclamation. In the original text, along with the signatures of the Bolshevik Central Committee, the Petersburg Committee, and the Military Organization, there appeared that of the Executive Commission of the Central Bureau of Trade Unions. Since the trade unions, at this point in the revolution, were still dominated by the Mensheviks, it is not surprising that this signature was missing from the June 17 version. With this omission, the new list of sponsoring organizations was solidly Bolshevik, while the text of the proclamation, as revised, was more closely in line with Bolshevik party policies as defined by Lenin. The way seemed clear for carrying out the Bolshevik plan. At this point, however, a new difficulty arose in the shape of the Anarchist-Communists.

The Anarchist-Communist Threat

Bolshevik attempts to control the restive and volatile workers and soldiers of Petrograd were threatened not only from the right and the center—the Provisional Government and the Petrograd Soviet—but also from the extreme left in the form of anarchist groups and individuals. On June 5 a group calling itself the "Anarchist-Communists" seized the printing press of a right-wing newspaper, the *Russkaia volia*; earlier, shortly after the February Revolution, the group had occupied an estate in the Vyborg district belonging to P. N. Durnovo, a former tsarist minister of internal affairs. Since that time, the Durnovo villa had served as the anarchists' operational base. The government had tolerated the occupation of the estate but reacted vigorously to seizure of the printing press; a regiment of garrison troops was sent to forcibly evict the anarchists. Determined to eliminate the group entirely, P. N. Pereverzev, the Menshevik minister of justice in the Provisional Government, on June 7 gave the Anarchist-Communists a twenty-four-hour deadline to vacate the Durnovo estate.[48]

Pereverzev's ultimatum met with resistance not only from the Anarchist-Communists themselves but also from many workers in Vyborg district factories who went out on sympathy strikes. More immediately useful to the anarchists were some fifty Kronstadt sailors, politically radical and spoiling for action, who showed up to help defend Anarchist-Communist headquarters. Faced with these new difficulties, the government softened its ultimatum, while in the Petrograd Soviet compromise measures were hurriedly worked out in an effort to head off a direct clash.

Largely neglected by both Soviet and most Western historians, the anarchist disturbances of June and July 1917 contributed a vital element to the turbulent and confused unfolding of the revolutionary situation. With regard to Stalin, the problem is important principally because it helped shape his views on revolutionary strategy and the role of the party.

For the Bolsheviks the Anarchist-Communists posed the threat of outflanking the party on the left and appealing to the workers with their flamboyant actions and radical slogans. It was to counter this threat that a meeting of members of the Bolshevik Central Committee, the Petersburg Committee, and party workers of the district organizations met on June 5 and adopted a resolution calling on the workers to abstain from "scattered" (razroznennykh) actions.[49]

Taking advantage of the reprieve granted them by the Provisional Government, the Anarchist-Communists on the afternoon of June 9 formed a "Provisional Revolutionary Committee," evidently to help organize preparations for a demonstration they planned to hold, also on June 10. Leaflets calling on the workers and soldiers to support this demonstration were being circulated in Petrograd and Kronstadt at the same time as Stalin's proclamation in its original version.[50]

Unlike the Bolsheviks, most of whom reluctantly accepted the cancellation of their June 10 demonstration, the Anarchist-Communists continued with plans for their own demonstration, the date for which was moved back to June 14. Since these plans threatened to interfere with Bolshevik preparations for the Soviet-sponsored demonstration on June 18, the Petersburg Committee took steps to prevent any demonstration before that date. On June 14 *Pravda* carried an announcement, which stated,

> The Petersburg Committee considers it necessary to announce decisively that all scattered [razroznennye] actions of individual units of soldiers and workers can do great harm to the cause of the revolution. Therefore any demonstrations whatsoever without the summons of the [Bolshevik] Central Committee, the Petersburg Committee, and the Military Organization are considered absolutely impermissible.[51]

As an indication that this decision enjoyed the support of the party leadership as a whole, the same issue of *Pravda* carried a signed article by Stalin entitled "Against Isolated [razroznennykh] Demonstrations," in which the same position was stated in the most uncompromising terms.[52] "It now transpires," Stalin wrote, that a new workers' demonstration is being "organized" at the Durnovo villa. We are informed that meetings of factory committee representatives, headed by the Anarchists, are taking place at the villa with a view to organizing a demonstration today. *If this is true, then we most emphatically condemn* all isolated, anarchic demonstrations. . . . [W]e regard such anarchic demonstrations as *disastrous to the cause of the workers' revolution.*

Stalin was particularly insistent on the need for all party members to refrain from taking part in the proposed demonstration:

To merge with the Anarchists and engage with them in reckless demonstrations which are doomed to failure beforehand is impermissible and criminal on the part of class-conscious workers.

To give his message a positive tone, Stalin held out the prospect of a much stronger, more imposing demonstration, under Bolshevik auspices, on June 18. "It is now our task," Stalin urged,

to see to it that the demonstration in Petrograd marches under our revolutionary slogans. We must therefore nip in the bud every attempt at anarchic action, in order the more energetically to prepare for the demonstration on June 18.

With characteristic heavy-handedness, Stalin repeated the message twice more before signing the article.

The combination of the Petersburg Committee's resolution and Stalin's authoritative statement achieved the desired result: no demonstration was held on June 14. For Stalin, the effect was to reinforce an attitude already characteristic of his concept of the proper relation between the party and the masses; only the party, in his view, had the right to lead the masses; attempts by other organizations or individuals to encroach on this right would be "disastrous to the cause of the workers' revolution," while support of such efforts by individual Bolsheviks was not merely "impermissible" but "criminal."

The Conference of Bolshevik Military Organizations

To Lenin, control of the armed forces was a vital element in his overall strategy. Stalin, working at the *Pravda* office under Lenin's immediate supervision, had ample opportunities to absorb his chief's point of view. A signed article by Stalin, "Yesterday and Today (Crisis of the Revolution)," published in *Pravda* on June 13, bore witness to the good use to which Stalin was putting his apprenticeship.[53] Skillfully and effectively the article analyzed the continuity in the Provisional Government's policy toward continuation of the war, especially

Kerensky's plans for a new offensive. The Mensheviks and the SR's, having entered the cabinet, were adapting their views to those of the Cadets, ostensibly discredited by the resignation of Milyukov and Guchkov but still intent on achieving a military victory and maintaining the alliance with France and England. The inevitable consequence of these developments, Stalin argued, was that the internal policies pursued by the Provisional Government, with the more and more open support of the moderate socialists, constituted an accelerating trend toward out-and-out counterrevolution.

Stalin's article served as a fitting prelude to his participation in the All-Russian Conference of Bolshevik Military Organizations, which opened in Petrograd on June 16. The mood of the more than one hundred delegates was highly militant; many of them felt that the time was ripe for an insurrectionary bid for power, and far from having to stir up their ardor, Lenin, in his address to the conference on June 20, found it necessary to urge restraint, caution, and patience. Even the normally unmilitary Zinoviev, caught up in the martial excitement of the conference, spoke of a choice between death on the battlefield or on the barricades.[54]

Stalin's assignment at the conference was a relatively minor one, reflecting Lenin's recurring need for a spokesman for his views on the national question. In keeping with this role, Stalin's address, presented on June 17, had as its subject the national question in relation to the armed forces, in particular the question of basing army units on the national principle.[55] After listening to Stalin's report, the delegates adopted a resolution framed along Leninist lines which recognized the right of each nationality to its own national formations but affirmed that

> the establishment of national regiments does not correspond to the interests of the toiling masses and may be used by the bourgeoisie for counter-revolutionary purposes. [56]

Here, perhaps, Lenin—and Stalin as his spokesman—came close to accepting the position on the national question taken by Dzerzhinsky and others at the April Conference.

The Demonstration of June 18

The presence of the military conference delegates in the capital gave added impetus to the Bolsheviks' preparations for the June 18 demonstration, since it put at their disposal the services of more than one hundred experienced and energetic agitators. With this reinforcement the Central Committee was able to make full and effective use of the short time remaining before the demonstration.

The weather on June 18 was fair and mild—a perfect June day, which helped the Bolsheviks achieve a massive turnout. Unofficial and government estimates agree that between four and five hundred thousand people marched in the demonstration. To the dismay of the Menshevik and SR leaders, the great majority of the marchers carried banners inscribed with slogans representing Bolshevik policies—"All Power to the Soviets," "An End to the Imperialist War," "Down with the Ten Capitalist Ministers"—rather than ones in support of the Soviet and the Provisional Government. The demonstration was orderly and peaceful; no shots were fired, no one was killed or injured. All the more impressive was the Bolshevik triumph, a triumph not only of policy but of control and mobilization of the masses. After June 18 no one in Petrograd could doubt that the Bolsheviks were making solid gains among the workers and soldiers in the capital.

The June 20 issue of *Pravda* carried analyses of the demonstration and its significance by both Lenin and Stalin. Though they agreed on the basic facts, the two men's interpretations differed in ways that cast a revealing light on their varying concepts of the revolution.

Lenin's article, entitled "The Eighteenth of June," put the demonstration in the historical perspective of an ongoing, steadily deepening revolutionary crisis.[57] "June 18," he wrote,

> was the first political demonstration of *action*, an explanation of how the various classes act, how they want to act and will act, in order to further the revolution—an action not given in a book or newspaper, but in the streets, not through leaders, but through the people.

The conclusion Lenin drew was that only the proletariat—read the Bolshevik party, speaking in the name of the proletariat—could lead Russia and the world out of their difficulties.

> A crisis of unprecedented scale has descended upon Russia and the whole of humanity. The only way out is to put trust in the most organized and advanced contingent of the working and exploited people, and support its policy.
>
> . . . .
>
> There is no way out unless the masses put complete confidence in their leader, the proletariat.

Lenin's article was sober, analytical, and marked by only the slightest touches of rhetorical color. In contrast, Stalin's article, entitled "At the Demonstration," attempted to convey something of the buoyant feeling of excitement and power which characterized the demon-stration.[58]

> The day is bright and sunny. The column of demonstrators is endless. From morn to eve the procession files towards the Field of Mars. An endless forest of banners. All factories and establishments are closed. Traf-fic is at a standstill. The demonstrators march past the graves [where victims of the February Revolution had been buried] with banners lowered and the *Marseillaise* and the *Internationale* give place to *You Have Fallen Victim* [the revolutionary movement's hymn for its honored dead].
> The air reverberates to the roar of voices. Every now and again resound the cries: "Down With the Ten Capitalist Ministers!" "All Power to the Soviet of Workers' and Soldiers' Deputies!" And in response loud and approving cheers ring out from all sides.

For Stalin the main conclusion to be drawn was that the Menshevik-SR policy of compromise with the bourgeois parties had proved itself bankrupt. "The overwhelming majority of the demon-strators," he wrote,

> expressed downright lack of confidence in the policy of compromise with the bourgeoisie. The demonstrators marched under the revolutionary slo-gans of our Party.

Whereas Lenin's article stressed the proletariat as the leader that the masses must follow if they were to escape from the impasse in which they found themselves, Stalin emphasized the primacy of the party in providing guidance to the workers and soldiers.

In their articles both Lenin and Stalin showed an uneasy awareness of the charges leveled against the Bolsheviks, in the Soviet and else-where, of plotting to seize power under cover of allegedly peaceful demonstrations. The differing ways in which the two writers dealt with this issue are instructive. Lenin brought up the charge only once, briefly, at the outset of his article:

> The demonstration in a few hours scattered to the winds, like a handful of dust, the empty talk about Bolshevik conspirators and showed with the utmost clarity that the vanguard of the working people of Russia, the industrial proletariat of the capital, and the overwhelming majority of troops support programs that our Party has always advocated.

This, incidentally, is Lenin's only reference to the party in the entire article. It represents the party as articulating the views of the indus-trial proletariat and soldiers but not dictating to them. To a far greater degree than Stalin, Lenin was able to identify the party with the masses, rather than seeing it as an agency for manipulating them.

Stalin took up the "plot" theme in the final paragraph of his article, treating it with the heavy sarcasm that was one of his favorite modes of discourse:

There is no possible room for doubt: the fairy tale about a Bolshevik "plot" has been utterly exposed. A party which enjoys the confidence of the overwhelming majority of the workers and soldiers of the capital has no need for "plots." Only an uneasy conscience, or political ignorance, could have suggested the "idea" of a Bolshevik "plot" to the "high-policy makers."

Stalin's words are double-edged: only an uneasy conscience, one can argue, would have led him—and Lenin—to cite the success of the June 18 demonstration as conclusive proof that no Bolshevik plot lay behind the party's preparations for the very different kind of demonstration that had been planned for June 10. Evidently the "plot" charges struck a sensitive nerve among the Bolshevik leaders. The continued refusal of Soviet historians to publish the protocols of the Bolshevik Central Committee for this period makes one suspect that these documents may contain evidence pointing to the very plot that Lenin and Stalin were at pains to deny.

Stalin in May and June: A Retrospective Look

After a slow start in May, Stalin moved closer to the center of the stage in June. By his personal contacts in the Military Organization, especially his collaboration with Smilga, Stalin achieved an influential relation with the organization whose planning was central to the main revolutionary events of June—the abortive demonstration of June 10 and its triumphant sequel, the peaceful demonstration of June 18. Stalin's ability to compose inflammatory proclamations was ideally suited to the occasion. No lengthy theoretical analyses were needed, nor was impassioned oratory called for—both areas in which Stalin was notably weak. Instead, his own brand of self-taught Marxism, expressed in the liturgical cadences of the Orthodox seminary, caught perfectly the mood of the workers and soldiers of wartime Petrograd. Smilga and the Military Organization provided the machinery needed to translate Stalin's rhetoric into mass action. It was a highly effective combination of talents.

Stalin's relations with Lenin took a new and unexpected turn in June. Instead of waiting for Lenin's directives, Stalin boldly assumed responsibility for the course of party policy and led a cautious but hopeful Lenin in his wake. The idea for the June 10 demonstration did not originate with Lenin, nor did he direct Stalin to write the proclamation that expressed its goals. Instead, Lenin found himself confronted with developments that might lead either to brilliant success or to abject failure, and he wavered between hope and skepticism.

When the Central Committee called off the June 10 demonstration, party discipline was imposed on Smilga but not on Stalin; instead, Stalin's proclamation was recycled and made to serve for the demonstration of June 18. Stalin's threat to resign from the Central Committee was not only a protest against the cancellation of the June 10 demonstration but an expression of lack of confidence in Lenin's judgment and an affirmation of his own competence to set the party's goals. It showed a Stalin determined to strike out on his own, if necessary in opposition to Lenin.

In terms of writing, June was a relatively productive month for Stalin. In addition to the proclamation, he wrote the official party directive on the Anarchist-Communists ("Against Isolated Demonstrations") as well as a trenchant analysis of the Provisional Government's policies ("Yesterday and Today"). A striking indication of Stalin's emergence as a prominent party spokesman, alongside Lenin, was his contribution to *Pravda* of a review of the June 18 demonstration which matched that of Lenin in the same issue but which expressed a recognizably independent point of view.

Stalin's rapid emergence as one of the Bolsheviks' leaders was facilitated by the situation facing his potential rivals. Kamenev, on whom he had leaned for support in his first steps back in March, had by now clearly defined his stance as that of a moderate, urging the need for caution and restraint. No laurels were to be gathered along that path; by the same token, Kamenev held no threat to Stalin's ambitions and might prove a useful ally in the future. Zinoviev, after some wavering, had taken his position on the cautious wing of the party, alongside Kamenev. What power he had in the party derived from his close association with Lenin; even less than Kamenev could he be seen as a rival to Stalin.

The threat posed by Trotsky was an entirely different matter, but the situation in June masked his potential as a danger to Stalin. He still remained outside the party, excluded from its policy formulation and intent on proving himself worthy of party membership. The idea that in a few short months he would rise to a position coequal with that of Lenin would have seemed preposterous to Stalin at the time.

For Stalin in June the road to triumph as a party leader appeared identical with that for success of a Bolshevik-led revolution. Developments in July did nothing to dissipate these bright visions, but they showed that the double-tracked road to the top might prove to be more winding and obstacle-strewn than had seemed likely on that warm Sunday afternoon in June when the last marchers filed past the reviewing stand.

The success of the June 18 demonstration from the Bolshevik point of view was the result of a number of factors which would not recur in later situations. The demonstration took place in fine weather, on a Sunday that had the character of a summer holiday. Politically its sponsorship included not only the Bolshevik party but also the Petrograd Soviet and the First All-Russian Congress of Soviets. As for the Provisional Government, it observed a cautious neutrality; it neither supported nor opposed the demonstration. The focus of its attention was elsewhere: June 18 was the day on which the Russian army, under its new commander in chief, General Brusilov, was about to launch its ill-fated summer offensive.

Whereas the moderate socialist parties supported the June 18 demonstration, the Cadets boycotted it, and there were no attempts by middle-class and conservative elements to interfere with it or to organize counterdemonstrations. It almost seemed that Stalin's forecast of June 6—"The bourgeoisie will be frightened at the sight of the armed workers and will hide"—had proved accurate.

To a large extent the success of the demonstration was due to the organized, purposeful work of the Bolshevik cadres. Party discipline was exemplary; workers and soldiers marched past the reviewing stand in orderly ranks, bearing aloft banners inscribed with slogans sponsored by the Bolsheviks.

For Stalin, the June 18 demonstration could only reinforce and deepen a concept of the party and its relation to the revolution which had been developing over the years. The party organization, in Stalin's view, was the key to successful action by the masses, whether it took the form of a demonstration in the streets or a general armed uprising culminating in revolution. Action by the workers or soldiers outside the party's control—"scattered" or "unorganized" demonstrations—threatened to disrupt the controls exercised by the party and must therefore be avoided. If the party remained united and exercised effective control over the masses, there would be little danger of counteraction by conservative or liberal groups. Stalin had none of Lenin's realistic sense of the social forces that could be expected to oppose a Bolshevik-led bid for power, just as he had little awareness of the need for socialist revolutions in the West to support a socialist revolution in Russia. Stalin's Marxism and his sense of social forces were too rudimentary to encompass the kind of strategic calculations which sophisticated Marxist thinkers like Trotsky and Lenin devised to justify their faith in the possibility of a proletarian revolution in Russia. For Stalin all that was needed was the strictly disciplined, tightly centralized party organization; action by the masses would follow automatically once the party machine swung into action. Stalin's concept of the revolution thus reflected both his strengths and his weaknesses. It laid heavy stress on the arts of organization and control, arts which he found congenial and of which he was later to develop a mastery; it made no demands for brilliance as a political theorist or as an orator capable of swaying a mass audience, talents that Stalin conspicuously lacked.

The success achieved by the Bolsheviks in the June 18 demonstration served for Stalin as a confirmation of these principles and determined once and for all his approach to the problem of the seizure of power. Not surprisingly, therefore, Stalin pinned his faith on these principles in the very different conditions that existed at the time the Bolshevik party made its bid for power in October.

The June 18 demonstration illustrates another fundamental trait of Stalin's psychology, the difficulty he experienced in foreseeing coming events, counterbalanced by his strength in exploiting a situation that he thoroughly understood as the result of earlier experiences. Faced by a novel situation, Stalin tended to be temporarily baffled; encountering a situation that repeated one of his earlier lessons, he could feel fully in command. The two demonstrations of June thus presented an ideal situation for Stalin. The canceled demonstration of June 10 served as a dress rehearsal—it alerted him to the general nature of the problem and showed him some of the principal elements to be manipulated. When the June 18 demonstration was mounted, everything fell into place. In October, however, there was to be no dress rehearsal; Stalin, like the other party leaders, was to have only one chance at the grand prize.

4 // JULY

The July Days and Their Aftermath

The Bolsheviks' Evaluation of the June 18 Demonstration

By Bolshevik standards the June 18 demonstration had been a great success, revealing the tremendous power latent in the capital's masses of workers and soldiers and their strong affinity for the slogans and policies of the Bolshevik party. The Mensheviks, who had originally proposed the demonstration, proved incapable of swaying it in the direction they desired, support for the Provisional Government and their own brand of moderate socialism. Paradoxically, however, the immediate sequel to the demonstration was a resurgence of popular support for the government and the adoption of a policy of tactical retreat by the Bolsheviks.

Had the Bolsheviks miscalculated? No, Stalin explained to the Sixth Party Congress on July 27; the reason lay in the intrusion of a new factor into the situation. "The comrades know," Stalin said,

> how the demonstrations of June 18 went off. Even the bourgeois papers said that the overwhelming majority of the demonstrators marched under the slogans of the Bolsheviks. The principal slogan was "All Power to the Soviets!" No fewer than 400,000 persons marched in the procession. . . . It

was the general conviction that the demonstration of June 18, which was more imposing than the demonstration of April 21, was bound to have its effect. And it should have had its effect . . . But that very day our armies launched an offensive, a successful offensive, and the "Blacks" [right-wing extremists] began a demonstration in the Nevsky Prospect in honor of it. That obliterated the moral victory gained by the Bolsheviks at the demonstration. It also obliterated the chances of the practical results. . . . The Provisional Government remained in power.[1]

Whatever one may think of Stalin's explanation for the shift in the popular mood (and there is independent evidence that the government's announcement of the Kerensky offensive *did* evoke a widespread, if ephemeral, outpouring of patriotic enthusiasm, especially among the well-to-do sections of society), his explanation is valuable for its revelation that some Bolsheviks, and presumably Stalin himself, saw the June 18 demonstration as a means of achieving "practical results," which might well include the overthrow of the Provisional Government. In Stalin's reasoning, the April 21 demonstrations had shaken the Provisional Government and forced it to sacrifice two key ministers; the far more impressive demonstration of June 18 should have had correspondingly impressive "practical results."

Thus, the Bolshevik leadership recognized that the immediate sequel to the June 18 demonstration would probably not be a further heightening of their influence and authority among the masses. Bolshevik strategy at this point, Stalin continued in his report to the Sixth Congress, stressed the importance of delay:

We decided to wait until the moment of the attack on the front was over, to give the offensive [an opportunity] definitely to fail in the eyes of the masses, not to yield to provocation and, as long as the offensive was under way, under no circumstances to demonstrate, to wait it out and allow the Provisional Government to exhaust itself.

Stalin said nothing of the wider considerations that might have prompted the Bolshevik leadership to observe caution in their strategy. It was Lenin who articulated this aspect of the situation most clearly, in a speech to a session of the conference of Bolshevik Military Organizations on June 20, at which he warned that

One false move on our part can wreck everything. . . . If we were now able to seize power it is naive to think that having taken it we would be able to hold it.

The problem, as Lenin saw it, was that the Bolsheviks did not yet enjoy sufficient influence among the masses and their elected representative bodies, the soviets. Lenin was particularly concerned to prevent attempts at an unsupported coup d'état:

> In order to gain power seriously (not by Blanquist methods), the proletarian party must fight for influence inside the Soviet.

But he expressed firm faith in the underlying social forces that he felt were bringing the socialist revolution closer:

> Events should not be anticipated. Time is on our side.[2]

Still under the influence of the shock that had led to his reversal of position on June 12, Lenin now advocated caution and restraint in terms virtually indistinguishable from those used by Kamenev. It was only with the greatest difficulty, however, that Lenin was able to impose a bridle on the impetuous advocates of immediate action in the Military Organization and the Petersburg Committee. At a meeting of the committee on June 20 there was strong pressure for a radical line, and two days later the left-wingers pushed further with their demands before an unofficial joint meeting of the party Central Committee, the Executive Commission of the Petersburg Committee, and the Military Organization. Undeterred by the leadership's official policy of caution, the proponents of immediate action in the Military Organization began systematic, though unacknowledged, preparations for a new demonstration, which they hoped would develop into a full-scale uprising.

Stalin evidently took no direct part in these debates, though he had already shown that his sympathies lay with the left wing. When he addressed the conference of military organizations on June 21 it was to deliver a report on the national minority regiments in the army, a subject in line with his public identification as the party's leading specialist on the national question.

Stalin's apparent restraint coincided with a strengthening of his political position within the soviet bureaucracy. At its final session, on June 24, the First All-Russian Congress of Soviets elected an all-Russian central executive committee (Russian initials VTsIK) to function as its policy-making body between congresses, and Stalin was one of thirty-four Bolsheviks named to this new body. As a member of the VTsIK Stalin was given the opportunity to participate in official gatherings and to observe at close quarters the working of a semigovernmental institution. For Stalin, this was congenial work, and it is suggestive that the muting of his sympathies with the left-wing hotheads coincided with his assumption of new responsibilities in the VTsIK.

Buildup for the Military Uprising

Definite plans for a military demonstration against the Provisional Government were under way at least as early as July 1, the date on which members of the All-Russian Bureau of Military Organizations learned that the First Machine Gun Regiment was planning to organize a demonstration. Podvoisky, leader of the Bolshevik Military Organization, later reported at the party's Sixth Congress that by July 2 the Military Organization was cognizant of plans for an uprising on the following day. In an exceptionally frank and revealing article published in 1932, V. I. Nevsky, another member of the Military Organization, disclosed that the organization's actions, though ostensibly aimed at holding back the troops, in line with the official Bolshevik policy of restraint, had actually contributed to the soldiers' readiness to demonstrate and to their belief that they would have Bolshevik support.[3]

, In so doing, the Military Organization was violating the spirit, if not the letter, of a Central Committee directive adopted on July 2, which categorically forbade the Military Organization to take part in preparations for the demonstration and which ordered it to take all necessary measures to prevent an outbreak.[4] Lenin was not present at this meeting, having left Petrograd on June 29 to recuperate from an illness, but the decision was fully in line with his views.

The July Days: Outbreak

With Lenin temporarily absent from the capital, Stalin had an opportunity to demonstrate his growing influence as one of the leaders of the Bolshevik party. The record of the period is incomplete and at times confused to the point of chaos, but the nature of Stalin's role emerges with reasonable clarity. It is that of a skilled negotiator, trusted in the VTsIK as well as in the Bolshevik Central Committee, trying to steer a cautious course for himself and for the party in a rapidly changing situation.

The initiative for the armed demonstrations that broke out on July 3 evidently came from the soldiers themselves, spurred on by the imminent threat of transfer from garrison duty in the capital to service in the front line, to stiffen the sagging offensive. Members of the Military Organization continued to provide encouragement and guidance for the insurgent troops, notwithstanding the fact that official Bolshevik policy, as formulated by the Central Committee on July 2, was to abstain from participation in an armed demonstration. Even as late as the afternoon of July 3, at a time when the troop movements in the street were already in full swing, the Bolshevik Central Committee voted against participation in the demonstration. A report to this effect was carried by Stalin to a joint meeting of the VTsIK and the Executive Committee of the Petrograd Soviet, at which the problem presented by the troop demonstrations was being hotly debated.

The sense of urgency which pervaded the joint meeting of the executive committees was due in part to the fact that the stability of the Provisional Government was being threatened not only on the streets but also from within. Late on July 2 Kerensky and two government ministers, Tsereteli and Tereshchenko, returned from Kiev following negotiations with the separatist Ukrainian Rada. The concessions to Ukrainian nationalism agreed to by the three-man commission were too much for the Cadet ministers in the cabinet, and three of them announced their resignation late on July 3.

Acutely aware of the danger that the weakened Provisional Government might succumb to new popular pressures, the joint meeting of the executive committees adopted a resolution banning *all* demonstrations, an action fully supported by Zinoviev and Kamenev. So strong was the soldiers' surge toward direct action, however, that the Bolsheviks' resolve to keep their hands off soon began to crumble. The Second All-City Petrograd Bolshevik Conference, meeting on the afternoon of the third to debate the question of establishing its own newspaper (a proposal strongly opposed by Lenin, who feared it as a threat to the party's centralized control), found itself confronted by the growing insurgency of the troops, especially the First Machine Gun Regiment, and voted not merely to support the demonstration but also to demand that the VTsIK assume power.

Encouraged by the conference's support, the soldiers redoubled their pressure on the Bolshevik leadership to sanction and lead their action. Early in the evening of the third the workers' section of the Petrograd Soviet, having learned of the conference's pro-demonstration decision, followed suit by voting to support the demonstrations. Cautiously, however, the workers' section decided that they would try to keep the movement in peaceful channels.

Now the pressure began to mount on central Bolshevik headquarters, located in the Kshesinskaya mansion. Hurried and informal debates were conducted with regard to the proper course of action, combined with unavailing efforts to calm the restless soldiers. Recognizing that the soldiers were determined come what may to march on the Provisional Government's meeting place in the Tauride Palace, the Military Organization finally agreed to lead a demonstration for the avowed purpose of presenting the soldiers' demands to the Provisional Government. Carried away by the contagious air of insurgency which pervaded the talks, even the usually cautious Zinoviev joined Trotsky, one of the soldiers' favorite orators, in demanding the peaceful transfer of power to the soviets. A formal vote to this effect was taken by the Central Committee.

The Kronstadt Sailors Join the Demonstration

There is general agreement among contemporary observers that the arrival in Petrograd of an armed contingent of sailors from the Kronstadt naval base early on July 4 made an exceptionally strong impact on the tension that gripped the capital. For this episode the historian is fortunate in having available the memoirs of F. F. Raskol'nikov (pseudonym of F. F. Il'in).[5]

In 1917 Raskol'nikov, a young midshipman in the Baltic Fleet, held the post of deputy chairman of the Kronstadt Soviet of Sailors' Deputies. An ardent Bolshevik, Raskol'nikov served as principal liaison man between the Kronstadt Soviet and Bolshevik headquarters in Petrograd. At Lenin's insistence, regular telephone contact had been established in May. In Raskol'nikov's words,

> We had a very good system whereby I rang Petersburg [Petrograd] every day and, asking to speak to Lenin, Zinoviev or Kamenev, reported to them everything that had happened at Kronstadt and received the instructions needed for our current work.[6]

On July 3 a group of soldiers from the First Machine Gun Regiment came to Kronstadt to urge the sailors to join the demonstrations that were planned or that were already in progress. Before the machine gunner delegates were permitted to address a meeting of sailors, Raskol'nikov called Bolshevik headquarters and was warned by Kamenev that the soldiers were ignoring the party's opposition to demonstrations and were already cruising the streets of Petrograd in armored cars mounted with machine guns. Kamenev reiterated the party's opposition to demonstrations.

Meanwhile, the soldiers at Kronstadt had succeeded in convoking an impromptu gathering of sailors and were urging them to join the action in Petrograd without delay.

In accordance with Kamenev's instructions Raskol'nikov called for restraint, pointing out the danger of provocation from right-wing elements. To gain time he proposed the establishment of an organizational commission to check on the situation in Petrograd and to ascertain the mood of the fleet. The sailors having reluctantly accepted the proposal, Raskol'nikov, as a newly elected member of the investigating commission, again telephoned Bolshevik headquarters for guidance and information. This time it was Zinoviev who answered the phone, to tell Raskol'nikov of the Central Committee's newly adopted decision to support the demonstrations planned for July 4 as armed, organized, and *peaceful* (Zinoviev stressed the word).

This decision, reported by Raskol'nikov to the sailors, was enthusiastically received, and the meeting unanimously decided to take part in a peaceful but armed demonstration on the following day.

The night of July 3 was taken up with preparations, and on the morning of July 4 an improvised flotilla assembled to take the armed sailors, joined by some workers and soldiers, to Petrograd. It was a formidable expedition, numbering some ten thousand demonstrators, of whom perhaps twenty-five hundred were sailors with rifles.[7]

In Raskol'nikov's account there is no suggestion that at any time did the leaders of the Kronstadt sailors or the sailors themselves consider taking part in an *unarmed* demonstration or that the question of whether or not the demonstrators should be armed was raised in the telephone contacts between Kronstadt and Bolshevik headquarters in Petrograd. Raskol'nikov provides the following rationale in favor of an armed demonstration:

> It was easy to foresee that an unarmed demonstration would have been dealt with by "armed force."

Furthermore,

> The need for arms, the only means of defense in the event of blood-letting, was also dictated by the circumstance that, while announcing a demonstration, we retained the right at any moment to turn it into an armed uprising.[8]

Thus, it was with a deliberately open-ended strategy that the sailors were led into the tumultuous situation in Petrograd on July 4.

The Question of Lenin's Real Aims

All during the hectic events of July 3 Lenin was absent from Petrograd, so that the debates, decisions, and reversals of decisions by the Bolshevik leadership were taken without the benefit of his immediate guidance. As to his real intentions in the crisis there is a fundamental split in the sources, Bolshevik historians maintaining that Lenin still favored a policy of caution and restraint, whereas the Menshevik memoirist N. N. Sukhanov asserted that Lenin was really aiming at the seizure of power, using the military demonstrations as his springboard.[9] The nonavailability of the protocols of the Bolshevik Central Committee for this period renders full certainty impossible, but the evidence indicates that even at the height of the action Lenin was still urging a policy of restraint. Hurriedly summoned back to the capital by his colleagues early on the morning of July 4, Lenin, shaky from illness, addressed a restless assembly of soldiers and sailors from the balcony of the Kshesinskaya mansion in an attempt to moderate their ardor. His advice was to maintain order, resist provocations, and return peacefully to their barracks.

Lenin's impromptu address, which was to be his last public appearance before the seizure of power in October, had little visible effect on his audience, but his continued advocacy of caution and restraint had a sobering influence on those in the party who favored an all-out test of strength with the Provisional Government. No one in the party was willing to challenge Lenin directly, and even those who privately hoped for a successful armed uprising were loath to assume its leadership in the absence of Lenin's sanction. Deprived of the kind of disciplined and organized party control which had helped make the June 18 demonstration a success, the troop movement on July 4 began to falter and lose momentum.

The Bolsheviks Accept Leadership in the Demonstrations

Part of the confusion which hangs over the July Days is due to the fact that *Pravda*'s editorial board found itself unable to keep pace with the rapidly changing situation and the sharp reversals of policy within various party bodies. The early morning edition of *Pravda* on July 4 was originally intended to feature an appeal drafted by Zinoviev and Kamenev calling on the masses to observe restraint, but when the Central Committee decided late on July 3 to support the demonstrations the appeal was pulled out of the matrix for the following day's edition without anything being substituted, so that the July 4 edition came out with a blank space prominently featured on the front page. Someone—possibly Stalin—had meanwhile drafted a proclamation calling attention to the internal difficulties besetting the Provisional Government and demanding its replacement by a "new power"—the Soviet of Workers', Soldiers', and Peasants' Deputies.[10]

Officially the July 4 proclamation is not claimed as the work of Stalin, and its real authorship must remain a matter for conjecture. It can be argued, however, that its basic line is consistent with that of the June 10 and 18 proclamations, the authorship of which is officially ascribed to Stalin. Whoever wrote it evidently believed that the long-awaited moment was at hand when the Provisional Government would go down in defeat before the triumphant masses.

If it was not Stalin who wrote the leaflet—and the evidence in favor of his authorship is at best slender—who was its author? The most likely candidate is S. Ya. Bagdatiev, who had called for the overthrow of the Provisional Government in April and who is reported to have written a leaflet over the signature of the Petersburg Committee calling for a demonstration on July 3.[11]

Armed with the new proclamation, Bolshevik agitators on the morning of July 4 hurried out to factories and barracks to supervise the election of delegates charged with carrying to the executive committees the demand for transfer of "All Power to the Soviets." While the revolutionary spirit of the workers remained high, however, the mood of the garrison troops was becoming less militant.[12]

The Provisional Government Prepares to Defend Itself

At the same time that the troops' militancy was dimming, the Provisional Government was initiating a series of moves for its own defense and the defeat of its most threatening adversary, the Bolshevik party. One of the first and, as events were to prove, most successful moves in this direction was a propaganda campaign aimed at discrediting Lenin. Late on the evening of July 3, P. N. Pereverzev, minister of justice, suggested that stories be put out alleging that Lenin had been accepting financial support from the German General Staff. Ever since Lenin's return in April, charges of Bolshevik disloyalty and subservience to German interests had circulated in the capital, and they had had a profound effect, especially in the army. By early July, investigators employed by the Provisional Government had unearthed some of the details surrounding Lenin's clandestine contacts with the Germans, and while the government's information was neither complete nor accurate, enough was known to provide the basis for a plausible prima facie case of treason on the part of Lenin and the Bolshevik party.

Pereverzev's suggestion was taken up with enthusiasm in the Provisional Government, and a former member of the Bolshevik party, Gregory Alexinsky, was persuaded to serve as sponsor for a collection of forged documents designed to prove Lenin's treachery. By the afternoon of July 4 Pereverzev's preparations were complete, and calls were made to all the city's newspaper editors to attend a press conference at which the story would be released.

Patriotism and a sense of duty were still potent factors among the army rank-and-file, and for many soldiers the idea of taking part in a direct assault on the government was repellent. During the afternoon of July 4, reports about Lenin's link with the Germans were presented to a number of garrison units, and the resultant swing in the troops' attitude away from the Bolshevik leader fully confirmed Pereverzev's judgment that this propaganda weapon could have a devastating effect on the Bolsheviks' standing and influence among the troops.

In this emergency—a real crisis for Lenin, since he could not be sure just how much the Provisional Government had been able to piece together with regard to his German dealings—the man who came to Lenin's aid was Stalin. It was Stalin, playing on the comradely feelings of a fellow Georgian, who went personally to N. S. Chkheidze, one of the chairmen of the VTsIK, with the urgent request that he take immediate action to block publication of the story. The feeling of solidarity within the "revolutionary democracy" of socialist parties, still regarded as including the Bolsheviks, was potent enough to persuade Chkheidze, reluctantly backed by the more skeptical Tseretelli, to accede to Stalin's plea. Nearly all the editors accepted Chkheidze's request that they kill the story, but one small afternoon tabloid, the *Zhivoe slovo*, carried it, under the heading "Lenin, Ganetsky & Co.— German Spies." Stalin's effort to block its publication had therefore failed in its primary aim, but there was an important secondary effect that profoundly strengthened his standing in the eyes of the party's leader. The question of whether or not the attempt to block the story succeeded was of secondary importance for Lenin—after all, the government had shown that it could easily find other ways to circulate the story, even if all the newspapers refused to print it. What was important for Lenin was that Stalin had stood firmly beside him at a moment of acute personal crisis. Probably no other action by Stalin throughout his long association with Lenin did so much to solidify his standing with the party leader, and the depth of Lenin's publicly expressed gratitude is a measure of the acute anxiety he felt at the prospect of seeing his entire revolutionary career torpedoed by disclosure of his financial links with the German General Staff.[13]

Pereverzev's effort to discredit Lenin was only one of the measures of self-defense adopted by the Provisional Government at the height of the July crisis. On the afternoon of July 4, the government ordered the disarming of workers and soldiers and drafted plans for the eviction of the Bolshevik Central Committee from its headquarters in the Kshesinskaya mansion. At the same time, urgent messages were sent out to a number of field unit commanders calling on them to come to the defense of the regime. These measures were taken with the support of the Soviet executive committees and the Mensheviks and SR's who controlled their policies. At a turbulent meeting of the executive committees, which lasted until dawn on the morning of the fourth, it was demanded that "demonstrations which bring shame to revolutionary Petrograd [must] be ended once and for all." When the meeting broke up, around 5 A.M., the Menshevik and SR delegates hurried off to the factories and barracks to explain the meeting's decision to the workers and soldiers.[14]

Throughout the afternoon of July 4, meanwhile, conservative and right-wing elements in Petrograd were firing on the workers' demonstrations, either to drive the workers to take cover or to provoke them into the use of arms so as to have an excuse for crushing them by force.

Lenin Enforces the Policy of Retreat

While the Provisional Government was trying to pull itself together, organize its defenses, and take steps to blunt the insurgent threat, the soldiers and workers who had been marching, assembling, and demonstrating for nearly two days and nights were beginning to show signs of weariness, uncertainty, and lack of leadership. The effect of the call for transfer of power to the soviets voiced in the Bolsheviks' July 4 proclamation had been blunted by Lenin's impromptu address to the soldiers and sailors advising them to return peacefully to their barracks. Whatever truth there may be in the reports that Lenin had been planning to use the July demonstrations as the basis for an assault on the Provisional Government, it is incontrovertible that by the morning of July 4 he had decided to call off the demonstrations and stage a general retreat. Notwithstanding the fact that the Bolshevik party at this time was far from disciplined or unified in its organization and policies, its members still looked to Lenin for guidance. Decisive for the party's tactical stance was the attitude adopted by the top echelon of Lenin's lieutenants, who were accustomed to taking their cue from Lenin. Two of these men, Zinoviev and Kamenev, needed no persuasion to adopt a policy of caution. Trotsky was not yet a member of the party during the July Days and had no voice in shaping its policies. If it was indeed Stalin who drafted the July 4 proclamation calling for the transfer of power to the soviets, he did so on his own authority, without the backing of Lenin or the party leadership. By the time the proclamation had been issued, in any event, the change to retreat was already in full swing.

With his alertness to shifts in the balance of social forces, Lenin had decided by the morning of July 4 that the insurgent wave had already crested and that a descent into an as yet unfathomed trough was inevitable. It must remain an open question just how far Lenin's gloomy prognosis was due to his evaluation of events in the streets of the capital and how much was due to his fear that the truth about his financial support from the German General Staff was in imminent danger of disclosure. Unmistakably clear, however, is his determination to impose a policy of general retreat on the party, beginning with his talk to the soldiers and sailors on the morning of July 4.

Bringing the Central Committee to accept the need for retreat presented few obstacles; far more difficult was the problem of reining in the firebrands of the Petersburg Committee and the Military Organization. Even in a party that enjoyed a considerable degree of local autonomy and independence in policy making, however, it was obviously essential that on such an important question as this, discipline must be enforced. But it took a series of sharp clashes, stretching over the next two days, before Lenin was able to obtain general compliance with the policy of retreat.

By the evening of July 4, the cumulative evidence pointing to the necessity for an immediate retreat on the part of the Bolsheviks had convinced all but the most fanatic advocates of an armed uprising. At 8 P.M. an enlarged session of the party's Central Committee was held in the Tauride Palace, with representatives of the Petersburg Committee, the Military Organization, and Trotsky's *Mezhraiontsy* group present. It was a stormy and somber session, but Stalin, in his speech to the Sixth Party Congress, smoothed over the rough spots and presented matters from an unconvincingly optimistic angle:

> It is decided that now that the revolutionary workers and soldiers have demonstrated their will, the action should be stopped. An appeal is drawn up on these lines: "The demonstration is over. . . . Our watchword is staunchness, restraint, calm."[15]

The Moderate Socialists Decide to Prop Up the Provisional Government

Earlier on the evening of the fourth, around 6 P.M., the executive committees of the soviets opened a joint meeting that was to have decisive significance for the fate of the Provisional Government, the Bolshevik party, and the revolution. A clear-cut choice confronted the Mensheviks and the SR's: either they must throw their support to the Provisional Government, still reeling under the impact of the Cadet ministers' resignation, or they must accede to the demonstrators' demand—backed by some members of the Bolshevik party—that they themselves take power in the name of the revolutionary masses.

Since no Bolsheviks were present at the meeting, it fell to the lot of a member of the *Mezhraiontsy* group, Lunacharsky, to introduce a proposal condemning the Provisional Government and demanding the transfer of power to the soviets. Sustained by their conviction that the revolution was essentially a middle-class, bourgeois phenomenon and that Russia was not yet prepared for a socialist revolution, the moderate socialists brushed aside Lunacharsky's proposal—as they had similar ones presented by various workers' delegations earlier that afternoon—and in the early morning hours of July 5 adopted a resolution voicing conditional support for the Provisional Government and asserting that should the question of transferring power to the soviets arise, "only a full meeting of the executive committees has the right to decide this question."[16] For the moderate socialists, this resolution represented the historic parting of the ways, their reluctant but nonetheless definite decision to tag along with the middle-class parties rather than risk their fate and that of Russia on the uncharted seas of a full-scale popular revolt led by the Bolsheviks.

The Bolsheviks on the Defensive

While the executive committees were holding their long, tense meeting, a decisive shift occurred in the balance of military power in Petrograd. Throughout July 3 and into the following day, insurgent troops had controlled the streets of the capital, bolstered by throngs of aroused workers carrying placards and slogans. By the afternoon of the fourth, the troop movement had begun to subside; the workers, however, still kept up their demonstrations, and as late as 8 P.M. a noisy group of them pushed into the meeting hall where the executive committees were in session, demanding that the soviets take power. It was with a tremendous feeling of relief, therefore, that the harried delegates in the executive committee session greeted the midnight arrival of troops of the Izmailovsky Regiment, straight from the northern front, from whence it had marched to the defense of the Provisional Government and the Soviet.

The shift in the military balance was accompanied by a sharp stepping up of the government's assault on the Bolsheviks. Early on the morning of July 5, a detachment of troops was sent to the printing press where *Pravda* was published with orders to wreck it, orders that the troops enthusiastically carried out. Some arrests were made, but none of *Pravda*'s editors, including Lenin and Stalin, were caught.[17] On the following days the campaign to throttle the Bolsheviks' press continued with raids on *Soldatskaia pravda* and *Trud*. With the help of sympathetic printers, however, the Bolsheviks were able to find a new press from which, on July 6, a substitute for *Pravda*, entitled *Listok pravdy*, was issued.

The next target for repression was the Kshesinskaya mansion, where the Bolsheviks had established their headquarters. An order to occupy the building was issued by the Provisional Government on

July 4, with the approval of the executive committees of the soviets. General P. A. Polovtsev, commander of the Petrograd Military District, at once began assembling a task force to execute the order. For its part the Bolshevik Military Organization, recognizing the imminence of an attack and forewarned by rumors of Polovtsev's preparations, set up patrols at the mansion and prepared to defend it by force of arms. Preparations were also made to defend the nearby Peter and Paul Fortress, where the Bolsheviks had established their reserve headquarters.

While government forces were preparing for the assault, the Bolshevik leadership, meeting on the afternoon of the fifth, reaffirmed their decision to conduct a tactical retreat. Zinoviev, now clearly identified as an opponent of further demonstrations, was sent by Lenin to the Peter and Paul Fortress to order its surrender, an order that the Military Organization ignored. The difficult task of negotiating the surrender of the forces defending the Kshesinskaya mansion was assigned to Stalin. In a talk with Tseretelli late on the afternoon of the fifth, Stalin sought assurances that there would be no bloodshed and that the Bolsheviks would be provided with new meeting quarters in return for an agreement to hand over the mansion without resistance. Stalin evidently believed that an agreement was reached along these lines; the moderate socialists, however, reneged on their promise to find alternate quarters for the Bolsheviks.[18]

Stalin was also called on to negotiate the disarming of a detachment of Kronstadt sailors who were defending the Peter and Paul Fortress. With little or no room for maneuver, Stalin's task was limited to securing the voluntary submission of the sailors and their agreement to return to Kronstadt peacefully and unarmed.[19]

Viewed from the standpoint of the Soviet and the Provisional Government, Stalin had played a useful role in these negotiations, and there seems little doubt that his services earned him some grudging respect in those quarters. It is probably for that reason that his name was not included in the list of Bolshevik leaders subject to arrest which the Provisional Government issued on July 6.

For the Bolsheviks, however, the outcome of Stalin's negotiations was a sharp worsening of their position—the loss of their centrally located headquarters, eviction from the Peter and Paul Fortress, and the graphic demonstration to the troops of their inability or unwillingness to lead or defend them.

Even after these setbacks, nevertheless, there were still some Bolsheviks who wanted to continue the struggle. There was a final flareup of the spirit of resistance among members of the Petersburg Committee at a session held on the afternoon of July 6, at which there was sentiment for calling a general strike. Lenin, who attended the meeting, not only firmly vetoed the strike proposal but personally drafted a back-to-work proclamation for distribution among the workers. At a hastily summoned meeting of the Central Committee that evening, Lenin announced a momentous change in the party's tactics: in view of the domination of the soviets by the Mensheviks and the SR's, he argued, the slogan "All Power to the Soviets" must be withdrawn in favor of one calling for the direct seizure of power by the Bolsheviks— not immediately, but at some later time when changed conditions made success a realistic possibility. Despite the harsh repression it faced, Lenin insisted, the Bolshevik party must meanwhile use every legal avenue open to it for political action.[20]

The Question of Lenin's Arrest and Trial

The order for the arrest of Lenin, Zinoviev, and Kamenev, which the Provisional Government had issued earlier on the sixth, provided a test of Lenin's new line. The question now was whether the use of legal means ought to include his submission to arrest and trial. Lenin himself was undecided at the outset of the debate, at one point going so far as to draft a letter to the Provisional Government offering to submit to arrest under certain conditions. There were weighty arguments on both sides of the question. A trial, it might be argued, could be used to attack the government—the history of the Russian revolutionary movement provided plenty of instances where tactics of that kind had been effectively employed by revolutionaries. A decision to avoid arrest, on the other hand, might be interpreted as an implied confession of guilt, and thus further damage the Bolsheviks' standing among the workers and soldiers. What guarantees were there, however, that if Lenin and his aides tamely submitted to arrest they would be given a fair trial, or that they would not be lynched by some fanatical anti-Bolshevik officer or guard? For Lenin there was always the additional unspoken worry: how much did the government really know about his German contacts? If there was a trial, the question would certainly be brought up, and there could be no assurance that he would be able successfully to defend his innocence.

In the first of what was to become a prolonged series of debates on this thorny question, the Central Committee on July 6 decided against permitting Lenin to submit to arrest. Preparations were immediately launched to find a secure hiding place for him and his indicted comrades. Once again Stalin was given an opportunity to earn Lenin's gratitude. It was in Stalin's rooms with the Alliluevs that Lenin and Zinoviev spent the tense days from July 7 to 11, in fear of imminent discovery. Stalin, with his bona fides firmly established in Soviet circles, was not molested, and served as contact man for the concealed Lenin. When Lenin finally decided that security demanded that he get out of the city, Stalin was one of the small group who accompanied him to the Maritime Station for the journey, in disguise and under an assumed name, to a small village, Razliv, in the vicinity of Petrograd, where the gendarmes and investigators of the Provisional Government would have difficulty in finding him.

There was probably never a moment in the nearly two-decade-long association between Lenin and Stalin when their personal relations were more warm and cordial than in the period between Lenin's flight from Petrograd in July and his further move, a month later, to a more secure hideout across the border into quasi-independent Finland. Throughout the July crisis Stalin had stood firmly beside him, rendering him invaluable personal services. It was Stalin who had publicly come to Lenin's defense against the government's charge of treason. It was Stalin who arranged for the temporary quarters where Lenin and Zinoviev took refuge July 7–11. Stalin was one of the small group of comrades who escorted Lenin to the Maritime Station on July 11.

Even Trotsky grudgingly acknowledged the closeness between the two men at this time. Lenin, he writes, "undoubtedly trusted him [Stalin] as a cautious conspirator."[21] But it was not mere recognition on Lenin's part of Stalin's conspiratorial talents; the bond between them at this point was stronger than Trotsky was prepared to admit. The immediate aftermath of the July Days was an organizational crisis for the Bolshevik party, but it was also an acute personal crisis for Lenin; and it was Stalin, more than anyone else, who helped him weather this storm. The credit that Stalin earned in Lenin's eyes during the July crisis was to remain for years a reserve against which he could draw in their personal relations, outweighing his many blunders and serving to conceal from Lenin until almost the end of his life the fact that on a number of important issues he and Stalin held fundamentally different views.

Impact of the Military Defeat

In his report to the Sixth Congress, Stalin asserted that Bolshevik policy immediately after the June 18 demonstration was to remain quiet, avoid further antigovernment actions, and await the moment when the newly launched offensive had run its course before resuming an active policy. Bolshevik behavior during the July Days hardly fitted into that strategy, a fact that strengthens the view that it was really the insurgent masses rather than the Bolshevik leadership who had precipitated that action. Late on the evening of July 6, when the Bolshevik rout was nearly complete—ousted from their headquarters, their newspapers banned, their principal leaders proscribed and fugitive—the first reports began to come in of a Russian defeat, the beginning of the inglorious end of the ill-starred Kerensky offensive which had been launched in June with so much fanfare and such high hopes. Had they been able to avoid identification with the excesses of the July Days, had they been able to stick to the strategy outlined by Stalin in his Sixth Congress speech, this was the moment at which the Bolsheviks could have capitalized on the military defeat, which rapidly assumed the dimensions of a full-scale disaster, a disaster for which the Kerensky government should have borne the primary responsibility. Instead, the Bolsheviks provided the excuse by which the government attempted, with some success, to explain away the military defeat. Press accounts in newspapers sympathetic to the government appeared on July 7 with accusations that the Bolsheviks had been a principal factor in the army's setback, through their advocacy of defeatism and their all-too-successful efforts at undermining military discipline.

The heated debate over the question of Lenin's arrest and trial was resumed on July 7 in Stalin's rooms at the Alliluevs' apartment. To explore the possibility of a guarantee of Lenin's security, someone—possibly Stalin—undertook to ascertain whether the soviets could offer such a guarantee. Receiving a negative response, Stalin, it is said, joined the majority of the Central Committee in opposing Lenin's submission to arrest and trial.[22]

Existing records of this important debate are inconsistent and confused. In some, Stalin is identified as the negotiator who sounded out the Executive Committee of the Soviet on the question of a guarantee; in others this role is assigned to Ordzhonikidze. On one point only is there nearly complete agreement, that of Stalin's position. Even Trotsky, citing Krupskaya in support, affirms that "Stalin held out more tenaciously [against Lenin's arrest and trial] than the others and was proved right."[23] Three weeks later, however, when this question came up once more for discussion, at the Sixth Congress, Stalin not only treated it as one not already decisively answered but even attempted to revive the project of obtaining guarantees for Lenin's safety from the Executive Committee of the Soviet.

Kerensky Takes Power; Lenin Slips Out of Petrograd

Throughout the government crisis of early July, Kerensky was the central figure in the Provisional Government, although he was not yet formally its leader. It was Kerensky whose actions had helped precipitate the double crisis that nearly brought down the government: by sponsoring the military offensive, thereby goading a number of military units in the Petrograd garrison into open revolt, and by negotiating the compromise with the Ukrainian nationalists, thereby provoking the Cadet ministers into the withdrawal that triggered the cabinet crisis.

Fittingly, then, it was Kerensky who emerged at the end of the July crisis as the formal and generally acknowledged leader of the Provisional Government. Prince George Lvov, a well-meaning but ineffective Cadet politician, resigned as premier on July 8, and Kerensky took his place on the following day. One of his first actions was to order a thorough investigation of the near-insurrection that had just ended. At about the same time, orders were issued to break up the First Machine Gun Regiment and send its members to front-line units.

Deprived of its founder and leader, harried and persecuted by the authorities, the Bolshevik party in the second half of July faced its greatest challenge. That it emerged from the ordeal strengthened, confident, and ready for action was due in large part to the hard work and unshaken faith of Sverdlov and Stalin.

For Stalin, the party's time of troubles was the opportunity for which he had been preparing himself. In March he had shown his eagerness to play a leading role for which he was totally unprepared. Since mid-April, however, he had been undergoing a crash apprenticeship in revolutionary tactics and principles at the hands of Lenin, master craftsman of the revolution. Now, armed with the theoretical knowledge he had previously lacked and schooled by participation alongside Lenin in a succession of crises, Stalin felt ready to step forward as the party's acting leader.

At one stroke, by ordering the arrest of Lenin, Zinoviev, and Kamenev, the government had cleared the path for Stalin's rise to power. Now, too, Stalin's shrewd political maneuvering, the wisdom of his decision to retain a footing in the Executive Committee of the Soviet through his Georgian contacts and his "honest broker" negotiations with the insurgents during the July Days, paid off handsomely. The omission of Stalin's name from the list of those to be arrested reflected not merely an underestimate of his political strength on the part of the government but a positive evaluation of his status by the moderate socialist leaders in the VTsIK.

It was a stroke of luck for Stalin that Trotsky took himself out of the running by volunteering for imprisonment on July 10, thereby removing a threat to Stalin's position as acting leader of the party.

Fate seemed to have taken a hand in furthering Stalin's cause. Now it was up to him to show how well he could use the opportunity thus provided.

The "Pencil Story": Stalin's Daydream

Any comprehensive attempt to trace Stalin's activities during the July Days of 1917 must take into account a curious report that first appeared in print toward the end of 1929. This report, which I call the "pencil story," was given by the popular poet Demian Bedny (pseudonym of Yefim Alekseevich Pridvorov) in one of his contributions to *Pravda*'s celebration of Stalin's fiftieth birthday, which fell on December 21, 1929. Two issues of *Pravda* were devoted to the anniversary, those of December 20 and 21, and Bedny contributed to both issues. In *Pravda* for December 20 he published an article entitled "Completely True," while in the issue of December 21 his contributions took the form of a poem, "I Am Sure," and an article entitled "Fragments."[24]

The pencil story occurs toward the end of "Fragments," the major part of which consists of a discussion of Stalin's use of the "mountain eagle" image to characterize Lenin. Almost as an afterthought, Bedny then shifts to events in 1917, "on the eve of the July Days," which establishes the date as July 3, 1917, Old Style. On that day, Bedny says, he was sitting in the editorial office of *Pravda* talking with Stalin. Suddenly the telephone rang and Stalin took the call. It proved to be from a sailor at the Kronstadt naval base who wanted Stalin's advice on a momentous question: should the sailors come armed to the demonstration in Petrograd then in preparation, or should they come without weapons?

Bedny found the situation extremely funny, not because of the question, which was serious enough, but because of Stalin's behavior in answering it. Puffing on his pipe and stroking his moustache, Stalin thought for a moment, then gave an answer that reduced Bedny to helpless laughter. "We scribblers," said Stalin, "always carry our weapons—our pens—with us wherever we go. As to your weapons, comrade, you can be the best judges of that."

As Bedny admiringly points out, Stalin had avoided recommending in so many words that the sailors come armed to the demonstration, but that was clearly his implication. In the event the demonstration turned out badly, no one could charge that Stalin had called for the use of armed force against the government. It was that aspect of Stalin's reply which earned Bedny's admiration for Stalin's "cunning."

"Fragments" was included in a collective volume published toward the end of 1929; in the following year, a second mass edition was published.[25] Thereafter, however, the article dropped out of sight. It was not included in Bedny's Collected Works (nineteen volumes, 1928–32), nor in the eight-volume Collected Works, published in 1965.

Before examining the treatment that historians of the revolution and biographers of Stalin have given the pencil story, it will be useful to consider Bedny's other major contribution to the celebration of Stalin's birthday, the article "Completely True." In this article Bedny uses a newspaper column by a Socialist Revolutionary émigré, Semyon Vereshchak, as the basis for a laudatory account of Stalin's reportedly courageous behavior as an inmate in the Baku prison in 1908.[26] At the bottom of the article appears the date February 7, 1928; an editorial note explains that "in connection with the fiftieth birthday of Comrade Stalin, the editorial board of Pravda considered it appropriate to remind the readers of Pravda of a feuilleton of Comrade D. Bedny which reflects in artistic form one of the moments in the heroic past of Comrade Stalin."

Contrary to what one biographer of Stalin has assumed, the 1928 date does not indicate prior publication in Pravda.[27] More cautiously, Tucker states, "Bedny's article was dated Feb. 7, 1928, but I have not been able to ascertain whether or not it appeared in print before the birthday celebration in 1929." In fact, Bedny's article did not appear in Pravda in February 1928; it was, however, included in volume 12 of his Collected Works, which came out in 1928.[28]

"Completely True," like the Vereshchak column on which it is based, has attracted favorable attention from Stalin's biographers because of its lively portrayal of the young Stalin's staunch behavior under the harsh conditions of prison existence. The fact that the story was told by an SR émigré, who would normally have had no reason to praise Stalin, has convinced a number of Stalin's biographers that the story must be substantially accurate. H. Montgomery Hyde, for example, calls it "one of the most vivid and at the same time most trustworthy [reminiscences] of the young Stalin to have survived."[29]

The first of Bedny's writings produced specifically for the birthday celebration, the poem "I Am Sure," is a slight thing, even by Bedny's customary lightweight standards; it amounts to little more than a plea of not being able to produce anything suitable for so momentous an occasion. It evidently served as a warm-up exercise, however, for an editorial note at the end states that the author did, nevertheless, write the article "Fragments," which follows immediately.

Most historians of the Russian Revolution have treated the pencil story with distrust or have ignored it entirely. A number of Stalin's biographers, on the other hand, have been attracted to it, in part because it lends a touch of color to the account of Stalin's activities in the July Days, in part because it brings out something of the man's character and behavior.

The first of Stalin's biographers to consider the pencil story was Trotsky, who called it "the enigmatic testimony of Demian Bedny," adding, "The story was probably stylized. But one senses a grain of truth in it." Thus, Trotsky accepted the story as essentially true, cautioning, however, that

> one must not exaggerate the significance of that episode. The question probably came from the Kronstadt Committee of the Party. As for the sailors, they would have gone out with their arms anyway.[30]

Trotsky's commentary marks the beginning of a tendency among Stalin's biographers to strengthen the pencil story by adding details in an attempt to fit it into the known framework of events. Thus, Trotsky provides the hypothesis that the question "probably came from the Kronstadt Committee of the Party"; that is, it was a question to which the Kronstadt Bolsheviks really wanted an answer. But Trotsky immediately undercuts this suggestion by commenting, "As for the sailors, they would have gone out with their arms anyway." Why, then, would the Kronstadt Committee raise the question in the first place? And why would they not identify themselves in making the call? And why would the call be directed to Stalin, at the editorial office of *Pravda*, rather than to the headquarters of the Bolshevik Central Committee in the Kshesinskaya mansion? Trotsky provides no answer to these questions.

Several biographers of Stalin, reluctant to abandon the pencil story but troubled by questions of this kind, have followed Trotsky's lead in adding details that were not in the original. Thus, Boris Souvarine writes,

> He [Stalin] assumed administrative work at the headquarters of the Party and of its journals, and was careful to say and do nothing which would commit him irrevocably. Demian Bedny relates with admiration the following example of his method.[31]

Souvarine then retells the pencil story. He sees it as evidence that Stalin assumed administrative tasks and slurs over the question of Stalin's relation to the Central Committee with the phrase, "at the headquarters of the party and of its journals." But the sailor's question was hardly of an administrative nature, nor would the sailors have been likely to call the *Pravda* editorial office in regard to a matter that required an authoritative ruling from the Central Committee.

Ulam performs a similar operation on the pencil story to increase its verisimilitude. "Stalin," he writes,

> a famous story has it, was the member of the Central Committee of whom the sailors inquired by telephone whether they should bring their rifles along.[32]

In Ulam's version, two significant "improvements" have been added: first, that Stalin was being consulted in his capacity as a member of the Central Committee; second, that it was "the sailors," that is, a significant body of them, not merely an unidentified individual, who were asking for Stalin's counsel.

Other biographers of Stalin who have given the pencil story some weight include Edward Ellis Smith, who notes that the story may be "unauthentic," but who nevertheless builds an elaborate structure on it, marred by a number of factual errors, for example, the date.[33] Ronald Hingley ignores the question of authenticity but brings out the relevance of the story to an understanding of Stalin's character:

> The [sailor's] query was embarrassing to Stalin. As an enthusiastic disruptor of the existing semi-order, he, of course, preferred armed to pacific protesters any day. After all, even under the Provisional Government incitement to armed insurrection was a punishable offense. Here was a delicate diplomatic problem which called into play both Stalin's sense of irony and his natural caution. Screwing up his face in an expression crafty in the ultimate degree, and stroking his mustache with his free hand, he spoke his Delphic reply into the telephone.[34]

Misled by Smith's errors, Hyde uses the story as the basis for asserting that the demonstration of July 4 began "with Stalin, on Lenin's initiative, summoning the sailors from the naval base at Kronstadt to a 'peaceful demonstration.'"[35] Alex de Jonge falls into the same trap.[36]

Several biographers of Stalin, including Tucker and Payne, pass over the pencil story in silence, evidently judging it to be worthless as a historical record. Understandable and even laudable as reflecting a strict sense of what constitutes valid historical evidence, this restraint is regrettable in that it leaves the puzzle of the pencil story unsolved. After all, the story *did* appear in Pravda; Stalin liked it well enough to see to its republication twice; and Trotsky had a point when he said, "One senses a grain of truth in it."

What, then, is the real meaning of the pencil story? To understand its significance, it is necessary to place it in the context of known events during the July Days. Of special relevance are the available data on contacts between Kronstadt and Bolshevik headquarters in

Petrograd. As noted above, the memoirs of Raskol'nikov are the best available source for this question.

It is obvious that Raskol'nikov's testimony conflicts at every point with the pencil story. The story does not give a true account of events in 1917; it is not merely "stylized," as Trotsky put it, but palpably false. It is noteworthy that the story did not appear in print until the end of 1929; it could not, in fact, have been published earlier because it would have made Stalin look ridiculous. Only after he had won a decisive victory over all his major political rivals could such a transparent fiction have been published. But Trotsky's assertion that "one senses a grain of truth in it" should not be disregarded. Something happened; the story was told, and it was published and republished with Stalin's implicit endorsement. The solution to Trotsky's "enigma" may be found in the sequence of Bedny's contributions to *Pravda* on December 20 and 21, 1929. The following reconstruction appears to be probable:

First, *Pravda*'s editors decided to go all out in celebrating Stalin's fiftieth birthday, devoting two issues to the event. In preparing their copy for the December 20 issue they came across Bedny's article, "Completely True," which he had submitted on February 7, 1928, but which at that time they considered unsuitable. In view of the heated political struggle then in progress, it would have been harmful to Stalin's interests to cite an SR émigré, even in praise of Stalin. Bedny's article was therefore consigned to the files, though Bedny liked it well enough to include it in volume 12 of his *Collected Works* later that year.

The situation was completely different in December 1929, when Stalin had emerged the victor in the struggle for power. Now there could be no danger in publishing the article. Thus, it was published in the issue for December 20. Stalin was understandably delighted. Bedny, who was a regular visitor to the *Pravda* offices, received a cordial invitation to meet Stalin, probably on the afternoon of December 20. In the euphoric mood engendered by his recent political victory, Stalin relaxed and disclosed some of his inner feelings.

The conversation began with a discussion of Stalin's concept of Lenin. With a poet's psychological insight, Bedny recognized that Stalin's image of Lenin as a "mountain eagle" revealed more about Stalin than it did about Lenin.[37]

Just as the visit was drawing to a close, Stalin's mind reverted to 1917, the July Days, and he told Bedny the pencil story, with the appropriate facial expressions and gestures. Bedny found Stalin's performance highly amusing, but he also recognized that the story was in some way important to Stalin.

Shortly after the visit, Bedny wrote an account of its two major topics, the mountain eagle image and the pencil story. Since the article had no overt unity, Bedny called it "Fragments." (The underlying unity, Stalin's psychology, could hardly be admitted publicly.)

Why did Stalin tell the pencil story, and what psychological needs did it meet for him? Two possibilities suggest themselves. First, the story soothed an old wound to Stalin's ego. Though he had been formally a member of the ruling inner circle of the Bolshevik party in July 1917, no one had thought to ask his opinion on such an urgent question as the appearance of a contingent of Kronstadt sailors in the July 4 demonstration. Instead, it was Kamenev and Zinoviev, two other members of the center, who received the calls from Raskol'nikov at Kronstadt and who gave him authoritative direction.

Raskol'nikov's memoirs, published in 1923 and republished in 1925, must have been acutely painful to Stalin because of their casual disregard of his existence in July 1917. In recompense, the pencil story portrays Stalin as the sole Bolshevik leader whom the Kronstadt sailors consulted. (*Pace* Souvarine, Ulam, et al., there is nothing in the story to indicate that the sailors were consulting Stalin in his capacity as a member of the CC; the clear import of the story is that Stalin answered the query about weapons on his own authority, without reference to his colleagues.)

It seems probable that the pencil story, with its focus on the question of arming the sailors, reflects a sense of guilt on Stalin's part concerning his role in disarming the sailors at the Peter and Paul Fortress on the morning of July 6, 1917. For obvious reasons, that was an episode in which he could take little pride. He had done his duty, in fulfillment of a task assigned to him by the CC, but there was nothing heroic about his action, nothing that ministered to his need for self-glorification. If, as the pencil story would have us believe, Stalin had refrained from advising the sailors to carry arms at the July 4 demonstration, then he bore no responsibility for arranging the surrender of their arms on July 6; that responsibility fell on others.

It is noteworthy that Bedny, with his insight into Stalin's psychology, made three major contributions to the Stalin cult of personality at the time of the fiftieth birthday celebration: first, the Baku prison story in "Completely True"; second, the mountain eagle image in "Fragments"; and third, the pencil story, also in "Fragments." Bedny's role in regard to the first two was simply that of reporter and commentator; no manipulation of the data was required. In the case of the pencil story, the situation was more complex. Simply to relate the facts—that Stalin in December 1929 had spun this tall tale about long-ago events—would not suffice. What was needed, Bedny must have realized, was to give the story the stamp of historical authenticity by altering the dates and making it appear that his visit with Stalin in the *Pravda* office took place at the time of the events described in the story.

It was not Bedny's fault that the pencil story suffered from a number of obvious weaknesses, the most glaring of which was its direct conflict with established historical facts. That weakness could be met for the time being by Bedny's assertion that the story was true (Bedny was in effect saying, "I was there"). Later, it would require the suppression of materials that invalidated it, especially Raskol'nikov's memoirs and those of his brother, Il'in-Zhenevsky; finally, it would strengthen Stalin's motive for extermination of the Il'in brothers.

The pencil story suffered, however, from another, less easily remediable weakness. It disclosed all too frankly a significant aspect of Stalin's situation in 1917, his physical isolation at the *Pravda* office and his failure to maintain close contact with the other members of the Bolshevik leadership. For Stalin in 1917, the *Pravda* office served as a refuge from the tumult and uproar of revolutionary events. It can thus be seen as one of a series of refuges which mark Stalin's career, from his isolated, one-man hut in Siberian exile in 1915–16 to his Kremlin office and Moscow-region dacha in the period of his full dictatorship.

For Stalin in 1917, however, the *Pravda* office was a refuge that became a trap. In July, as later in October, Stalin remained outside the mainstream of events and missed some of the crucial developments of the revolution. It was in large part because the pencil story disclosed this aspect of Stalin's situation in 1917 that it was found unsuitable for use by Soviet biographers and historians, even during the period of Stalin's cult of personality.

For the insight it can provide into Stalin's mentality and unconscious motivation, however, the pencil story is a valuable historical document. It makes available to us one of Stalin's earliest recorded daydreams. Its telling to Bedny and its publication in *Pravda* mark the moment in Stalin's career when he instinctively felt that his recent political victory gave him power not only to determine the future course of Soviet policy but also to revise the past, to correct the historical record, to expunge evidence he found distasteful, and to substitute his own version of what should have happened, free of the fear that anyone would dare to contradict him. It was to take more than ten years and the lives of countless victims, including the Il'in brothers, before Stalin had fully achieved this goal. By that time the pencil story had been largely forgotten, ignored by Stalin's court historians and surviving elsewhere as a historical curiosity.

Historians of 1917 have been right to ignore the pencil story; its overt meaning tells us nothing useful about the history of the revolution. On the other hand, those biographers of Stalin who have attempted to use the story as evidence, however distorted, of Stalin's actions in 1917 have been misled. Seen as a mental construct dating from a period long after the events it purports to describe, it has value not for our historical understanding of 1917 but for our psychological understanding of Stalin as he was at the end of 1929.

Mid-July: Stalin Emergent

For the Bolshevik party as a whole, the July Days and their aftermath represented a serious though not fatal setback. For Stalin, however, they meant a sudden, entirely unexpected emergence as one of the party's top and most active leaders. The reasons had little to do with Stalin's own capabilities; they were due in large part to the removal of those who stood in his way, either actually, like Lenin, Zinoviev, and Kamenev, or potentially, like Trotsky. By its order for the arrest of some of the Bolsheviks' top leaders, the Provisional Government temporarily muffled the voice of Lenin. Zinoviev, forced into hiding with Lenin, dropped out of active participation in the formulation of policy. Kamenev, jailed, lost the opportunity to influence either Stalin or the party as a whole. Trotsky, jailed at his own request, not yet formally a Bolshevik, presented no immediate threat to Stalin as writer, orator, or party leader.

The only potential rival facing Stalin was Sverdlov, but the latter chose to pursue a complementary rather than a competing role. Mainly concerned with management of the party machine, Sverdlov was content to leave the visible and vocal leadership of the party to Stalin.

The period from Lenin's departure from Petrograd on July 12 to the end of the Sixth Party Congress in early August, therefore, was a windfall for Stalin in which his dreams of glory seemed miraculously to have materialized. Not until the end of the 1920s was he to have such a clear field in which to demonstrate his leadership capacity.

Stalin and Sverdlov in Control

What was the relationship between Stalin and Sverdlov at this point? Was there a division of labor, or did they collaborate on the tasks facing the party? In his biography of Stalin, Trotsky assumed that they collaborated. "The daily leadership," he wrote, fell to Sverdlov and Stalin as the most influential members of the Central Committee remaining at liberty. The mass movement had in the meantime weakened considerably. Half of the party had gone underground. The preponderance of the machine had grown correspondingly. Inside of the machine the role of Stalin grew automatically. That law operates automatically throughout his entire political biography and forms, as it were, its mainspring.[38]

Several factors combined to lead Trotsky to that conclusion—a mistaken one, in my judgment. Most influential was Trotsky's experience during the 1920s with Stalin's masterful employment of the party machine in the struggle for power. Projecting that experience back onto the revolution, Trotsky believed he had found a recurring pattern in Stalin's career. Always intent on finding the "law" underlying surface appearances, Trotsky equated the situation facing the party in July 1917 with the entirely different one that existed after Stalin's appointment as general secretary in April 1922.

To suppose that Stalin collaborated with Sverdlov in managing the party machinery in mid-July 1917 would mean believing that as early as 1917 Stalin recognized the importance of the machine and understood how to manipulate it. Nothing in the historical record supports that conclusion, however, and there is much to refute it. Sverdlov was the first party official to master the skill of organizational control of the party machine, and his very mastery left little opportunity for Stalin to collaborate with him or learn from him. In July 1917, Stalin served as the top active party leader, while Sverdlov tended to the daily grind of party management. Even at the Sixth Party Congress Sverdlov spoke only on organizational questions, leaving the policy questions to Stalin, or, as Sverdlov himself put it in his second report to the congress,

> The report of Comrade Stalin has fully illuminated the activity of the Central Committee. There remains for me to limit myself to the narrow sphere of the organizational activity of the Central Committee.[39]

In 1917 Stalin was still searching for power through imitation of Lenin as top party leader and policy maker, little suspecting that the key to success was unobtrusively present in the organizational work of Sverdlov.

Lenin Redefines the Party Line: The "July Theses"

Though forced into hiding, Lenin had no intention of yielding his right to define the Bolshevik party line. On July 10, his last full day in Petrograd, he dashed off an article, "The Most Recent Political Situation (Four Theses)," in which he defined the existing balance of power and the response that he believed the party should make.[40] The article constituted in effect a major realignment of Bolshevik policies toward the Provisional Government, the other socialist parties, and the soviets.

In Lenin's view, a military dictatorship had taken power "with the deliberate or semi-deliberate assistance of Kerensky." The leaders of the Mensheviks and the SR's had "completely betrayed the revolution by putting it into the hands of counter-revolutionaries and by turning themselves, their parties, and the Soviets into mere fig-leaves of the counter-revolution." Under these conditions,

> all hopes for a peaceful development of the Russian revolution have vanished for good.

Lenin saw only two possible outcomes:

> either complete victory for the military dictatorship, or victory for the workers' armed uprising.

Thus, Lenin's immediate reaction to the party's setback was to greatly extend his vision of the future possibilities open to the party. This was the first time since the February Revolution that he had posited an armed uprising as the next step for which the party should prepare itself.

Lenin's most startling conclusion concerned the soviets, or rather the slogan, "All Power to the Soviets," which the Bolsheviks had been using with increasing response since mid-April. This slogan, Lenin now argued,

> was a slogan for peaceful development of the revolution, which was possible in April, May, June, and up to July 5–9, i.e., up to the time when actual power passed into the hands of the military dictatorship. *This slogan is no longer correct,* for it does not take into account that power has changed hands and that the revolution has in fact been completely betrayed by the SR's and Mensheviks.

The party's role, therefore, was to

> gather forces, reorganize them, and resolutely prepare for the armed uprising . . . [whose aim] can only be to transfer power to the proletariat, supported by the poor peasants, with a view to putting our Party program into effect.

As to the party, it must revert to its practices of 1912–14, combining legal with illegal activities, making use of every legally permitted opportunity but under no "constitutional or 'peaceful' illusion."

The textological history of Lenin's July 10 article is complex, but an analysis of it is necessary in order to understand Stalin's activities and policies at this time. Stalin, as we shall see, admitted under questioning at a party conference on July 16 that he did not have Lenin's theses with him, and for many years it was believed that they were lost. Meanwhile the article, "The Most Recent Political Situation," stripped of its subtitle, "Four Theses," and toned down by the removal of all references to an armed uprising, appeared in the July 20 issue of *Proletarskoe delo*, the organ of the Bolshevik fraction of the Kronstadt Soviet. This text, with an altered heading, "The Political Mood" (*Politicheskoe nastroenie*), was signed with the initial *W* and was not recognized as substantially the Lenin article until 1959, when A. M. Sovokin published an article on the Bolshevik Central Committee meeting of July 13–14.[41]

The original manuscript of Lenin's article had meanwhile been found in the party archives not long after his death and was published in 1926.[42] Kamenev, who edited the volume, failed to note the crossed-out subtitle and also failed to recognize the article as the supposedly lost "July Theses." The manuscript, as published in 1926, showed editorial changes, the most important of which was the replacement of the expression "armed uprising" with the words "a determined struggle of the workers." Kamenev assumed that the changes had been made by Lenin himself for the purpose of evading government censorship and thus making possible the publication of the article, adding, however, "The article did not appear in the press."

Sovokin asserts that it was Stalin who made the editorial changes. "It has been established," he writes,

> by indications on the manuscript of V. I. Lenin's article, that J. V. Stalin prepared it for publication. Guided by indications given in the article, Stalin, for conspiratorial considerations, changed the expression "armed uprising" to "a resolute struggle" and deleted the end of the article.[43]

Sovokin does not mention the crossing out of the subtitle, "Four Theses." Was this also part of Stalin's "editorial preparation" of the article for publication? It would seem highly probable, since it was Stalin's failure to produce the "theses" on demand which sparked a partial repudiation of Lenin's new policy line at a Petrograd Bolshevik conference July 16–20.

Stalin was entrusted with the task of presenting and defending Lenin's new policy. The first opportunity arose on July 13 and 14, when the Central Committee held an enlarged meeting, including delegates from the Military Organization, several Moscow organizations of the party, and possibly Trotsky's *Mezhraiontsy* group.

The protocols of this important meeting remain unpublished—
Sovokin says, "They have not been found"—and Stalin's part in the
proceedings is unknown, but the results speak for themselves. Instead
of endorsing Lenin's theses, the meeting adopted a half-way position,
in effect rejecting the Leninist analysis:

> On the key question of relations with the soviet, the CC chose to sit on
> the fence . . . unlike Lenin . . . this meeting apparently concluded that the
> correct path to power was still a peaceful one through the Soviet.[44]

While concrete proof of Stalin's contribution to this outcome is
lacking, his subsequent position indicates that he disagreed with
Lenin on the role of the soviets and gave only lip service to Lenin's
demand for a change of orientation.

The question came up again on July 16 at a conference of the
Petersburg Committee, resuming now after the interruption of the
July Days. The protocols of this conference, which were published in
1927, throw a revealing light on Stalin's behavior as spokesman of
Lenin's new line.[45]

Resumption of the Second Petrograd All-City Bolshevik Conference

On the morning of July 16, a handful of Petrograd Bolshevik delegates
assembled to continue and conclude the all-city conference that had
begun on July 1 but that had been interrupted by the July Days.
Stalin, as the ranking party leader, was scheduled to deliver two
reports: one on the current situation, the other for the Central Committee on its actions during the July Days.

The agenda called for the report on the current situation to be
presented first, but on the morning of July 16 Stalin objected that
because so few delegates were present the report would not be given.
After some debate, a compromise was agreed on under which Stalin
would present the CC report first, then the report on the current
situation. (Eventually seventy-two delegates showed up.)

In his "Report by the Central Committee on the July Events,"
delivered at the morning session, Stalin endeavored to refute the
charge that the Bolsheviks had

> incited and organized the demonstration of July 3 and 4, with the object of
> compelling the Central Executive Committee of the Soviets to take power,
> and if they refused to do so of seizing power ourselves.[46]

His defense took the form of a chronology of the events of July 3–5,
beginning with the sudden intrusion into the Bolshevik all-city con-

ference of two representatives of the First Machine Gun Regiment early on the third and ending with the surrender of the Peter and Paul Fortress on the fifth. In speaking of the party's tactics, Stalin made no reference to Lenin. When he came to the surrender of the fortress, however, Stalin stressed his own role. Faced with a demand from an SR, Kuzmin, for the evacuation of the fortress, Stalin said,

> The Central Committee of our party decided to do everything in its power to avoid bloodshed. It delegated me to the Fortress of Peter and Paul where I succeeded in persuading the sailors garrisoned there not to accept battle, since the situation had taken such a turn that we might find ourselves face to face not with the counter-revolution but with the right wing of the democracy [i.e., the SR's].

"It is clear to me," Stalin continued,

> that the right wing wanted bloodshed so as to administer a "lesson" to the workers, soldiers and sailors. We prevented them from carrying out their plan.[47]

Stalin thus cast himself in an honorable role. His was the only name of an individual Bolshevik leader mentioned in the entire report. Even when he came to the charge of disloyalty directed against Lenin, Stalin omitted any reference to Lenin:

> As to the infamous slander that our leaders are backed by German gold, the Central Committee considers this accusation to be completely groundless and not serious.[48]

During his report, Stalin was asked about the Central Committee's attitude toward the appearance in court of Lenin and Zinoviev to stand trial on the charge of treason. In reply, Stalin asserted the innocence of the party leaders but said it had been decided that they should not submit to trial, since

> the Bolshevik fraction of the Central Executive Committee has no guarantee that our comrades would not be torn to pieces by illegal bands in view of the rabid calumny that is being carried on against us.

Here, too, however, Stalin contrived to stress his personal contribution to the decision:

> I personally raised the question of an appearance [in court] with Lieber and Anisimov and they answered that they could not give any guarantee whatsoever.[49]

In his report on the July Days, Stalin minimized the importance of

Lenin's guidance and highlighted his own direct participation in events—significantly, as a member of the Executive Committee of the Soviet rather than of the Bolshevik CC.

At the evening session of July 16, Stalin presented the report "On the Current Situation."[50] It was to provide the basis for this report that Lenin had written "The Most Recent Political Situation (Four Theses)." A comparison of Stalin's July 16 report with Lenin's July 10 article reveals that Stalin either failed to grasp Lenin's concepts or was unwilling to lend them his support. In place of Lenin's clear-cut analysis of power relationships, Stalin offered a confused medley of ideas in which his own efforts at analysis appeared side by side with disjointed fragments from Lenin's theses. In place of Lenin's stark alternatives— either a right-wing military dictatorship or an armed uprising by the workers and poorest peasants—Stalin portrayed a confused and inconsistent future:

> The peaceful period of development of the revolution has come to an end. A new period has begun, a period of sharp conflicts, clashes, collisions. Times will be turbulent, crisis will follow crisis.

On the question of the party's attitude toward the soviets, Stalin failed to give a clear-cut answer. He raised the question toward the end of his report but then simply turned away from it, suggesting that the party extend an offer of unification to the left-wing socialists in the soviets; the Menshevik-Internationalists, led by Martov; and the Left SR's, led by Kamkov. Completely missing was Lenin's sharp break with the soviets and his demand for withdrawal of the slogan "All Power to the Soviets." In its place, Stalin reverted to his stance of March and April.

The editors of Stalin's *Works* have made numerous changes in the text, one of which might mislead the incautious reader into believing that Stalin did in fact support Lenin's negative position on the soviets. According to the text in Stalin's *Works*, he said,

> The working class has proved to be more sensible than its enemies thought. When it realized that *the Soviets* had betrayed it, it declined to accept battle on July 4 and 5.[51]

What Stalin actually said, according to the protocols of the conference published in 1927, was,

> When it [the working class] realized that *the right wing of the revolution* [i.e., the Mensheviks and the SR's] had betrayed it. . . .[52]

In making this suggestion, Stalin again stressed his own part in events. "On July 5," he said,

> when the Central Committee of our party issued a call to end the demon-
> strations, at a session of the Central Executive Committee I said, the
> counter-revolution is on the march, it is strangling us, but you [i.e., the
> Mensheviks and the SR's] will be next, give us a hand in fighting the
> counter-revolution. When this proposal was presented . . . they laughed at
> us: what kind of unity can there be with people who have disfigured
> themselves with blood and espionage. On July 5 and 6 it became com-
> pletely clear that the Mensheviks and SR's were against us in alliance with
> the counter-revolution. Now we must reject in the most decisive manner
> the idea of union with the allies of the counter-revolution whose hands are
> stained with the blood of workers and soldiers. We should help those
> Mensheviks and SR's who want to fight the counter-revolution, to break
> away from the defencists, the betrayers of the revolution. I propose to you
> the plan of uniting with the left flank of the revolution.[53]

The key issues that Stalin had ignored or slurred over in his report
were brought into sharp focus in the discussion that followed by
delegates whose questions indicate that word of Lenin's new stance
had spread through the party ranks. The first questioner was a delegate named Mazlovsky, who asked whether the party, in the event of
future conflicts, would lead "an armed protest."[54] In reply, Stalin
failed to endorse Lenin's call for a nationwide armed uprising; instead,
he spoke of the likelihood of "armed uprisings" in the future and said
the party "must not wash its hands of them," but instead of providing
a chart for the future he reverted to the July Days, arguing that the
party had been right in refusing to make a bid for power.

> We could have taken power on July 3 and 4; we could have compelled the
> Central Executive Committee of the Soviet to sanction our taking power.
> But the question is, could we have retained power? The front, the prov-
> inces, the Soviets would have risen against us. Power which did not rest
> upon the provinces would have proved to be baseless. By taking power
> under such circumstances we would have disgraced ourselves.

Next, a delegate named Ivanov asked Stalin,

> What is our attitude toward the slogan "Power to the Soviets"? Is it time to
> call for "dictatorship of the proletariat"?

Cornered, Stalin finally responded with what was essentially
Lenin's position, though with a few added touches of his own:

> When a crisis of power is resolved, it means that a certain class has come to power—in this case, the bourgeoisie. Can we then continue to adhere to the old slogan, "All power to the Soviets!"? Of course not. To transfer power to the soviets, which in fact are tacitly working hand-in-glove with the bourgeoisie, would mean helping the enemy. If we win, we can transfer power only to the working class, supported by the poorer strata of the rural population. We must advocate another, a more expedient form of organization of the Soviets of Workers' and Peasants' Deputies. The form of power remains as before, but we change the class content of the slogan and we say in the language of the class struggle: All power to the workers and poor peasants, who will conduct a revolutionary policy.

Again, Stalin failed to make Lenin's point about the soviets, nor did he clearly express Lenin's call for preparations for an armed uprising.

After an impassioned but inconclusive discussion, a group of delegates asked that Lenin's theses be read. To his embarrassment, Stalin was forced to admit that he did not have them with him but said that they boiled down to three points: (1) the counterrevolution has triumphed; (2) the Mensheviks and the SR's have betrayed the revolution; (3) the slogan "All Power to the Soviets," under present conditions, was a "quixotic" slogan; power must be transferred to classes, not to institutions.[55]

This was at best a highly oversimplified summary of Lenin's theses; completely missing was his call for preparations for an armed uprising in place of reliance on the soviets.

In his concluding remarks, Stalin repeated his own concept of the attitude the party should adopt toward the soviets. "We are unequivocally in favor," he said,

> of those soviets where we have a majority, and we shall try to set up such soviets. We cannot, however, give power to soviets which are defending a union with the counter-revolution.

Stalin then presented an eleven-point draft resolution, "On the Current Situation." Far from withdrawing the slogan "All Power to the Soviets," Stalin, in the first point, called for

> the concentration of all power in the hands of revolutionary workers' and peasants' soviets.[56]

It was now late in the evening, and the delegates decided to take a break, resuming their discussion on the evening of July 17. The most remarkable thing about this session was the complete absence of Stalin. He neither took part in the discussion nor defended the resolution he had introduced. The awkward matter of Lenin's missing theses was raised at the very outset by a group of delegates from the Vyborg district who again asked that the theses be presented. In Stalin's absence, it was the chairman of the session, Gleb Bokii, who replied that

> the theses of Comrade Lenin are not available to the presidium [of the conference].[57]

In Stalin's absence, it fell primarily to Volodarsky to defend the resolution on the current situation and cope with the criticisms and suggestions for change offered by various delegates. At the conclusion of the debate, but before a vote was taken, Narchuk, on behalf of a group of delegates from the Vyborg district, announced that they would refrain from voting, "since the theses of Comrade Lenin were not presented and the reporter [i.e., Stalin] did not defend the resolution." The reproof to Stalin was unmistakable. The results were clear in the voting: 28 in favor, 3 against, 28 abstaining.

Stalin reappeared at the final session of the conference, on the evening of July 20, taking an active part in the discussion of such topics as the municipal elections in Petrograd and preparations for the coming party congress. Overall, however, he could not take pride in his performance at the conference. He had neither offered the delegates a clear lead of his own nor faithfully discharged his responsibilities as stand-in for Lenin.

Lenin Explains His Strategy

The double rebuff to Lenin's new line—at the enlarged meeting of the CC July 14–16 and the Second Petrograd Bolshevik conference July 16–20—forced him to reconsider, not his overall strategy—of that he was completely confident—but his method of presenting it to the party. Clearly, there were doubts and misgivings to be overcome, especially in regard to the soviets.

At some undetermined date in mid-July, therefore, Lenin addressed himself to the task of explaining his new policy in fuller detail. The result was the article "On Slogans," which constitutes Lenin's most explicit statement on the role of the soviets.[58]

The slogan "All Power to the Soviets," Lenin now argued, had been correct for an earlier stage of the revolution—"say, from February 27 to July 4"—but "it has patently ceased to be correct now." The slogan, in Lenin's view, had been appropriate only in regard to "the peaceful path for the progress of the revolution." That period had ended "suddenly" on July 4 when "power passed into the hands of the counterrevolution"—and Lenin reminded his readers that "the issue of power is the fundamental issue of every revolution." Under these conditions,

> The slogan calling for the transfer of state power to the Soviets would now sound quixotic or misleading. Objectively it would be deceiving the public.

(N.B.: Lenin's use of the term "quixotic," which Stalin picked up in his reply to questions at the Second All-City Conference on July 14, helps to place Lenin's article shortly before that date.)

How was the power of the counterrevolution to be overcome? Lenin's answer was clear.

> No one, no force can overthrow the bourgeois counterrevolution except the revolutionary proletariat. . . . The only solution is for power to be in the hands of the proletariat, and for the latter to be supported by the poor peasants and semi-proletarians.

Only when such a revolution had taken place, in Lenin's view, would the opportunity and the need for soviets arise again,

> but *not* the present soviets, not organs collaborating with the bourgeoisie, but organs of revolutionary struggle against the bourgeoisie. It is true that even then we shall be in favor of building the whole state on the model of the soviets. It is not a question of soviets in general, but combating the *present* counter-revolution and the treachery of the present soviets.

Lenin steadfastly opposed any role for the existing soviets:

> The present soviets have failed, have suffered complete defeat, because they are dominated by the Socialist Revolutionary and Menshevik parties.

It must remain an open question whether Lenin could have secured the adoption of his sharp turn in strategy had he been able to lead the discussion in person. His success in putting through his radical policy on the national question against stubborn opposition at the April Conference is proof that he had the power, by persuasion, prestige, and political manipulation, to impose his will on the party. In April, however, Stalin had acted effectively on Lenin's side. In mid-July Stalin gave only reluctant and grudging support to Lenin.

Lenin's condemnation of the existing soviets and his refusal to admit the possibility of their regeneration along Bolshevik-approved lines continued from his first statement of this position on July 10 for another two months. Not until his article "One of the Fundamental Questions of the Revolution" was published on September 14 did he retreat from his position. The question may be raised whether Lenin ever fully understood the appeal of the soviets to those who elected them—workers, peasants, soldiers. Basically, Lenin regarded the soviets as a tactical device to be used or discarded at will. For Lenin, the slogan "All Power to the Soviets," one of the party's most popular, could be advanced or withdrawn on purely tactical considerations.

In the preparation and execution of the Bolshevik seizure of power in October, Lenin was again to show his disregard for the soviets and his impatience with those who differed from him on this point. His mid-July demand for withdrawal of the slogan "All Power to the Soviets" failed, in part because of Stalin's insubordination, but also because it went against the grain of many party members and workers.

Stalin on the Role of the Soviets

In an article published in *Pravda* on November 26, 1924, as part of the triumvirate's polemic against Trotsky, Stalin asserted that "after the July defeat, disagreement did indeed arise between the Central Committee and Lenin on the question of the future of the soviets."[59]

> It is known that Lenin, wishing to concentrate the Party's attention on the task of preparing the uprising outside the soviets, warned against any infatuation with the latter, for he was of the opinion that, having been defiled by the defencists, they had become useless. The Central Committee and the Sixth Party Congress took a more cautious line and decided that there were no grounds for excluding the possibility that the Soviets would revive.

Did Stalin in 1924 accurately report the attitude of the party leadership, other than Lenin, toward the soviets in mid-July 1917, or was his statement colored by his knowledge of later events, especially the Bolshevik seizure of power in the name of the soviets in October 1917? Contemporary evidence from mid-July 1917 indicates that at that time Stalin was not unwilling to follow Lenin's lead in repudiating the soviets as hopelessly compromised. In an unsigned article published in *Rabochii i soldat* on July 17, 1917, Stalin wrote,

> Yesterday the defencists renounced even the pitiful "control" over the government which they had—and reduced the "Soviets" to the role of useless rubber stamps of the counterrevolution.[60]

Stalin's continuing doubts about Lenin's uncompromising rejection of the soviets were made clear, however, in an article he published on July 20, 1917, "What Do the Capitalists Want?"[61] "The fact is," Stalin wrote,

> that the soviets, before which the capitalists grovelled yesterday, and which are now defeated, have still retained a modicum of power and now

the capitalists want to strip from the soviets those last crumbs in order to strengthen their own power more fundamentally.

By July 27, just as the Sixth Party Congress was getting under way, Stalin had clarified his ideas on the soviets, broken with Lenin on this point, and was, in effect, giving renewed support to the slogan "All Power to the Soviets."

Stalin's turnabout was made public on July 27 in his article "The Constituent Assembly Elections."[62] Here Stalin called for agreement between the Bolshevik party and "non-party groups of propertyless peasants" and "non-party organizations of soldiers and sailors." The article provided a "model platform"

which might serve as a basis of agreement with such non-party organizations of peasants and soldiers.

Point 20, the final one in the platform, reads as follows:

Lastly, we are in favor of all power in the country being turned over to revolutionary Soviets of workers and peasants, for only such power can lead the country out of the impasse into which it has been driven by the war, the economic disruption, and the high cost of living, and by the capitalists and landlords who are fattening on the people's need.

Was There a Military Conference July 21–22, 1917?

According to Trotsky,

On the 21st and 22nd of July [1917] an exceptionally important conference, which remained unnoticed by the authorities and the press, was held in Petrograd.[63]

"The conference," Trotsky continues,

was attended by representatives of 29 front-line regiments, of 90 Petrograd factories, of Kronstadt sailors and of several surrounding garrisons.

"It would seem," Trotsky reluctantly conceded,

that the leading roles in this remarkable conference were played by Sverdlov and Stalin.

Except for Trotsky's statement, however, there appears to be no record of this "exceptionally important conference." Not only did it remain "unnoticed by the authorities and the press," it has remained unnoticed by historians and biographers of Stalin, other than Trotsky, down to the present. Was the conference, then, a figment of Trotsky's imagination?

The most likely explanation is that Trotsky misdated the military conference of *June* 21–22, 1917. The June conference, at which Stalin spoke on the national question in relation to the armed forces, is well documented and attracted plenty of attention by "the authorities and the press."

Trotsky's error is instructive for the light it throws on his work habits. Having misdated the conference, he tried to adjust it to the situation prevailing in mid-July; that is, the period of the emergence of Stalin and Sverdlov as leaders of the party. The effect is to put the reader of Trotsky's biography of Stalin on guard and to reinforce the lesson that Trotsky's knowledge of events during the period of his imprisonment was unreliable.

The Sixth Party Congress

Preparation: Lenin Meets Stalin

Lenin had good cause to be concerned about Stalin's stubborn refusal to toe the party line, as defined by Lenin, in regard to such a fundamental question as the role of the soviets. Since his written words had proved unavailing, it might be expected that he would make an effort to see Stalin in person and try to win him over. In any case, the imminent opening of the Sixth Party Congress on July 26 presented a challenge to Lenin to reassert his authority and to ensure that Stalin, as his spokesman, would faithfully present his views on the major questions facing the party.

A meeting between the two men shortly before July 26 would therefore be logical, and there is archival evidence that one took place.[64] Unfortunately, the Soviet reference provides no details—neither the place of meeting nor the subjects discussed. Presumably Stalin met Lenin at his hideout in Finland, and almost certainly they discussed strategy for the congress, but until the archival reference is published in full, we can only speculate on its content.

A clue to the substance of the discussion is provided by an article, "Constitutional Illusions," which Lenin wrote on July 26, shortly after his talk with Stalin.[65] This is another in the series of articles, beginning with "The Most Recent Political Situation," in which Lenin hammered home his conviction that the bourgeoisie, led by the Cadets, had established a military dictatorship to which the moderate socialist leaders in the Petrograd Soviet were rendering support.

Lenin mentioned the soviets only in passing; the soviets, he wrote,

> are trembling for their own fate as they receive message after message that the Cossacks may come and smash them up. The Black Hundred [right-

wing extremists] and Cadet force, which led the hounding of the Bolsheviks, is beginning to hound the soviets.

Lenin saw nothing positive in the soviets and foresaw no place for them in his strategy of revolution. The article, one of Lenin's most uncompromising, took aim against exactly such "constitutional illusions" as Stalin had manifested in his article of July 24, "What Do the Capitalists Want?"

Lenin's diatribes did have an effect on Stalin, as can be seen from the latter's article, "The New Government," published on July 26.[66] Here Stalin went a long way toward accepting Lenin's conviction that the soviets had hopelessly compromised themselves. "The Cadets," he wrote,

> wanted the government strengthened at the expense of the Soviets, and they wanted it to be independent of the Soviets. The Soviets, led by "bad shepherds," have conceded this, thus signing their own death warrant.

But with characteristic stubbornness Stalin stopped short of fully endorsing Lenin's negative appraisal of the soviets. "The Central Executive Committee," Stalin wrote,

> the representative of all the Soviets, is now following the lead of the Provisional Government and is masking the latter's counter-revolutionary physiognomy with revolutionary phrases.
>
> Roles, evidently, have changed, and not in favor of the Soviets.

On the Eve: The Delegates Convene

On July 25, the day before the Sixth Congress was to open, a meeting was held to discuss procedures for the congress. Fifty delegates were present, of whom thirty had the right to vote, the remaining twenty having consultative rights only. M. S. Ol'minsky, a party member since 1898 and a representative of the Moscow organization of the party, presided at the meeting, but Sverdlov was its principal organizer; it was his proposals that were discussed and, with virtually no dissent, adopted.

The protocols of the meeting, published in *Rabochii i soldat* at the time and reprinted with the congress protocols in 1958,[67] made no reference to Stalin's participation, a fact that raises some doubt about the widely expressed view that Stalin shared with Sverdlov responsibility for organizing the congress. Stalin's apparent absence from this important meeting and Sverdlov's dominant role point to the conclusion that the organizational aspect of the congress was fully in

Sverdlov's hands, with Stalin neither offering nor being asked to assist him.

The Opening Session

The Sixth Congress opened on the evening of July 26. Party members in the Vyborg district had worked out the logistical arrangements—lodging, subsistence, transportation, provision of a meeting place—despite the fears of some delegates that it would be impossible to hold the congress in Petrograd in view of the Provisional Government's hostile attitude.

Stalin did not attend the opening session, just as he had missed the preparatory meeting on the preceding day. Again, it was Sverdlov who provided organizational direction, presenting the regulations of the congress and its agenda. After discussion, the delegates unanimously elected a five-man presidium consisting of Sverdlov, Ol'minsky, Lenin, Yurenev, and Stalin—two of whose members would later die in Stalin's purge. Bokii proposed the election of Lenin as honorary chairman, a proposal that was adopted unanimously. On Sverdlov's proposal the delegates then voted to name five additional honorary chairmen: Zinoviev, Kamenev, Trotsky, Kollontai, and Lunacharsky. Thus, the *Mezhraiontsy* made their formal entry into the congress, along with the Leninist Old Guard and the party's leading token female.

The Second Session: Stalin Is Late

The possibility that Stalin was engaged in image building is suggested by an incident that took place on the morning of July 27. At the designated hour of 10 A.M., only a handful of delegates—far less than a quorum—had showed up. Sverdlov was present but left when it became clear that no business could be conducted for the time being. A group of delegates—some thirty-four in all—thereupon drew up and signed a formal protest against the tardiness of their comrades. In their protest the signatories proposed the adoption of a sign-in sheet for delegates, including the time of arrival.

The principal item of business for the second session was the report for the Central Committee, which Stalin was to present. Was his tardiness inadvertent, or was it a deliberate maneuver designed to increase his stature in the eyes of the delegates? The suspicion that it was the latter is enhanced by a curious passage in one of Stalin's later writings in which he defined his concept of political greatness.[68] The occasion was a reminiscence of Stalin's first encounter with Lenin, at the Tammerfors Conference in December 1905. "Usually," Stalin wrote,

> a great man comes late to a meeting so that his appearance may be awaited with bated breath. Then, just before the great man enters the warning goes round, "Hush . . . silence . . . he's coming." The rite did not seem to me superfluous, because it created an impressive and inspired response. How great was my disappointment to see that Lenin had arrived at the conference before the other delegates were there and had settled himself somewhere in a corner and was unassumingly carrying on a conversation, a most ordinary conversation, with the most ordinary delegates. I will not conceal from you that at that time this seemed to me to be rather a violation of certain essential rules.

It was a violation that Stalin had no intention of repeating, to judge by his late arrival at the second session. The trouble, from Stalin's point of view, was that the Bolshevik party had not yet been through the Stalin school of the thirties and had not yet learned to play its part in the ritual of charismatic leadership and devoted followers which was Stalin's concept.

The Report for the Central Committee

Had Sverdlov planned to chair the second session, as he had the first, and as he was to do in the great majority of the remaining thirteen sessions of the congress? The protocols are silent on this question; they simply omit naming any chairman for the second session. It fell to the lot of M. S. Ol'minsky to lead off.

The session opened at 10:45 A.M., three-quarters of an hour late, with Ol'minsky's reading of the statement of protest by the thirty-four delegates who had arrived on time. After a short greeting to the congress from a Latvian factory, Stalin delivered the report for the CC.

As so often in Bolshevik history, there is a tangled web of textual evidence which must be unraveled before we consider the substance of Stalin's report. The report exists in two major variants, which for convenience can be designated A and B. Variant A is the text as given in the first (1919) edition of the protocols and, with minor factual corrections, in all subsequent editions (1927, 1934, 1958).[69] Variant A was also printed in the 1925 collection of Stalin's speeches and writings from 1917.[70] This is an important benchmark, for it shows that in 1925 Stalin acknowledged the validity of the text published in the 1919 edition of the congress protocols.

It was not this text, however, but variant B that the editors of Stalin's *Sochineniya* used in 1946.[71] In terms of original date of publication this variant has priority, since it first appeared shortly after the report was delivered, in *Rabochii i soldat* for July 30 and August 8, 1917. As first published, however, variant B dealt only with the July crisis, omitting those sections of Stalin's report which covered May and June. For volume 3 of Stalin's *Sochineniya*, therefore, the editors simply lifted the appropriate sections from variant A and tacked them on at the beginning. The editors also used their blue pencils to delete or add materials they considered appropriate.

Comparison of the two variants indicates that B is, in all probability, an early draft of the report, with A representing approximately the text as delivered at the congress by Stalin. Variant B is less polished, less comprehensive, closer to the original documents on which Stalin's report was based. From internal evidence it appears that these included a log of events for the July Days which must have been maintained at party headquarters by one of the secretaries.

Since variant A is in nearly all respects a better product, and since it was eventually recognized as the official text, the question arises, why was variant B published in 1917, and why did the editors of Stalin's *Sochineniya* use it instead of variant A? A reasonable hypothesis would be that variant B represents Stalin's original draft, whereas variant A is an edited and revised text. Edited and revised by whom? Not by Stalin himself, evidently, since in that case he would have provided the revised text, not the draft, to *Rabochii i soldat*. Similarly, the editors of his *Sochineniya* in 1946 would have used the improved, revised text. Someone other than Stalin, therefore, revised the rough draft of the report before it was delivered. Who?

Suspicion falls first of all on Lenin, whom we have seen meeting with Stalin shortly before July 26. The report as delivered by Stalin on July 27, however, expresses points of view which Stalin is known to have held but with which Lenin disagreed. If Lenin did see the draft of Stalin's report before it was delivered, therefore, he was unable to win Stalin over to his point of view.

Other likely candidates for the role of editor are Sverdlov and Bukharin, both present at the congress and both well prepared to render Stalin this service. Bukharin had just arrived in Petrograd, however. He had to prepare his own report on the international situation and could hardly have found time to edit Stalin's draft.

That leaves Sverdlov as the most likely candidate for the role of editor. It would appear highly probable, in any case, that Sverdlov, as acting joint leader of the party, would have had a chance to read Stalin's rough draft.

Stalin's report (using variant A) opened with a concise and well-organized analysis of the current stage of the revolution. "Before I go on to the report on the political activity of the CC for the past two and a half months," Stalin said,

> I consider it necessary to note a basic fact, defining the activity of the CC. I have in mind the fact of the development of our revolution, raising the question of intervention in the sphere of economic relations in the form of control over production, the transfer of land into the hands of the peasants, the transfer of power from the hands of the bourgeoisie into the hands of the Soviets of workers' and peasants' deputies. All of this defines the profound character of our revolution. It has begun to take on the character of a socialist workers' revolution. Under the pressure of this fact the bourgeoisie has begun to organize itself and to wait for a suitable moment for an attack. Such a moment is considered the moment of retreat on the front, or, more accurately, the moment of retreat if Germany succeeds in attacking us.[72]

This passage, coming at the beginning of Stalin's report and in effect summarizing its conclusion, creates the impression of an editorial insertion. Omission of the passage from the text as given in Stalin's *Sochineniya* strengthens the view that it was not written by Stalin himself. Emphasis on the transfer of power to the soviets rules out Lenin as its author. Again, Sverdlov appears to be the most likely candidate.

Stalin then took up the CC's activities in May, in a passage I have already quoted (see pp. 105–6). As we have seen, Stalin defined three major areas of party work in May: the reelection to the soviets, the campaign of protest against the death sentence at the front, and the municipal elections in Petrograd.

Stalin's account of the CC's activities in June centered around the major demonstrations mounted in that month, the abortive one of June 10 and the successful one of June 18. This section of Stalin's report has also been used earlier (see pp. 137–38). There are no significant textual differences between the various versions of the report which are available.

"I now come," Stalin continued, "to what is most interesting to you [the delegates], the events of 3–5 July."

Stalin began his account with the arrival, at 3 P.M. on July 3, of two representatives of the First Machine Gun Regiment at the Petrograd City Conference of Bolsheviks, which was meeting in the Kshesinskaya mansion. In response to the soldiers' announcement of their plans for a demonstration, Volodarsky informed them that the party had decided not to demonstrate.

At this point, the two variants of Stalin's report differ significantly. Variant *A* quotes Volodarsky as telling the soldiers, " 'The party has decided not to demonstrate, and party members of the regiment must not dare to disobey the party's decision.' "[73] Variant *B* strikes a less authoritative tone. After stating that Volodarsky told the soldiers of the party's decision not to demonstrate, *B* adds the following explanation:

> For the CC it was clear that both the bourgeoisie and the Black Hundreds wanted to provoke us into an uprising in order to fasten on us responsibility for the risky offensive. We had decided to wait for the moment of the attack at the front, to allow the attack to be thoroughly discredited in the eyes of the masses, not to yield to provocation and, while the attack was in progress, not to demonstrate under any circumstances, to wait and allow the Provisional Government to exhaust itself.[74]

Only after this explanation, in variant *B*, does Stalin's report give Volodarsky's warning to the soldiers, and in notably less brusque terms:

> Comrade Volodarsky answered the delegates that the party had [made] a decision not to demonstrate and members of the party in their regiment must obey this decision. The delegates of the regiment departed with a protest.[75]

At 4 P.M., Stalin continued, the Bolshevik Central Committee, meeting in the Tauride Palace, formally endorsed the decision not to demonstrate. Stalin, on the instructions of the CC, reported this decision to the Bureau of the Central Executive Committee (CEC) of the Soviet.

At this point, variant *A* takes on a personal note as Stalin states,

> I gave them all the facts, informed them that delegates of the machine-gun regiment had sent their delegates to the plants and factories. I suggested that the Bureau take all means to ensure that the action [*vystuplenie*] did not take place. This statement, on our demand, was recorded in the protocols. Messrs. SR's and Mensheviks, who now accuse us of preparing a demonstration, forget about this.[76]

In place of this graphic personal account, variant *B* has the following brief summary:

> On the instructions of the Central Committee of the party, Comrade Stalin presents to the Bureau of the Central Executive Committee of the Soviet a statement about everything which has taken place, including the decision [not to demonstrate].[77]

Here, it would seem, Stalin touched up and made more graphic the rough draft of his report. It is odd, however, that the editors of his *Sochineniya* chose the dry, colorless text of variant *B* in this passage. Both variants of Stalin's report then proceed with an hour-by-hour chronicle of the mounting tension in Petrograd as columns of workers joined the soldiers' demonstration. In a highly significant insertion, however, variant *A* gives the following information, completely lacking from variant *B*:

> Incidentally, concerning Lenin. He was not present; he left on 29 June and returned to Petrograd only on 4 July, in the morning, only after our decision to intervene in the demonstration had already been taken. Lenin approved of our decision.[78]

The striking thing about this passage is its bare, almost perfunctory character. It says nothing about the party leaders' decision to send a message to Lenin urging him to return to Petrograd nor about his impromptu address to the demonstrators on the morning of July 4. Far from playing a leadership role, Lenin in this portrayal is limited to endorsing a decision already taken by the party CC.

What are we to make of this grudging and minimal portrayal? A plausible conjecture would be that someone—Sverdlov, perhaps—insisted that Stalin add a statement about Lenin's participation in the events of July 4 but that Stalin did so only to the barest minimum and with the obvious intent of reducing as far as possible Lenin's part in decision making. In Stalin's version, "we," that is, the leaders on the spot, had reached a sound decision well in advance of Lenin's return.

In preparing Stalin's report for presentation, the editor cut out much of the detail that had appeared in the rough draft. In its place the edited text stressed the attack on Lenin as a German agent, calling it "the turning point" in the July events. In this connection Stalin mentioned his telephone request to kill the story, but asserted that the call was to Tseretelli. (In actual fact, as we have seen on p. 146, the call was to Chkheidze, though Tseretelli was also consulted.)

Variant *A* gives details on the negotiations of July 6 which are missing from variant *B*:

> On 6 July our comrades Kamenev and Zinoviev conducted conversations with Liber about the protection of members of the party and party organizers from hooligan attacks, on the re-establishment of *Pravda's* editorial office, etc. The conversations ended in an agreement in accordance with which armored cars would be withdrawn from the Kshesinskaya mansion. The bridges would be lowered, those soldiers remaining in the Peter and Paul Fortress would depart unhindered, and a guard would be established

at the Kshesinskaya mansion. But the agreement was not kept, since behind the back of the Central Executive Committee a military clique, having established a right-wing dictatorship, began to act.[79]

Variant *A* also includes (as *B* does not) Stalin's curiously muted account of his own part in these abortive negotiations:

> I went to the CEC with a proposal to end the matter without bloodshed. In answer to my question, What do you want? Will you fire on us? We are not rising against the soviet . . . Bogdanov answered that they wanted to avoid bloodshed. We went to the staff. The military received us in an unfriendly way, they said the order had already been given. I got the impression that these gentlemen wanted at all costs to carry out a bloodletting.[80]

The report said nothing about Stalin's part in arranging the disarming and surrender of the Kronstadt sailors. Variant *A* concludes with a defense of the party's behavior during the July Days, to the effect that "our party always moved with the masses." The party's actions had served to limit the bloodshed; it had played the part of a "regulator." This essentially defensive summing up is another obvious editorial insertion into Stalin's report. The rough draft, variant *B*, closes instead with an analysis of the fateful consequences for the Mensheviks and the SR's of their decision to turn against the Bolsheviks and side with the bourgeois parties:

> It became clear that in betraying the Bolsheviks the SR's and Mensheviks have betrayed themselves, have betrayed the revolution and have unleashed and unbridled the forces of counterrevolution.[81]

The Discussion of Stalin's Report

The pressures under which the Sixth Congress operated are reflected in the debate that followed Stalin's report. Twenty-nine delegates asked to speak, but a majority voted to cut off the discussion after only eight had spoken. A prominent theme was that the Central Committee report had concentrated exclusively on events in Petrograd, to the detriment of the provinces.

A number of delegates raised questions about the CC's conduct at the time of the June 10 demonstration. Manuilsky was the most critical, characterizing the CC's sudden reversals as "hysterical decisions [which] only compromise our Central organ."[82]

The CC's actions during the July Days also came in for criticism. S. N. Ravich, a thirty-eight-year-old delegate from the Petrograd organization, faulted the party leadership for negotiating with the CEC to end the demonstration, rather than by a direct appeal to the workers.[83] (Ravich's future in Stalin's Russia was not a happy one; after a number of oppositional actions he joined the Trotskyite faction and was ousted from the party in 1928; following temporary readmission he was ousted again in 1935. Sentenced to the camps in the Great Purge, he managed somehow to survive until 1955.)[84]

With regard to the slogan "All Power to the Soviets," the most striking thing about the debate was that no one showed an awareness of Lenin's demand that it be withdrawn. Milyutin asserted that the slogan "has now become generally recognized and only those people abandon it who fear to take power, who betray it in the name of civic peace"—a thrust against the Mensheviks and the SR's but inadvertently grazing Lenin as well.[85]

Even before Stalin had a chance to reply, V. P. Nogin, a member of the Central Committee, defended the CC against the charge that it had given too much attention to Petrograd and had neglected to inform the provinces of its plans.[86] Petrograd, he affirmed, "is the center of the revolutionary movement." Nogin conceded, however, that there were some errors in the CC's record, especially its repeated decision not to conduct demonstrations at a time when the masses spontaneously demonstrated, forcing the CC to alter its decision. Nogin also reminded the delegates of the CC's lack of technical facilities for keeping the provinces abreast of current developments in the capital.

Stalin Replies to the Debate

Following Nogin's defense of the CC, the session chairman (Ol'minsky?) called for a vote on a motion to end the discussion. A majority of the delegates, anxious to get on with the proceedings, voted in favor of closure.

At this point the historian has only one text at his disposal, that of the congress protocols. The editors of Stalin's *Works* use the congress text, with editorial changes that are sometimes significant. Stalin's statements have the ring of authority. He spoke firmly but with a new degree of flexibility. He opened with a strong defense of the CC's policies:

> Comrades, no one has criticized the political line of the Central Committee or objected to its slogans. The Central Committee put forward three major slogans: All power to the Soviets, [workers'] control over production, and confiscation of the landed estates. These slogans won sympathy among the masses of the workers and among the soldiers. They proved to

be correct, and by waging the fight on that basis we retained the support of the masses. I consider this a major fact in the Central Committee's favor. If it issues correct slogans at the most difficult moments, that shows that in the main the Central Committee is right.[87]

There was nothing here about withdrawal of the slogan "All Power to the Soviets"; Stalin simply ignored the whole direction of Lenin's strategy since mid-July.

Turning to specific criticisms, Stalin replied first to the charge that the CC had concentrated too much on Petrograd and had neglected the provinces. With uncustomary moderation, Stalin granted the justice of the charge:

> The reproach of isolation from the provinces is not without foundation. But it was simply impossible to cover all actions.
>
> The charge that the CC virtually became the Petersburg Committee is to some extent justified. This is a fact. But it is here, in Petrograd, that the policy of Russia is being hammered out. It is here that the directing forces of the revolution are located. The provinces react to what is done in Petrograd. This is because the Provisional Government is here, in whose hands all power is concentrated. Here is the Central Executive Committee, the voice of the entire organized democracy.[88]

No trace here of Lenin's bold assertion that the Provisional Government had been replaced by a right-wing military dictatorship; no echo of his call for repudiation of the CEC together with the entire soviet network.

Other weighty considerations, Stalin argued, forced the CC to act boldly, without consulting the provinces:

> events are moving fast, an open struggle is in progress, and there is no assurance that the existing government may not disappear any day. Under such circumstances, to wait until our friends in the provinces catch up with us would be senseless.

Significantly, Stalin pointed to the *modus operandi* of the Central Executive Committee of the Soviet, which

> decides questions of the revolution without consulting the provinces. The whole government apparatus is in their hands. And what have we got? Our only force is in the revolutionary workers and soldiers [*Works* 3:180 has "And what have we got? The apparatus of the Central Committee"]. To demand of the Central Committee that it take no steps without first consulting the provinces is tantamount to demanding that the Central Committee should not march ahead of events but trail behind them. But then it would not be a Central Committee. Only by following the method

which we did follow could the Central Committee keep abreast of the situation.

Stalin's defense of the CC was reasonable and well founded. The moderation of his tone and his willingness to grant the validity of the charges against the CC may reflect the fact that he had often been in the opposite situation as a provincial party worker critical of the policies laid down by the party's central leadership. Now he was seeing just how difficult it was to coordinate policies at the center with those in the provinces.

Ignoring the criticism of the CC's vacillation at the time of the June 12 demonstration, Stalin dealt briefly with the events of July 3–5. He admitted that there was failure but insisted that what had taken place was a demonstration (*demonstratsiya*), not an uprising (*vosstanie*).

As to Manuilsky's reproach that the CC had failed to put out leaflets explaining the events of July 3–5, Stalin reminded the delegates that

> our printing press had been wrecked and it was physically impossible to get anything printed in other printing plants, as this would have exposed them to the danger of being wrecked like ours.

He ended on an optimistic note:

> All the same, things here are not so bad; if in some of the districts we were arrested, in others we found a welcome and were greeted with extraordinary enthusiasm. And now, too, the spirit of the Petrograd workers is splendid and the prestige of the Bolsheviks is immense.

With that inspiring message Stalin concluded his reply to the discussion, but he still had something to add. "I should like," he said, "to raise a few questions." First was a proposal to prepare a manifesto explaining the facts about the slander of the party leaders. (Lenin was not specifically mentioned.) The commission charged with drafting this manifesto, Stalin suggested, should also issue a proclamation to the revolutionary workers and soldiers of Germany, France, England, and so on, informing them of the events of July 3–5.

Stalin's second point was to reopen the question of a trial for Lenin and Zinoviev. "Just now," he said, "it is still unclear who holds power"—a statement that would have shocked Lenin. Even more startling was Stalin's conclusion:

> If at the head [of the government] there will be a power which can guarantee our comrades against violence, which will have at least some honor, they will appear.[89]

Thus, Stalin of his own free will reopened a question that had seemingly been disposed of before the congress. The delegates were unsure of how to deal with the question but voted to add it to the agenda. They also voted to set up a commission to prepare the manifesto and proclamation called for by Stalin, naming him a member of the commission, together with Bukharin, Sokol'nikov, Ol'minsky, Manuilsky, and Skrypnik.

The Third Session

The third session of the congress opened on the afternoon of July 27, with Sverdlov presiding. The first item on the agenda was the question raised by Stalin of the appearance in court of Lenin and Zinoviev. Of the nine delegates who spoke on this topic, only three—Volodarsky, Manuilsky, and Lashevich—considered it desirable that the party leaders submit to arrest. Their chief spokesman, Volodarsky, explained that their position was based on the assumption that a trial would turn into a countertrial of the Provisional Government, and he offered a resolution to that effect. The majority of speakers, however, strongly opposed the idea of a trial under existing conditions. Ordzhonikidze, Dzerzhinsky, and Skrypnik, who led off the debate, were especially firm.

Bukharin argued that under existing conditions there could be no guarantee that the trial would be fair or that the accused would be secure against violence. A resolution to this effect, which Bukharin introduced, was approved unanimously, in preference to one offered by Volodarsky and a much stronger one proposed by A. G. Shlikhter, a veteran of the revolutionary movement. A noteworthy feature of Bukharin's resolution was the inclusion of Trotsky's name, along with those of Lenin and Zinoviev, as one of the party leaders to whom the congress sent its greetings—the first reference at the congress to Trotsky in this capacity.

Stalin took no part in the discussion of the question he had raised; if he had hoped to sway the congress toward approving Lenin's submission to arrest, the mood of the delegates ruled out such a decision.

With that question disposed of, at least for the time being, Sverdlov proceeded to give the organizational report for the Central Committee. Of particular interest in the present context is a brief statement at the end:

The report by comrade Stalin has fully clarified the work of the Central Committee.[90]

Sverdlov's report highlighted the rapid growth of the party, from 78 party organizations with 80,000 members in April to 162 organizations and 200,000 members in July. Adding 10,000 from Siberia, 4,000 for the Minsk region, and 26,000 for the military organizations, Sverdlov reached a grand total of 240,000 party members.

Like other delegates, Sverdlov took up the question of relations between the CC and the Petersburg Committee, offering a fresh argument that directly involved Stalin. The CC, said Sverdlov, had in fact led the party as a whole, including the provincial centers, in large part through the editorials and news reporting in *Pravda*. "The Central Committee," he said,

> through *Pravda* ensured both the intellectual and the organizational leadership of the party. In *Pravda* the comrades found answers to all theoretical questions.

Conspicuously overlooking Stalin's role as a member of *Pravda's* editorial board, Sverdlov continued,

> Lenin and Zinoviev set forth all their views in *Pravda*.[91]

Following Sverdlov, Smilga gave the financial report for the CC, noting at the outset that he would have to limit himself to approximate figures because government security forces had seized the documents on which his report was to have been based.

There was no debate on Sverdlov's and Smilga's reports; instead, the third session continued with three brief statements on the relation of the CC to the provinces and to the Petersburg Committee. A nearly unanimous vote of approval for Sverdlov's and Smilga's reports brought the session to a close.

Regional Reports: Fourth to Eighth Sessions

Beginning with the fourth session, on the evening of July 27, and continuing through the seventh session, on the evening of the following day, the delegates listened to reports by representatives of regional organizations of the party, beginning with Volodarsky for the Petersburg Committee, continuing with Yurenev for the *Mezhraiontsy* and Kaminsky for the Ukraine, all on July 27; followed by Podbel'sky for Moscow, Podvoisky for the Military Organization in Petrograd, Yaroslavsky for the military organizations in Russia as a whole, Myasnikov for Minsk, Larin for the Menshevik-Internationalists, and Rimsha for the Riga front, all on the morning of July 28; followed by Zalezhsky for Helsingfors, Flerovsky for Kronstadt, Bubnov for the Moscow *oblast*, Preobrazhensky for the Urals, Shumiatsky for western

Siberia, and Mostovenko for the Rumanian front, all on the afternoon of July 28; and concluding with Dizhbit for the Baltic provinces, Vasil'ev-Yuzhin for the Volga district, Kapsukas for Lithuania, Epshtein (Yakovlev) for the Donetsk *oblast*, Anisimov for Grozny, and Kavtaradze for the Transcaucasus on the evening of July 28. Stalin was silent throughout these reports.

The eighth session, on July 29, was a short one; immediately after its opening a recess was called. The editors of the 1958 edition of the congress protocols link this development with a decree adopted by the Provisional Government on July 28 empowering the ministers of the army, navy, and internal affairs to close conferences dangerous to the war effort and state security, a decree framed in general terms but clearly aimed at the Bolsheviks. The editors also suggest that on this occasion the "small congress," composed of the congress presidium and members of the Central Committee, elected the new Central Committee.[92] Sovokin disputes this, defining the "small congress" as "the presidium and representation of the most important party organization and which was concerned with a number of especially important questions and a few organizational questions."[93] This leaves open the possibility that the election of the new CC—an "organizational question"—took place at this session.

The Ninth Session: Report by Bukharin

Delegates at the ninth session of the congress, on the afternoon of July 30, heard two major reports, one on the war and the international situation by Bukharin, the other on the political situation by Stalin.

Bukharin was a rising star in the party. Born in 1888, he joined the party in 1906. This was his first appearance as a speaker at a party congress. The choice of Bukharin as the party's spokesman on one of the most important issues facing the nation reflected his growing popularity as well as his emergence as one of the party's ablest, most articulate theorists and strategists. Even Lenin admitted being influenced by him; the work on which Lenin was engaged in August, "State and Revolution," was an exploration of questions which Bukharin had raised in 1915—questions about the organization of a future socialist society and its development.

In familiar Bolshevik terms, Bukharin traced the origins of the war to international imperialist rivalries; only worldwide proletarian revolution, he asserted, could end it. Revolution might come first either in Russia, in the form of a proletarian-peasant uprising, or in western Europe and elsewhere. If Russia took the lead—and Bukharin treated that as no more than a possibility—it would thereby assume an obligation to declare a revolutionary war on behalf of the proletariat in other countries. Even if its army was incapable of launching an offensive, it would have to wage a defensive revolutionary war. In that event, Bukharin said,

> we will have the right to announce to the proletariat of the entire world that we are waging a sacred war in the interests of the entire proletariat. By means of such a revolutionary war we shall ignite the flames of the world socialist revolution.[94]

With those words Bukharin established a position that was to bring him into direct conflict with Lenin in the spring of 1918. He also presented a strategy sharply differing from the one Stalin would offer in *his* report on the current situation. In his concluding remarks, however, after a brief and inconclusive debate on his report, Bukharin attempted to link his position with that of Lenin:

> In the present stage of the Russian revolution, the poorest sector of the peasantry, by the force of objective factors, will be our allies—and it gives us the basis to say that the Russian revolution has laid the foundation for the world revolution.[95]

Stalin's "Report on the Political Situation"

After a short break, the delegates reassembled to hear Stalin's "Report on the Political Situation." As was the case for his report for the Central Committee, the textual history of this second report is complex.*

---

*Two variants are available, which can be designated C and D. Variant C is the text as published in the 1919 and all subsequent editions of the party protocols; variant D is the text as published in *Proletarii*, no. 3 on August 16, 1917, and reprinted in an appendix to the 1958 edition of the protocols (pp. 281–85). Variant C was also published verbatim in the 1925 collection of Stalin's writings and speeches from 1917, *Na putiakh k Oktiabriu* (pp. 122–29). Unlike the situation with regard to Stalin's report for the CC, however, the text used by the editors of Stalin's *Sochineniya* is an amalgam of both variants, with the usual editorial changes. Thus, there appears to be no evidence pointing to a reworking of Stalin's original draft; rather, it seems probable that *both* variants represent the text that Stalin read at the congress, with variant D sometimes giving a better exposition, sometimes the reverse. Here I shall draw on both variants, assuming that the sum of both represents approximately what Stalin said at the congress.

Did Stalin in fact write the report, or did he merely read a text prepared by Lenin? The question has been raised by Sovokin, who marshals a mass of evidence purporting to prove that both Stalin's report and the resolution "On the Political Situation," which the congress adopted, were the work of Lenin, with Stalin merely serving as his mouthpiece.[96] If this conclusion is correct—and I find Sovokin's argument persuasive—then the question Stalin's biographer must raise is not, what can we learn about Stalin's ideas from the report, but how should we envisage the relationship between him and Lenin at this point and how effectively did he serve as Lenin's mouthpiece at the congress? Evidence cited by Sovokin indicates that shortly before the congress Lenin wrote a series of theses to serve as the basis for the "Report on the Political Situation." These have not been found, but Sovokin believes that a reasonably accurate version of them was obtained by A. Z. Shumiatsky, a delegate to the congress from the Central Siberian Bureau of the party, and published in the newspapers, *Krasnoyarskii rabochii*. Stalin, as we have seen (p. 175), met with Lenin shortly before the congress; this meeting would appear to be the most likely occasion on which Lenin could have given Stalin a copy of his theses.

The principal themes of the report are those familiar from Lenin's writings of mid-July: the sharp turn of events following the July Days; the establishment of a military dictatorship combining right-wing political figures with the army high command and supported by the moderate socialist parties; the end of the period of peaceful development of the revolution, as well as any possibility of a peaceful transfer of power to the soviets; the loss of power by the soviets; and the need for the party to prepare for the overthrow of the right-wing dictatorship by a new revolution led by the urban proletariat and supported by the poorer strata of the peasantry.[97]

The report was noteworthy for the frankness of its analysis of Russia's structure:

> It is our misfortune that Russia is a country of the petty bourgeoisie and that it still follows the Menshevik and Socialist Revolutionaries, who are compromising with the Cadets. And until the peasantry become disillusioned with the idea of compromise with the bourgeoisie, we will suffer and the revolution will go haltingly.

This being the case, the reporter felt it necessary to address the question of how a proletarian revolution could be made in a petty bourgeois country:

> Some comrades argue that since capitalism is poorly developed in our country, it would be utopian to raise the question of a socialist revolution.

They would be right if there were no war, if there were no economic disruption, if the foundations of the national economy were not shaken.

Furthermore,

The question of intervening in the economic sphere is arising in all countries as something essential in time of war.

Unlike Germany, however, where "this question is being settled without the direct and active participation of the masses," in Russia the workers were being drawn directly into the economic life of the country, thereby "raising the practical question of the socialist revolution."

Answering the question raised by Rykov at the April Conference—could backward, petty bourgeois Russia take the lead in carrying out a socialist revolution?—the reporter asserted,

It would be rank pedantry to assert that Russia should "wait" with socialist changes until Europe "begins." That country "begins" which has the greater opportunities.

Thus, the reporter swept away as "rank pedantry" the scruples of literal-minded Marxists who insisted that Russia was not ready for a socialist revolution.

As to the form the revolution would take, the reporter foresaw a national uprising:

Overthrow of the dictatorship of the imperialist bourgeoisie—that is what the immediate slogan of the party must be. The realization of this slogan is possible only if there is a powerful upsurge on a nation-wide scale.

The main forces of the new movement will be the urban proletariat and the poorer strata of peasantry. It is they that will take power in the event of victory.

Lenin's strategy included the possibility of proletarian revolutions in the west, as one of its essential components. As published in the August 1917 issue of *Proletarii* (variant D), this theme, only glancingly touched on in the congress protocols (variant C), is given crucial significance:

Seizing power is not difficult. It is necessary to hold onto it in order to effect a socialist transformation. This requires support from the revolutionary workers of the west. Recent events have disclosed with special clarity the close ties between the imperialists of Russia and the imperialists of the west. From this, however, it follows that the tie between the Russian workers and the revolutionary workers of the west must be just as close. *Without such a tie and support it will be easy for the united imperialists of Russia and the west to strangle the Russian revolution.*

Therefore the task of the party is: together with strengthening and broadening the proletarian army in Russia, to strengthen and broaden the tie of this army with the revolutionary workers in the west.[98]

This key passage shows that the basic idea later thought to be characteristic of Trotsky's theory of revolution was fully shared by Lenin in 1917.

Discussion of Stalin's Report: The Ninth and Tenth Sessions

If the report presented by Stalin was actually written by Lenin, a number of the delegates were unaware of that fact, to judge by the vigor with which they tore it apart in the discussion.[99] "The leap proposed by comrade Stalin," said N. S. Angarsky (Klestov), a Moscow delegate, "is not a Marxist tactic but a tactic of despair." Preobrazhensky said he could not agree with the assertion about the inevitability of new outbreaks. Yurenev found "a series of radical contradictions" in the report.

The center of the attack was Stalin's call for withdrawal of the slogan "All Power to the Soviets." As Volodarsky put it, "It is wrong to stigmatize the form just because the content has proved unsuccessful."

Debate was still raging when the chairman brought the ninth session to a close, and it picked up where it had left off when the tenth session opened at 10 A.M. on July 31. A group of delegates led by V. N. Podbel'sky, a Moscow delegate, had drawn up a list of questions to which they wanted Stalin to respond, all related in one way or another to the party's attitude toward the soviets:

1. What form of fighting organization of the working class does the reporter [Stalin] propose instead of the soviets of workers' deputies?
2. What is to be our practical relationship to the existing soviets of workers' deputies?
3. [What is to be] our relationship to the soviets of workers' deputies in which we now have a majority?
4. [What is the] concrete definition of the concept, "the poorest peasantry," and [how should we] define the form of its organization in connection with our relationship to the existing soviets of peasants' deputies?[100]

In replying, Stalin had his first opportunity to enter personally into the debate, and he handled himself rather well. His main argument was that classes, not organizational forms, were decisive. The party's new line was to demand the transfer of power to the workers and poor peasants; it was not calling for the overthrow of the soviets but simply shifting its strategy from the soviets as institutions to specific classes.

Support for Stalin's position was voiced by G. Ya. Sokol'nikov, a delegate from the Moscow *oblast*. Harking back to Lenin's formulation in 1905, he called the soviets "organs of uprising"; only in that capacity were they suitable vehicles for the assumption of power by the workers. V. P. Nogin disagreed: the slogan "All Power to the Soviets," he said, "remains valid and will attract the masses to us."

In all, some dozen speakers were given the opportunity to air their views before the chairman called on Stalin for the concluding remarks. His position was close to that of Lenin: the existing soviets were nothing more than bodies for the organization of the masses; their political power no longer existed. Nevertheless, he favored remaining in the existing soviets, and in the Central Executive Committee. Even control of all the soviets, Stalin warned, would not give power to the Bolsheviks; the existing government must first be overthrown. Once the party had taken power, it would be able to organize the government. Basing his analysis squarely on Lenin's, Stalin named three factors on which the party must base its strategy: the Russian proletariat, the peasantry, and the European proletariat.[101]

The tenth session closed with the election of a seven-man editorial commission to prepare the final draft of the resolution on the political situation; Stalin, inevitably, was named a member, together with Bukharin, Bubnov, Sokol'nikov, Milyutin, Nogin, and Lomov. In electing this body, the delegates were taking into account a certain difference of opinion which had developed between the main body of delegates, who supported Stalin's and Lenin's position, and the delegates from Moscow, who favored using an alternative text.

The Eleventh Session: Reports on the Party Press and the Economic Situation

On the evening of July 31, the delegates assembled for the eleventh session. No chairman is indicated in the protocols, but Sverdlov was evidently in charge, to judge by his authoritative instructions at the close of the session. Stalin was either absent or silent; the protocols contain no reference to him.

Two major reports occupied the delegates' attention: Kharitonov on the party press and Milyutin on the economic situation.[102] According to Kharitonov, the number of the party journals and newspapers after the July Days stood at the same figure—forty-one—as before. Eight newspapers, including *Pravda*, had been closed by the government; but of those, five, again including *Pravda*, had reappeared under different names—a simple device, the effectiveness of which is an accurate index of the government's weakness.

Milyutin's report stressed the imminence of a major catastrophe. Government expenditures on the army, he said, were the principal cause; in the first half of 1917 the figure had reached ten and one-half billion rubles; he forecast a figure over twenty billion for the entire year, an estimate on the low side, considering the rapidly worsening position of both the army and the government.

The economic plight of the working class, already serious, would get still worse, according to Milyutin. There would be a sharp increase in the number of strikes; the Bolsheviks, unlike the Mensheviks and the SR's, must support the strikers. When the political and economic crisis reached its climax, the party's principles, including workers' control, would emerge victorious. But Milyutin gave no indication of how the party should meet this challenge.

In closing the session, Sverdlov pointed to the need for work in the sections charged with preparing resolutions; a majority of the delegates agreed and voted to cancel the session scheduled for 9 A.M. on the following day. August 1, therefore, was a day of intense editorial labor by the editorial commissions, among whose members was Stalin.

The Twelfth Session

The delegates reassembled at 11 A.M. on August 2 for one of the congress's most demanding sessions. A single topic dominated the discussion: preparation of new party statutes, to replace the ones adopted at the Second Congress in 1903. Sverdlov, presiding, called on Kharitonov to present the draft of the new statutes.[103]

Several points, Kharitonov said, had provoked controversy in the drafting commission, among them Article 13 concerning the Central Committee. Its size was to be raised to twenty-one members; from this body a smaller group, designated the "narrow composition" (*uzkii sostav*) would be established, but for reasons of security its location would not be disclosed. It was in this conspiratorial form that the party's top policy-making body, forerunner of the Politburo, made its first documented appearance in party history. There had also been debate, Kharitonov said, on Article 4, dealing with expulsion from the party—another omen of things to come.

Sverdlov then called on S. M. Zaks (Gladkov) to read the draft statutes article by article. Discussion of articles 1 (definition of party members), 2 (admission of new members), and 3 (party dues) produced no surprises; these three articles were adopted as drafted by the commission. Expulsion from the party (Article 4) was to be performed by local party bodies, with the possibility of appeals to *raion* or *oblast* conferences; the ultimate authority was to be the party congress. In the discussion of Article 4, Sverdlov made one of his rare substantive contributions, adding the Central Committee as one of the "higher party bodies" to which expulsion could be referred. Unwilling to see the authority of the party congress diluted in this way, a majority of delegates voted against Sverdlov's proposal.

Discussion of other articles was uneventful. No one spoke on the *uzkii sostav*, either in opposition or in support; evidently the delegates accepted this centralizing move as necessary and desirable.

At Preobrazhensky's suggestion, a discussion of the party's attitude toward the question of national minorities was held; Stalin took no part in the discussion, nor did anyone call for his opinion, notwithstanding his semiofficial standing as party expert on this question.

The Fifteenth Session: Stalin Presents the Resolution "On the Political Situation"

The final session of the congress, which met on the afternoon of August 3, was one of the congress's most important, both for Stalin and for the party as a whole. Sverdlov again chaired the session, which opened with a report on the trade unions by N. P. Glebov (Avilov), a delegate from the Petrograd organization who was to serve in the first Bolshevik cabinet as commissar of posts and telegraphs. Glebov presented a draft resolution "On the Tasks of the Trade Union Movement," but before it was submitted to a vote Sverdlov called on Skrypnik to present a co-report, "The Party and the Trade Unions." There was virtually no discussion of these reports, though several delegates attempted to get one started; instead, a majority of the delegates voted in favor of the proposal by Nogin to turn over the draft resolutions to the Central Committee for final editing.

Sverdlov found time for an unscheduled report on the party's national policies in the Transcaucasus, delivered by A. Iusuf-zade, a delegate from Baku. As on the day before, Stalin was absent from the discussion, evidently preferring the role of acting party leader to that of expert on the national question. Nor had Stalin anything to say on unification of the party with left Mensheviks, a topic presented by Yanson, a member of Trotsky's *Mezhraionka* group.

The report entitled "On the Political Situation," which Stalin presented at the fifteenth session, was a revised draft of the one he had presented at the ninth session (p. 191). In the absence of the original text (omitted from the protocols), Sovokin has presented evidence pointing to the conclusion that the revision served to bring the text more fully into line with Lenin's ideas and that the resolution presented by Stalin was in fact Lenin's work.[104] Even if one accepts Sovokin's argument, however (and he makes a strong case), Stalin still faced the need to defend Lenin's position as he presented the resolution article by article.[105]

Article 1 set forth in concise terms Lenin's conclusion that Russia was now ruled by

a dictatorship of the counter-revolutionary imperialist bourgeoisie, based on a military clique from the army high command and provided with a revolutionary cover by the leaders of petty bourgeois socialism.

Article 2 provided Lenin's class analysis of the Provisional Government and its relationship with the Soviet of Workers' and Soldiers' Deputies. Only the support rendered the government by the SR and Menshevik leaders of the Soviet, in Lenin's view, saved the government and prevented the peaceful transfer of power to the soviets.

A. J. Ioffe, a *Mezhraionets*, proposed adding a reference to "the voluntary refusal of the leaders of the proletariat to take power," but Stalin argued that while there had indeed been such a refusal,

what is important for us is the objective fact, the insufficient consciousness rather than the subjective motive, the unwillingness of the leaders to take power.

On the basis of this fairly subtle distinction Stalin opposed Ioffe's amendment, and the delegates voted it down.

An obscure nonvoting delegate named Pavlovich (neither his initials nor his organization are indicated in the protocols) proposed adding "for example" or "mainly" before the reference to "capitalist pillage," on the grounds that pillage of military supplies was only one of the forms of bourgeois pillage. Stalin conceded the point's validity but suggested adding the words "in the main"; the delegates supported his proposal.

Ravich wanted to stress the role of "international imperialism" in the revolution, specifically in regard to the bourgeoisie's assumption of power—an unnecessary addition, Stalin replied, since the role of Allied capital was already cited in the preceding article. A majority of the delegates agreed.

Article 3 cited the "petty bourgeois character of the predominant masses of the population of Russia" as one of the principal reasons for the people's dreams of peaceful cooperation between workers and capitalists, peasants and landowners. There was no discussion; the article was accepted as read.

Article 4 depicted the decline of the soviets under the leadership of the petty bourgeois parties. The soviets had "ceased to be organs of uprising as well as organs of governmental power." The soviets supported the bourgeoisie in delaying the Constituent Assembly, hindering the transfer of land to the peasantry, sabotaging any attempt to combat the economic crisis, and preparing an offensive.

Sverdlov suggested replacing the word "supported," in regard to the offensive, by "approved by the majority of the soviets," a change that Stalin found acceptable and that the delegates approved.

Article 5 summarized in Leninist terms the course of the class struggle as manifested in the June demonstrations and the "spontaneous movement of July 3–4," culminating in the shift of the petty bourgeois parties to a coalition with the Cadets and an "open struggle against the revolutionary proletariat and the revolutionary troops." The same obscure Pavlovich suggested adding a reference to "revolutionary troops" at the beginning of the article, but Stalin opposed the suggestion as unnecessary and the delegates agreed. Stalin also successfully opposed several verbal changes offered by Yurenev, a *Mezhraionets*.

Article 6 reiterated Lenin's concept of an "imperialist dictatorship" as the actual wielder of power, coupling with it a description of the Central Executive Committee of the soviets as "completely powerless and inactive." Stalin then proposed adding to Article 6 the following passage, which the editing committee had deleted from Article 7:

> The Soviets are undergoing an excruciating agony, demoralized as a consequence of the fact that they did not take governmental power at the appropriate time.

V. I. Solov'ev, a twenty-seven-year-old delegate from the Moscow district organization, argued against Stalin's proposal on the grounds that its description of the soviets was not applicable to the provincial soviets, which were continuing to develop, but Stalin stuck to his guns:

> Not only in Petrograd but also in the provinces the soviets have lost their power. Just let them now try to arrest or remove from office any functionary, as used to happen! The counterrevolution is stronger in the capital, but it is also on the attack in the provinces.

The delegates approved Stalin's suggestion, which did not prevent Yurenev from trying to soften its harsh characterization of the soviets by deleting the reference to their "demoralization." Again, Stalin held firm. "Comrades," he said, the demoralization of the soviets is an objective fact, and it is not for us Bolsheviks to hide the facts.

It was a rhetorical trick, but it worked: the delegates approved Stalin's proposal, and with it the text of Article 6 as amended.

Article 7 set forth Lenin's demand for the replacement of the slogan "All Power to the Soviets," with the unwieldy slogan "Complete Liquidation of the Dictatorship of the Counterrevolutionary Bourgeoisie."

In the discussion Skrypnik called for an even sharper formulation of the need for struggle against the counterrevolution in order to mark the difference between the party and those Skrypnik called "opportunists." Good-humoredly, Stalin agreed in principle but pointed out that Skrypnik had not made a specific proposal. Smilga remedied that lack by suggesting the addition of a sentence which the drafting committee had deleted:

Only the revolutionary proletariat, on condition of its being supported by the poorest peasantry, has the power to fulfill this task, which constitutes the task of a new revolution in Russia.

After further comments by Skrypnik and Nogin (Stalin took no part in the debate), Article 7 was approved with Smilga's amendment.

The thrust of Article 8 was the definition of the party's role in the revolutionary upsurge. Under its leadership, the proletariat must organize and prepare for the moment when a general national crisis and a profound mass uprising create favorable conditions for the shift of the urban and rural poor to the side of the workers against the bourgeoisie.

Yurenev proposed sharpening the article's reference to the soviets, a proposal Stalin accepted and the delegates approved. Solov'ev called for the deletion of the adjective "all-national" in reference to the approaching crisis, a proposal Stalin opposed, saying,

In that particular spot we want to indicate specifically the extent of that crisis, its all-national character.

The delegates followed Stalin.

Article 9, the final section of the resolution, constituted the culmination of everything that had gone before. "The task of the revolutionary classes," it stated,

is then to strain all forces for taking governmental power into their hands and for directing it, in alliance with the revolutionary proletariat of the advance countries, toward peace and toward a socialist reconstruction of society.

Preobrazhensky suggested a more cautious conclusion:

for directing it toward peace and, on condition of proletarian revolutions taking place in the West, toward socialism.

Preobrazhensky's suggestion anticipated the position Trotsky would later be accused of taking; at the moment Preobrazhensky made it, however, it was party orthodoxy shared by Lenin; the delegates had already approved Bukharin's resolution, "On the Current Moment and the War," which clearly implied the necessity of an international proletarian revolution as a precondition for the overthrow of capitalism in Russia.[106] Nonetheless, Preobrazhensky's suggestion triggered a response from Stalin which has become famous. "The possibility is not excluded," Stalin said,

> that Russia will be the country which paves the way to socialism. Up until now there is no country which enjoys such freedoms as there are in Russia, which has tried to establish workers' control over production. Furthermore, the basis of our revolution is broader than in western Europe, where the proletariat confronts the bourgeoisie in complete isolation. With us the proletariat is supported by the poorest strata of the peasantry. Finally, in Germany the apparatus of government power works incomparably better than the imperfect apparatus of our bourgeoisie which is a dependency of European capital. We must reject the out-of-date view that only Europe can show us the way. There is dogmatic Marxism and creative Marxism. I stand on the ground of the latter.[107]

Just as Preobrazhensky's proposal prefigured the Trotskyite stance of the mid-twenties, so Stalin's rejoinder anticipated the later theory of "Socialism in One Country." Stalin's position was not, however, completely novel; Lenin had said more or less the same thing in reply to Rykov at the April Conference (see p. 78), but with one significant difference: in his reply to Preobrazhensky, Stalin shifted the discussion to the higher ground of "creative Marxism," an astonishing claim that went further than Lenin or any other of the party's leaders. The protocols give no indication that anyone recognized Stalin's boldness; they merely record the decisive vote against Preobrazhensky's proposal.

Harking back to Article 8, Yurenev proposed changing the word "battle" (*boi*) to "action" (*vystuplenie*), in order to remove the "criminal" (i.e., antigovernmental) connotation of "battle." Stalin disagreed:

the congress cannot proceed on the basis of the "criminality" of this or that expression. If we replace the word "battle" by "action," the impression would be created that we are renouncing all action (demonstrations, strikes, etc.), whereas we wish to restrain the proletariat only from battle to which the bourgeoisie hopes to provoke it.

Yurenev's proposal was rejected. That just about wound up the discussion; Stalin did not reply to two proposals by Skrypnik, and the delegates approved Article 9 as amended.

In an abrupt shift of ground, Stalin next proposed a slate of party leaders as candidates for the Constituent Assembly: Lenin, Zinoviev, Kollontai, Trotsky, Lunacharsky—an odd grouping: why was Kamenev omitted, or Bukharin? Why was Lunacharsky included? That the proposal was an influence-building maneuver on Stalin's part seems probable; we will find Stalin performing a similar action in October, a few days before the seizure of power. The protocols record "strong applause" but no vote, indicating the tactical nature of Stalin's proposal.

The question of what to call the congress received the delegates' attention briefly. Yurenev proposed designating it the "Petersburg Congress," in order not to arouse unnecessary conflict with the Menshevik-Internationalists, who could hardly be expected to accept this purely Bolshevik congress as the one following the Fifth Congress, at which the Mensheviks had been represented in force. It was Stalin who argued in favor of boldly calling it the Sixth Congress, claiming that the Bolsheviks represented the majority of the proletariat. The congress protocols allot this proposal to Preobrazhensky, but the editors of the 1958 edition, citing contemporary press accounts, assert that the proposal was made by Stalin.[108] In any event, the delegates accepted the proposal.

Trotsky Joins the Leadership

The closed session at which the new Central Committee was chosen, Sverdlov informed the delegates, had adopted a resolution to publish the names of the new CC "in case of the normal conclusion of the congress," that is, in case the government did not disrupt its proceedings. Put to a vote, the proposal was defeated. Clearly, the sense of the congress was to maintain secrecy about its chosen leaders. Some publicity was desirable, however; Ordzhonikidze offered a proposal to publish the names of the four members of the CC who received the largest number of votes. I consider it essential to do this in order to express the solidarity of the congress with the elected leaders of the party.[109]

Was Ordzhonikidze aware that the top four members of the CC elected at the April Conference had constituted the inner core of the CC, its *uzkii sostav?* Were the delegates aware? The protocols leave these questions unanswered; they merely note the "noisy applause" that greeted Ordzhonikidze's proposal, and its prompt implementation. Lenin, it was announced, had received 133 votes out of a possible 134, Zinoviev 132, and Kamenev and Trotsky 131 each.

Up to this point, the congress had gone well for Stalin—he had delivered two of the major reports and had acquitted himself well as spokesman for Lenin's policies. Disclosure of the top four leaders of the party, however, with Trotsky's name displacing that of Stalin, must have been a nasty shock. Whatever their personal relations had been up to this point—and the seeds of enmity had already been planted—this setback to Stalin's aspirations could only foster resentment and hostility.

Another jolt to Stalin's ego was administered by Sverdlov when he called on Nogin rather than Stalin to deliver the congress's concluding statement. Briefly but eloquently, Nogin contrasted the difficulties the party faced under existing conditions with the glorious future that awaited it as the architect of a new socialist society. The honor was international in scope, said Nogin:

> Our congress is first and foremost a congress of internationalists' action, the first congress taking steps toward socialism.

"Noisy applause" greeted this statement, followed by the singing of the "Internationale." Using its newly approved designation, Sverdlov then declared the Sixth Congress closed.

The New Central Committee

According to the editors of the 1958 edition of the congress protocols, "The list of members of the CC elected at the VI Party Congress has not yet been found."[110] According to the same source, Stalin later, in response to a questionnaire by Istpart, stated that "it would seem" that the number of CC members was twenty-three. K. A. Kozlov, a congress delegate whose notes are among the sources used by the 1958 editors, stated there were twenty-one full members and ten candidate members. As to specific individuals, the 1958 edition lists the following full members:

V. I. Lenin
Artem (F. A. Sergeev)
Ya. A. Berzin
A. S. Bubnov
F. E. Dzerzhinsky
A. M. Kollontai
M. K. Muranov
V. P. Nogin
Ya. M. Sverdlov
I. V. Stalin
M. S. Uritsky
S. G. Shaumian

Candidate members, according to the same source, included the following:

P. A. Dzhaparidze
A. S. Kiselev
G. I. Lomov
N. A. Skrypnik
Ye. D. Stasova

This listing, on the face of it, is radically defective, since it omits three of the four new CC members receiving the highest number of votes— Zinoviev, Kamenev, and Trotsky. Even adding these names, however, there are still six or eight (depending on whose total figure we accept) unaccounted for. The official multivolume *History of the Communist Party of the Soviet Union* is more reliable; to the 1958 list it adds not only Zinoviev, Kamenev, and Trotsky, but also Bukharin, Krestinsky, Milyutin, Rykov, Smilga, and Sokol'nikov—that is, it includes the names of a number of party leaders whom Stalin later purged.[111] As candidate members the same source lists (in addition to those named in the 1958 edition of the protocols) the following:

A. A. Ioffe
A. Lomov
Ye. A. Preobrazhensky
V. N. Yakovleva

Again, the later purging of individuals accounts for most of the names missing from the 1958 list.

Stalin at the Sixth Congress: A Balance Sheet

How effectively did Stalin conduct himself at the Sixth Party Congress? The answer to that question depends on the yardstick used to measure his performance. If the criterion is faithfulness to Lenin's views and obedience in voicing them, Stalin earns a respectable but hardly outstanding score. On the main points of Lenin's analysis—dictatorship of the "counterrevolutionary bourgeoisie"; withdrawal of the slogan "All Power to the Soviets"; preparation of an armed uprising based on the workers and poor peasants, leading to a socialist revolution—Stalin performed well.

On the negative side was Stalin's move, early in the congress, to reopen the question of Lenin's standing trial and his suggestion that, given suitable guarantees as to his safety, he should submit to arrest and trial. When the question was debated in the aftermath of the July Days, Stalin had stood foursquare against Lenin's submission to trial. Why did he later waver on this issue? Could Stalin have seen Lenin's arrest and trial under a more favorable light by late July? Coinciding as it did with his emergence as one of the party's top leaders, is there a possibility that Stalin, perhaps not consciously, welcomed a scenario in which his path to the summit was at least temporarily cleared by Lenin's elimination?

That Stalin might have been thinking along these lines is indicated by his astonishing statement on "creative Marxism." To claim the right to interpret Marxism "creatively" is equivalent to claiming the right to top leadership of the party, for there is no attribute of leadership more sacred than the right to define current strategy in terms of basic Marxist doctrine. Lenin freely exercised this right—his claim to party preeminence depended on it. But Lenin was almost always able to find something in Marx's writings, of which he was an avid and knowledgeable reader, to justify his innovations. Stalin, far less well versed in the Marxist scriptures, took the shortcut of "creativity" to justify his stance.

It would have been easy for Stalin to cite Lenin as his authority—after all, it was Lenin's views that he was defending. At no time during the Sixth Congress, however, did Stalin refer to Lenin in this capacity, and the editorial insertion of a reference to Lenin in the report for the Central Committee (see p. 182) was brief and grudging in the extreme.

In his statement at party gatherings immediately after the July Days, Stalin had showed an unwillingness to accept Lenin's downgrading of the soviets. A few weeks later, at the Sixth Party Congress, he had made some adjustments to Lenin's position. Having rejected the soviets as the basic mechanism of the revolution, Lenin was now calling for a general armed uprising of workers and poor peasants. In accepting this vision, Stalin was embracing a strategy that differed significantly from the course events were to take in October.

Trotsky's appearance at the Sixth Congress was symbolic rather than physical, but no less effective for that; his gamble on courting arrest had paid off handsomely, as the vote for the CC showed. Had he been present at the congress Trotsky would have had to take part in discussion, define his priorities on controversial issues, submit to questions. Absent, Trotsky loomed larger than life.

For Stalin, Trotsky's entry into the party was a most unwelcome development. With his customary caution, Stalin had included Trotsky's name in his list of candidates for the Constituent Assembly, but he could not rejoice in Trotsky's swift rise to eminence in the party.

Trotsky was to remain in jail until early September; Lenin did not return to Petrograd until early October. For Stalin, the month of August was to be his last opportunity to show his potential as party leader.

5 / / AUGUST

The month of August should have been a high point in Stalin's career. By default or design, the other party leaders were out of action or silenced, leaving him a clear field in which to perform. Instead, August for Stalin was a period of missed opportunities, faulty judgments, and a relapse into obscurity, for reasons well defined by Trotsky:

> The revival of the mass movement and the return to activity of the CC members who had been temporarily removed from it naturally threw Stalin out of the position of prominence he held during the July congress. From then on, his activities were carried on in obscurity, unknown to the masses, unnoted by the enemy.[1]

Citing a four-volume chronicle of the revolution published by Istpart in 1924, Trotsky adds,

> Stalin was not mentioned even once. Stalin's name is not even in the index of approximately 500 proper names. In other words, throughout those two months [August and September], the press did not take cognizance of anything he did or of a single speech he gave, and not one of the more or less prominent participants in the events of those days mentioned his name even once.[2]

Sources for Party History in August and Early September

For the historian of the revolution and the biographer of Stalin, August 1917 is an oasis of documentation in the desert of missing or nonavailable sources. Beginning with the Central Committee session of August 4 and continuing into the early months of 1918, we have a series of well-kept, orderly protocols of the CC's meetings—forty-six in all, of which more than half—twenty-nine—took place before the Bolshevik seizure of power.

In addition to the CC protocols, we have Stalin's writings. During August Stalin made twenty contributions to the party press, varying from brief notes to fairly extensive articles and editorials. These were published, and presumably written, on an almost day-to-day basis. The longest interval of silence between items is four days (August 9–13).

A striking feature of Stalin's output in August is that none of the writings carried any indication of authorship. Not until September 6 did Stalin again begin using his party pseudonym, either in full or in abbreviation ("K.St." on September 6, "K. Stalin" on September 9, "K." on September 12). Thus, in August he failed to take advantage of one of the legitimate means available to him of keeping his name before the public and marking out his own specific analysis of the revolution. Trotsky, himself a brilliant journalist, delivered a withering but not unjustified verdict on Stalin's journalistic endeavors in August and September:

> There is practically nothing to say about Stalin's newspaper work during that period. He was the editor of the central organ, not because he was a writer by nature, but because he was not an orator, and simply did not fall into any public activity. He did not write a single notable article; did not pose a single new subject for discussion; did not introduce a single slogan into general circulation. His comments on events were impersonal, and strictly within the framework of current Party views. He was a Party member assigned to a newspaper, not a revolutionary publicist.[3]

Deutscher gives faint praise to Stalin's newspaper work during this period for its "simple and incisive style" but cannot avoid a downgrading:

> Stalin's writings were really the small change of Bolshevik propaganda.[4]

Formation and Functions of the *Uzkii Sostav*

The most important organizational task facing the new Central Committee was the establishment of the *uzkii sostav*, the policy-making organ of the party, as provided for in the new party statutes. This matter was taken up at the first postcongress session of the CC on August 4.[5] Stalin was present, as were Sverdlov, Bukharin, and Dzerzhinsky.

It was decided to fix the size of the *uzkii sostav* at eleven members (a proposal for a somewhat smaller body of nine members was voted down). In a display of the organizational talents he was developing, Stalin proposed that the *uzkii sostav* operate in accordance with a division of functions among its members. The proposal was adopted.

Membership of the *uzkii sostav* was settled at the following CC session, on August 5.[6] Stalin and Sverdlov were obvious choices; the other members were Sokol'nikov, Dzerzhinsky, Milyutin, Uritsky, Ioffe, Muranov, Bubnov, Stasova, and Shaumian (not yet in Petrograd; until his arrival, Smilga). In choosing these individuals, the CC was acting in accordance with the principle that physical presence was indispensable for membership, rather than prestige or stature. Stalin was the only carry-over from the "April Bureau."

Was the *uzkii sostav* a precursor of the Politburo, as Adam Ulam has suggested?[7] The answer must be a qualified "yes," in view of the fact that it was charged with functions of leadership and policy making similar to those of the later Politburo. In its membership, however, the *uzkii sostav* showed an almost willful disregard for the realities of power in the party. It was too large and too diverse to serve as an effective policy-making body. Omission of the party's real leaders— Lenin, Zinoviev, Kamenev, Trotsky—and the inclusion of third- or fourth-ranking figures such as Milyutin and Muranov rendered it incapable of providing genuine leadership.

As matters turned out, the *uzkii sostav* led a short and not particularly noteworthy existence. The protocols record only seven sessions—on August 6, 8, 13, 14, 16, 20, and 23; thereafter its policy-making functions were taken over by the full CC. Except for his suggestion at the August 4 session, Stalin made no contribution to the work of the *uzkii sostav* which the secretary thought sufficiently important to include in the protocols. The eclipse of the *uzkii sostav*, with its variegated membership and its failure to include the party's real leaders, was inevitable once these leaders resumed full-scale activity in September.

Establishment of the Secretariat

At its session on August 6, the Central Committee took a decision in regard to the Secretariat.[8] That body was to deal with the organizational side of party work and to be composed of five members, all drawn from the CC. Thus, the CC established an early precedent for the interlocking relationship between the two bodies. Those named as Secretariat members were Dzerzhinsky, Ioffe, Sverdlov, Muranov, and Stasova. No chairman was designated, but it was a foregone conclusion that Sverdlov would hold that position, *de facto* if not *de jure*.

Inasmuch as the Secretariat managed the organizational side of the CC's work, it was inevitable that it would eventually become the dominant body in the party. The smooth functioning of the Secretariat under Sverdlov served to mask the inner workings of the party's machinery. Certainly Stalin, in 1917, had no inkling of the uses to which the Secretariat could be put in building a personal machine. His failure to recognize its potential usefulness, reflected in his neglect of the opportunity to serve on the Secretariat (if he had wanted to, he could easily have pushed aside secondary figures such as Ioffe or Muranov), provides strong evidence of the gap between his ambition and his ability to win the commanding position from which that ambition could be realized.

Reorganizing the Party Press

One of the questions taken up by the Central Committee at its meeting on August 4 was the reorganization of the party's publications.[9] Action by the Provisional Government had led to the temporary closing down of *Pravda*. Meanwhile, the Military Organization was continuing to publish *Soldat*, and the Petersburg Committee was pressing hard for the right to publish its own newspaper.

Under these circumstances, the CC decided to take over *Soldat* as the party's official organ; neither the MO nor the PK, it was decided, should have its own newspaper. In the vote for the editorial board Stalin received the highest number of votes, 13, followed by Sokol'nikov and Milyutin, each of whom received 12 votes, making Stalin the senior editor.

The CC then took up the question of including Trotsky on the editorial board if he should be released from jail. By a slim margin (11 against, 10 for), the proposal was defeated. For Stalin, however, the reprieve was only temporary; freed on September 4, Trotsky showed up at a meeting of the CC two days later and was promptly named a member of the editorial board.

Party Publications

The question of party publications was taken up by the *uzkii sostav* at its eighth session held on August 20.[10] Stalin figured in a number of the assignments handed out. He was named a member of the five-man editorial board of *Vperëd*, designed to serve as a popular propaganda organ of the CC. He was also chosen to serve on the editorial board of the party's theoretical journal, *Prosveshchenie*, whose editorial line was defined as that of the Zimmerwald left wing. The party publishing house, *Rabochii*, was to be directed by the editorial board already set for *Vperëd*, including Stalin.

Stalin's membership on the editorial board of *Prosveshchenie* was extremely brief, however. Trotsky writes:

> On the 6th of September—after my liberation from prison—Stalin and Ryazanov were replaced on the editorial board of the theoretical journal by Kamenev and me.[11]

Thus, another item was added to the growing list of Stalin's grievances against Trotsky, all the more galling for Stalin in that it showed the party's low estimate of his ability as a theorist in comparison with Trotsky and Kamenev. Deutscher comments:

> After the [Sixth] Congress, when the imprisoned leaders, first Kamenev, then Trotsky, Lunacharsky and others were gradually released, Stalin again withdrew into the twilight of the *coulisse*.[12]

Kamenev under Suspicion

The first of the imprisoned Bolshevik leaders to be freed on bail was Kamenev, during the first week in August. It was to be nearly another month, however, before he resumed full-scale activity in the Bolshevik party and the Petrograd Soviet. The reason was a new charge against him. At its session on August 4, the CC heard a report by Nogin that rumors were circulating that Kamenev had collaborated with the Kiev office of the Okhrana, the tsarist secret police.[13] If substantiated, the rumors would have put an inglorious end to Kamenev's political career.

On August 10, the accusation was published by the Ministry of Justice and the bourgeois press. In view of the fact that Kamenev was a member of the Central Executive Committee (CEC) of the Soviet, that body had established a commission to investigate the rumors. At its session on August 6, the Bolshevik CC ordered Stalin to contact the commission.[14]

Kamenev was formally cleared of the charge on August 30 and immediately resumed full-scale political action, attending a session of the *uzkii sostav* on the day of his exoneration as well as taking on active participation in the Soviet CEC.

Kamenev Seizes the Initiative

At a session of the Central Executive Committee on August 31 Kamenev introduced a resolution, "On Power," which immediately became a rallying point for the Bolsheviks and for the radical left wing of the moderate socialist parties.[15] Consideration and adoption of Kamenev's resolution was the sole item on the agenda of an enlarged meeting of the Bolshevik Central Committee on August 31, with representatives of the Bolshevik fraction of the CEC and of the Petrograd Soviet.[16]

In his resolution, Kamenev called for a fundamental reorganization of state power. The Cadet party was to be excluded from the government, as were representatives of the upper classes in general. The government's policies of "compromise and irresponsibility" must be "fundamentally altered." The Provisional Government must be replaced by one "consisting of representatives of the revolutionary proletariat and peasantry." The new government must take the following measures:

(1) decreeing a democratic republic;

(2) immediate abolition of private property in gentry land without redemption and transfer of the land to management by peasant committees until a decision by the Constituent Assembly, with provision of tools for the poorest peasants;

(3) introduction of workers' control over production and distribution on a nation-wide scale. Nationalization of the most important branches of the economy, including oil, coal, and metallurgy. Ruthless taxation of large-scale capital and property and the confiscation of war profits;

(4) proclamation of the secret treaties as invalid and the immediate proposal to all the peoples of the belligerent nations of a general democratic peace.

"Immediate measures" to be taken included:

(1) The halting of all repression of the working class and its organs. Abolition of the death penalty at the front and restoration of full freedom of agitation and of all democratic organizations in the army. Purge of the counter-revolutionary high command.

(2) Electability of commissars and other officials by local organizations.

(3) Establishment in practice of the rights of nations living in Russia; first of all, satisfaction of the demands of Finland and Ukraine.

(4) Abolition of the State Council and the State Duma; immediate convocation of the Constituent Assembly.

(5) Abolition of all class privileges; full equality of citizens.[17]

Kamenev had done a thorough job. All that was missing from his resolution was an explicit call for a new revolution.

On August 31, the Bolshevik CC adopted Kamenev's resolution without change.[18] Stalin was present at the session that discussed and adopted it. The protocols record no individual statements, merely asserting that "all those present took part in the discussion." It is noteworthy, however, that Stalin's first recorded absence in August from sessions of the CC took place on the evening of the same day, August 31, and that he also missed the session of September 3. By his vigorous initiative Kamenev had put Stalin in the shade, and it is not surprising that Stalin's attendance at CC sessions became irregular.

It was not only the Bolsheviks, however, who adopted Kamenev's resolution. Later on the night of August 31, the Petrograd Soviet held a debate on the resolution which lasted through the night and which ended at 5:30 A.M. on September 1 with the rejection of an alternative SR proposal and the adoption of Kamenev's resolution.[19] As Rabino-witch points out,

> The August 31 session marked the first occasion on which a clear majority of the deputies present voted with the Bolsheviks on any political issue.

The leftward shift still fell short, however, of affecting the top policy-making echelon in the Soviet. In a lengthy session that ended on September 2, the All-Russian Central Executive Committee rejected Kamenev's resolution as well as an alternative presented by Martov on behalf of the Menshevik-Internationalists, adopting instead a resolution drafted by the centrist Mensheviks and the SR's which favored the early convocation of the Constituent Assembly but which meanwhile pledged support to Kerensky's newly hatched five-man Directory.[20] The Bolshevik spokesmen in the debate were Kamenev and Ryazanov; Stalin, if present, kept silent.

Did Stalin collaborate with Kamenev in the preparation of the August 30 resolution? That possibility is suggested by an editorial, "We Demand!" published in the August 28 edition of *Rabochii put'*, unsigned but attributed to Stalin by the editors of his *Works*.[21]

Comparison of Stalin's editorial with Kamenev's resolution reveals a high degree of similarity. Virtually every point in Stalin's program reappears in Kamenev's resolution. The principal differences lie in the organization and formulation of points. By shifting the proposals on land, workers' control, and peace to a more prominent position, Kamenev sharpened the focus on three of the Bolsheviks' principal slogans. Reflecting his greater familiarity with governmental agencies and practices, Kamenev included a number of points entirely lacking from Stalin's list, for example, the electability of local government officials, abolition of the State Council and State Duma, and abolition of all class privileges.

The major difference between the two documents, however, lay in the use to which each was put. For all its comprehensiveness, Stalin's editorial remained a paper document, lacking even the author's signature to give it a personal stamp. By contrast, Kamenev's resolution was immediately absorbed into the political life of revolutionary Petrograd, first in the Bolshevik CC, then in the Petrograd Soviet, followed by full debate, though not adoption, in the Central Executive Committee.

What exactly was Stalin's role in this episode? The near identity of the two documents virtually rules out the possibility of coincidence. Did Stalin prepare a rough draft, which Kamenev then polished and presented publicly? Or did Stalin obtain a working draft of the document from Kamenev, directly or indirectly, and then present it as his own, cautiously hiding behind the screen of anonymity?

Whichever explanation one prefers, the episode is not one in which Stalin could take pride. If he did indeed have a hand in the document's preparation, why did he not acknowledge his part authorship, either by signing the August 28 editorial or by publicly identifying himself as coauthor of the resolution? To do so would have lent it added weight and authority—after all, Stalin was by now an established member of the Bolsheviks' leadership, and a Kamenev-Stalin resolution, openly sponsored by both men, would have carried more weight than one presented by either man alone.

In this episode, one fact stands out prominently: Stalin's caution, his reluctance to commit himself publicly, coupled with a willingness to let others take the risk and, if matters turned out favorably, reap the rewards of publicity and recognition.

By the end of August the tempo of revolutionary events was beginning to accelerate, creating conditions that favored those willing to gamble on an unknown future. This was not Stalin's style, however. The qualities and attributes that had hitherto served him were devalued in the climactic phase of the revolution now rapidly taking shape.

The Reemergence of Zinoviev

Zinoviev remained in hiding throughout most of August. At its ninth session, on August 30, the Central Committee took up a proposal by Zinoviev that he be authorized to return to party activities.[22] The CC, in response, decided to mount a campaign demanding the freeing of party leaders arrested in July and "the return to their posts of the prosecuted leaders of the working class—Lenin, Zinoviev, et al."

Zinoviev made his first postindictment appearance at a meeting of the CC on the evening of August 31. He had already begun to contribute to the party press: On August 30 an unsigned article by Zinoviev, "What Not to Do," appeared in *Rabochii put'*.[23] Its thrust was to discourage the party in its preparations for an armed uprising, citing the example of the Paris Commune of 1871 as a warning.

Stalin, as senior editor, passed the article for publication without comment, an action that Trotsky regarded as characteristic of Stalin's lack of full support for the party line. Lenin was quick to rebut Zinoviev's caution in an article written on September 3.[24] Trotsky comments,

> Without mentioning Zinoviev, Lenin wrote on September 3, "The reference to the Commune is superficial and even foolish . . . the Commune could not at once offer to the people all that the Bolsheviks can offer them when they become the government: namely, land to the peasants, immediate peace prospects."
>
> The blow against Zinoviev rebounded at the editor of the newspaper. But Stalin kept silent. Anonymously, he was ready to support any Right Wing polemic against Lenin. But he was careful not to involve himself in it. At the first sign of danger he stepped aside.[25]

The Ruckus with the Military Organization

Meanwhile, Stalin had stirred up a hornets' nest with the Military Organization. At its meeting on August 13, the CC named Stalin to break the news to the MO that its newspaper, *Soldat*, was going to be taken over by the CC as the official party organ.[26] This would not have been an easy assignment under the most favorable conditions, but Stalin, by his arrogant and overbearing behavior, managed to make it far worse.

The meeting with the MO took place on August 13. According to a formal complaint by the MO to the CC, filed on the fifteenth,

> Comrade Stalin stated that there was no point in his holding talks with representatives of the Central Bureau of the MO; that, once a resolution had been adopted by the CC, it must be carried out without any discussion.

Smilga, said the MO, made a similar statement with regard to the funds belonging to *Soldat*. The MO characterized such behavior as "inadmissible"; such measures, it said, are not accidental, but from the moment of the change from the former composition of the CC have developed into an outright system of persecution and repression of an extremely strange character. . . . The Central Buro of the Military Organization demands from the CC the *immediate normal regulation of the question as to the forms* of the mutual relations of these two organizations, considering that the existing state of affairs hinders the work of the Central Buro of the Military Organization in accordance with the tasks assigned to it by the All-Russian Conference of Military Organizations.[27]

Strong language, directed unmistakably at Stalin. It is not surprising that the MO declaration of August 15 remained buried in the archives during the period of Stalin's power; its preservation and publication is a stroke of luck for the historian, showing as it does how far the Stalin of 1917 had already taken on character traits commonly thought of as dating from a much later point in his career.

The MO's blistering declaration was taken up by the *uzkii sostav* on August 16.[28] It flatly rejected the MO's demand for autonomy but pointedly refrained from endorsing Stalin's high-handed actions; instead, it showed a desire to mollify the MO. "The publication of a newspaper for the soldiers," said the CC,

> is recognized as desirable. Such a newspaper is *Soldat*. The CC entrusts the publication of this newspaper to the existing editorial board and delegates to it a member of the CC with the right of veto. Naming the editorial board is a prerogative of the CC. The Military Buro can propose the makeup of the editorial board to the CC. For talks with the Military Buro and the establishment of correct relations between them and the CC the CC designates Sverdlov and Dzerzhinsky. They are also directed to provide temporary supervision of the editorship of *Soldat*.

Stalin's behavior in this incident shows how far he had already moved in his self-identification with the unchallengeable authority of the party. In August 1917, however, his claim to power could still be challenged and curbed. The CC, by its handling of the case, delivered an implied reproof to Stalin for his failure to carry out the task to which he had been assigned, the takeover of *Soldat*. The MO's protest echoed the reference to Stalin's undesirable "personal characteristics" of March (see p. 11).

For Stalin's current status in the party, the most significant aspect of the matter was the CC's decision to send Sverdlov and Dzerzhinsky to probe the situation. This was not the first time Sverdlov had been called on to clean up one of Stalin's messes; in 1913 he had been sent by Lenin to rectify the situation in *Pravda's* editorial office resulting from policies initiated by Stalin of which Lenin disapproved.

The August episode served to refresh Sverdlov's impression of Stalin's weaknesses and faults of character. When Sverdlov helped to choose the team for the seizure of power in October, this shadow over Stalin may well have been a significant factor.

The Kornilov Mutiny

By the end of the Sixth Congress, Stalin had assimilated the broad outlines of Lenin's concept of current power relationships. In the events of August Stalin found evidence to confirm his and Lenin's view that a right-wing military dictatorship had been or was in the process of being established. It was in this context that Stalin viewed the Moscow State Conference, which opened on August 12 with some twenty-five hundred participants. In an article published on August 15 Stalin asserted,

> There is no reason for doubt. Matters are moving toward the establishment and legalization of a military dictatorship.[29]

It was under the influence of this concept that Stalin viewed the conflict that broke out toward the end of August between Kerensky, acting head of the government, and General Lavr Kornilov, commander in chief of the army. In an unsigned editorial published on August 28, Stalin minimized the significance of the conflict:

> The fight now going on between the coalition government and the Kornilov party is a contest not between revolution and counter-revolution but between two different methods of counter-revolutionary policy.[30]

Stalin continued to advance that explanation in his journalistic writings of late August and early September. Lacking in Stalin's analysis was any recognition of the leading role the party might play in using the conflict for its own purposes.

Lenin's reaction was significantly different. In the rapidly deepening gulf between Kerensky and the army high command Lenin saw the opening of a dazzling prospect for the Bolshevik party. On August 18 and 19 he wrote,

> Our task now would be to *take power* and to proclaim ourself the government in the name of peace, land for the peasants, and the convocation of the Constituent Assembly. . . .
> . . . Should a spontaneous movement break out in Moscow today, the slogan would be precisely to seize power.[31]

When Lenin learned, on August 30, of the open conflict between

Kerensky and Kornilov, he was jubilant. In a confidential message to the CC he wrote,

> The Kornilov revolt is a most unexpected (unexpected at such a moment and in such a form) and downright unbelievably sharp turn in events. . . . Like every sharp turn it calls for a revision and change of tactics. And, as with every revision, we must become extra cautious not to become unprincipled.

What Lenin had in mind was a sharp distinction between *supporting* Kerensky and *fighting* Kornilov. "We shall fight," Lenin wrote;

> we are fighting Kornilov, *just as* Kerensky's *troops do*, but we must not support Kerensky. *On the contrary*, we expose his weakness. That is the difference. It is rather a subtle difference, but it is highly essential and must not be forgotten.[32]

This strategy, Lenin believed, could lead the party to power. But caution and secrecy were imperative:

> we must speak of this as little as possible in our propaganda (remembering that even tomorrow events may put power into our hands, *and then we shall not relinquish it*).[33]

The key, Lenin argued, was action by the masses, galvanized into action by Bolshevik propaganda and agitation:

> Now is the time for *action*; the war against Kerensky must be conducted in a revolutionary way, by drawing the masses in, by arousing them, by inflaming them.[34]

Not for a moment did Lenin forget the war:

> In the war against the Germans, *action* is required right now; *immediate and unconditional peace must be offered* on *precise* terms. If this is done, either a speedy peace *can* be attained, or *the war can be turned into a revolutionary war*.[35]

Lenin's letter to the Central Committee was not intended for publication and therefore presented no problem to Stalin in his capacity as senior editor of the party organ. Nonetheless, the letter did create an awkward situation for Stalin in its emphasis on the imperative need for stirring up the masses against the Kerensky regime, a need that could only be met by party leaders with oratorical skills that Stalin lacked—but that Trotsky, more than anyone else, possessed in full measure.

From the moment when Lenin's letter of August 30 was received and read by the Central Committee, a new phase of the revolution opened, one in which Stalin's innate caution, his dislike for sudden shifts in policy, even his smoldering distrust of Lenin's guidance, all contributed to place him at a disadvantage.

Stalin's disadvantage was compounded by the reemergence of Lenin's senior lieutenants, Kamenev and Zinoviev, into active political life and by the meteoric rise of Trotsky. Meanwhile, ignored by Stalin and seemingly relegated to a merely administrative role was the real master of the party machine, Sverdlov, who worked tirelessly at the task of marshaling the party's human resources on behalf of the policies laid down by Lenin. Without realizing it, Stalin was being outflanked and outmaneuvered.

6 // SEPTEMBER-OCTOBER

Lenin on the Attack

The Kornilov mutiny represented a historic turning point in the Russian Revolution—the point at which the Provisional Government lost control of the army and, with that loss, the power to shape events. It also marked the opening of a split between Lenin and Stalin in their evaluation of the current situation and their views on the tactics the Bolshevik party should pursue in the changed circumstances.

For Stalin, the Kornilov mutiny represented nothing new or significant. In an August 28 editorial he wrote:

> It is a fact that Kornilov's present action is *merely the continuation* of the notorious machinations of the counter-revolutionary higher army officers.[1]

A few days later, Stalin called for a "break with the bourgeoisie and landlords" and for the "formation of a government of workers and peasants."[2]

That was the formula which Stalin continued to advocate in his journalistic writings in late August and early September. Lacking in Stalin's concept was any recognition of the leading role the party could play by entering directly into the revolutionary process, mastering it, and imposing a Bolshevik strategy on it. For all his proud boast at the Sixth Congress that he stood on the basis of "creative" Marxism, Stalin in August and early September showed no awareness of the party's potential for decisive action, at a time when the Provisional Government had dealt itself a mortal wound through Kerensky's inept handling of the Kornilov mutiny.

On September 3 Stalin published an unsigned editorial, "The Crisis and the Directory," in which he asserted that Kerensky's newly formed five-man Directory was in reality a screen for the dominance of the Cadets—a screen made plausible by the support given to Kerensky by the moderate socialist parties. "An implacable struggle," Stalin asserted,

> must be waged against the influence of the Socialist-Revolutionaries on the masses, work must be carried on tirelessly to rally the peasants and soldiers around the banner of the party of the proletariat.[3]

Stalin's conclusion, like his analysis, amounted to little more than a paraphrase of a longer article by Lenin, "From a Publicist's Diary," published two days earlier in *Rabochii*.[4]

Stalin missed the Central Committee session on September 3 for unknown reasons—he was not ill, nor was he absent from the capital. The most important business facing the CC was the consideration of Lenin's "Letter to the Central Committee of the RSDLP," written on August 30, in which he laid out the dual strategy of vigorously entering into the struggle against Kornilov while putting increased pressure on Kerensky.[5]

The protocols record only that Lenin's letter "was read."[6] Evidently no significant discussion took place. Lenin's boldness and daring found little if any response from a majority of members of the CC, including Stalin.

Lenin Throws Down the Gage: The Central Committee Meeting of September 15

By mid-September Lenin had reached the conclusion that the time was ripe for the Bolshevik party to seize power in the name of the workers and peasants. Still in hiding (a secret telegram from the head of the Petrograd Militia ordering his "immediate arrest" was sent out on September 14),[7] Lenin was forced to communicate with the Central Committee by letters hand-carried by liaison agents.

Between September 12 and 14, Lenin wrote a letter to the CC with copies to the Petersburg and Moscow party committees, "The Bolsheviks Must Seize Power."[8] A day or so later he sent a second letter, addressed only to the CC, "Marxism and Uprising."[9] The CC considered these letters and the challenge they posed at a meeting on September 15.[10] According to Daniels,

> Smilga, the Bolshevik chief in Helsingfors, took Lenin's letters to Petrograd on the 15th and turned them over to Krupskaya, who had remained in the city. She gave them to Stalin, who read them to members of the Central Committee assembled in Sverdlov's apartment.[11]

Deutscher also asserts that it was Stalin who brought Lenin's letters to the CC session of September 15.[12] Despite the fundamental importance of the problem raised by Lenin's letters, the protocols record statements on them by only two members of the CC during the debate, first Stalin, then Kamenev.

> Comrade Stalin proposes sending the letters to the most important [party] organizations with the suggestion that they be discussed. It is decided to postpone this to the next CC session.[13]

Thereupon someone proposed keeping only one copy of the letters. This proposal was adopted, six to four, with six abstentions.

For Kamenev, the program outlined in Lenin's letters was downright dangerous:

> Comrade Kamenev moved the adoption of the following resolution. After considering Lenin's letters, the CC rejects the practical proposals they contain, calls on all organizations to follow CC instructions alone and affirms once again that the CC regards any kind of demonstration in the streets as quite impermissible at the present moment. At the same time the CC makes a request to Comrade Lenin to elaborate in a special brochure on the question he raised in his letters of a new assessment of the current situation and the Party's policy.

This resolution was defeated; the protocols do not give the exact breakdown of the voting. The final action recorded in the protocols was the adoption of the following decision:

> CC members in charge of work in the Military Organization and the Petersburg Committee are instructed to take measures to prevent demonstrations of any kind in barracks and factories.[14]

This is slim evidence for the line-up of members of the CC, and much effort has been expended in an attempt to make out the actual stance of individual members of the CC in regard to Lenin's letters. What is clear is that the CC as a whole showed no willingness to act in accordance with Lenin's wishes. Kamenev's position is the only firmly established fact in the situation: he was unalterably opposed. Stalin's position is more enigmatic: did his proposal indicate support of Lenin and the desire to increase pressure on the CC to adopt the course of action demanded by Lenin, or was it a stalling move, aimed at gaining time while not rejecting Lenin's demands outright? Soviet historians of the Stalin school had no doubt on this score. For example, Yaroslavsky writes:

> Stalin passed severe strictures on Kamenev and thwarted his plans. [There is no evidence to support this assertion.] He proposed that Lenin's letters be discussed immediately [this is a barefaced lie] and that copies of them be sent to the most important Party organizations *for their guidance* [italics added. Stalin's proposal was for *discussion* of the letters, not for their use as "guidance"]. The Central Committee adopted these proposals [another outright lie].

Conscious, however, of the thinness of the case for Stalin's acceptance of Lenin's demands, Yaroslavsky adds:

> Stalin at this period devoted great attention to the preparation of armed uprising, to the formation of a Red Guard, and the arming of the workers.[15]

The contemporary record provides no support for this assertion. More cautiously, the editors of Stalin's *Works* simply state:

> At a meeting of the Central Committee of the Party, J. V. Stalin opposes Kamenev's demand that V. I. Lenin's letters . . . should be burned, and recommends that they should be circulated for discussion among the bigger Party organizations.[16]

For Trotsky, Stalin's motives were clear. Citing "the latest [Soviet] commentary," which

> declares that the purpose of Stalin's proposal was to organize the influence of local Party Committees on the CC and to urge it to carry out Lenin's directive,

Trotsky argues,

> Had such been the case, Stalin would have come right out in defense of Lenin's proposals and would have countered Kamenev's resolutions with—his own! But that was far from his thought. Most of the Committeemen in the provinces were more Rightist than the Central Committee. To send them Lenin's letters without the Central Committee's endorsement was tantamount to expressing disapproval of them. Stalin's proposal was made to gain time and in the event of a conflict to secure the possibility of pleading that the local Committees were balking.

To support his analysis, Trotsky points out that

Stalin did not even put in an appearance at the next session [of the CC] which met no sooner than five days later [September 25] and the question of the letters was not even included in the order of the day. The hotter the atmosphere, the colder are Stalin's maneuverings.[17]

Deutscher tries to mitigate the harshness of Trotsky's evaluation, writing,

Stalin suggested that the letters should be submitted to the major [Party] organizations for discussion, which suggested that he supported Lenin since any wide discussion of the matter would have tended to commit the Party to pass from argument to action. . . . In any case, Stalin's proposal was not accepted.[18]

One way of identifying Stalin's attitude toward Lenin's proposals is to note his behavior as senior editor of *Rabochii put'*. Roy Medvedev writes,

The sources show that during the decisive days of September and October 1917, when Lenin was urging immediate preparation for an insurrection, *Pravda* [i.e., *Rabochii put'*], edited by Stalin, did not carry some of Lenin's articles, or else cut entire paragraphs from them. This behavior on the part of *Pravda*, along with a certain "moderation" in the upper echelons of the Party, provoked sharp protests from him; he even began to communicate with Party organizations over the head of the Central Committee.[19]

A revealing light on Stalin's indecisiveness and procrastination is thrown by the contrasting behavior of Sverdlov. Without waiting for the CC to make up its mind, Sverdlov, for whom Lenin's word was law, took immediate steps to inform the workers at the Putilov factory of the substance of Lenin's letters to the CC.[20]

Stalin and the Pre-Parliament

Stalin missed the next session of the Central Committee, which took place on September 20.[21] There had evidently been criticism of his work as editor: "Several comrades," reported Sokol'nikov, "had complained about the tone of the Central Organ [*Rabochii put'*] and about certain expressions in articles, etc." The CC put off a detailed discussion of the matter but affirmed that "the general direction [of the Central Organ] fully coincides with the line of the CC."

Encouraged, no doubt, by this expression of support for his editorial work, Stalin attended the next meeting of the CC, on September 21.[22] Here the question of Bolshevik attendance at the Democratic Conference and the Pre-Parliament was the principal item on the agenda. Despite Lenin's insistence on a boycott, the CC decided "not to withdraw from the Democratic Conference but merely to recall members of our party from the presidium."

At a conference of the Bolshevik group in the Democratic Conference, held on September 21, Stalin supported Lenin's call for a boycott, in opposition to Kamenev and Rykov, who favored attendance.[23] It was Trotsky, however, who earned Lenin's approbation; learning of Trotsky's advocacy of the boycott at the September 21 meeting, Lenin wrote, "Trotsky was for the boycott. Bravo, Comrade Trotsky!"[24] The conference nevertheless voted 77 to 50 to take part in the Pre-Parliament, and at its session of September 21 the CC confirmed this decision.[25]

Trotsky's Mounting Prominence

With the release from jail of some of the party's top leaders, Stalin's brief eminence was increasingly threatened. At the CC session of September 23 (which Stalin did not attend), both Kamenev and Zinoviev put in an appearance, but it was Trotsky who dominated the session.[26] First, Trotsky's report on the Democratic Conference was formally adopted after a "critical analysis." Next, it was decided to appoint Trotsky and Sokol'nikov to a commission of the Democratic Conference charged with working out the text of an appeal to all nations.

Trotsky was also named, along with Rykov and Kamenev, to serve on the presidium of the Pre-Parliament. It was Trotsky who was chosen to speak at a commission of the Democratic Conference, elected to negotiate with ministers in the attempt to form a new government. Trotsky's services were again enlisted, together with those of Sokol'nikov, Bubnov, and Ioffe, to prepare a resolution on the Pre-Parliament for the forthcoming party gathering.

Trotsky's rapid rise in the party was due in large part to his skill as a speaker and writer. When the CC met again on September 24 (with Stalin present), Trotsky was chosen as Bolshevik candidate for chairman of the Petrograd Soviet, while Rykov was to be put forward for membership on the presidium.[27] At the same session, Sverdlov was designated to serve on the commission to prepare the projected Second Congress of Soviets. It was small consolation to Stalin to find his name included with twenty-four others as party nominees for the Constituent Assembly.[28]

The CC Meetings of October 5 and 7: Setting Up Party Machinery

At the CC session of October 5—the first he had attended in two weeks—Stalin successfully proposed the holding on October 10 of a party gathering with representatives of the CC and members of the Petrograd and Moscow party organizations, timed to coincide with the Northern Region Congress of Soviets.[29] The idea was not original with Stalin, however. The Soviet historian Ye. N. Gorodetsky, citing archival evidence, quotes a letter to the CC of October 5 from G. I. Bokii, secretary of the Petersburg Committee, which reads,

> Considering the present moment critical for the revolution and considering that extremely great responsibility now falls on our party for the further course of events, the E[xecutive] C[ommittee (IK)] of the PK considers necessary the immediate calling of a meeting of the CC with Petersburg and Moscow workers in order to indicate the political line of our party.

On the back of this document, Gorodetsky notes,

> in the writing of Ya. M. Sverdlov is written: The CC on receiving the proposal of the IK PK has decided to call a meeting of the CC with workers from the localities. The executive commission will be informed in good time concerning the time and place of the meeting. It is proposed to time the meeting for the Northern Oblast Congress of Soviets.[30]

Stalin's modest achievement was promptly overshadowed, moreover, by the omission of his name from a commission to prepare a draft program for the forthcoming party congress, the members of which were Lenin, Bukharin, Trotsky, Kamenev, Sokol'nikov, and Kollontai.[31]

The highlight of the CC session of October 7, which Stalin attended, was the naming of Trotsky, Sverdlov, and Bubnov to serve on and organize an information bureau under the CC "for the struggle against counterrevolution."[32]

Trotsky later recalled Stalin's role in the establishment of this committee:

> That very day [October 7], at the CC session it was decided to organize an Information Bureau on Fighting the Counter-Revolution. The deliberately foggy name covered a concrete task: reconnaissance and preparation of the insurrection. Sverdlov, Bubnov, and I were delegated to organize that Bureau. In view of the laconic nature of the protocol and the absence of other documents, the author [i.e., Trotsky] is compelled to resort to his own memory at this time. Stalin declined to participate in the Bureau,

suggesting Bubnov, a man of little authority, in place of himself. His attitude was one of reserve, if not of skepticism, toward the idea itself. He was in favor of an insurrection. But he did not believe that the workers and soldiers were ready for action. He lived isolated not only from the masses, but even from their Soviet representatives, and was content with the refracted impressions of the Party machine.[33]

Stalin's refusal to get involved with the technical preparations for an uprising was one of the critical factors by which he cut himself off from the seizure of power. Agreed in principle to the idea of an insurrection, he evidently wanted to avoid committing himself too deeply to a risky project whose outcome was unknown.

The combination of Trotsky and Sverdlov was a powerful one, joining the party's most brilliant and effective orator with its master organizer. The team of Sverdlov and Trotsky was to dominate the climactic events of October, culminating in the seizure of power on the twenty-fifth. Stalin's role in the Bolshevik Revolution would be determined by what he could contribute to, and what he would be asked to contribute, by this team. It was Stalin's misfortune that neither Sverdlov nor Trotsky had a high regard for his abilities, nor would either man turn to Stalin for help in an emergency. Stalin's role in the seizure of power would therefore depend primarily on his own perspicacity and energy, his ability to keep pace with the trend of events, and his grasp of the strategy as defined by Lenin and implemented by party members working under the close supervision of Trotsky and Sverdlov.

Rabinowitch downgrades the importance of the Information Bureau, although he notes its subsequent strengthening:

> Nevsky and Podvoisky from the Military Organization and Latsis and Moskvin from the Petersburg Committee were subsequently named to the Bureau as well. There is no evidence that the Bureau functioned actively; for the time being the Central Committee's primary objective in establishing such a body seems to have been to undercut the operation initiated by the Executive Commission [of the Petersburg committee].[34]

But for Stalin, the incident represented another missed opportunity.

The CC Session of October 10: Insurrection on the Agenda

The most famous, most fateful session of the Bolshevik CC took place on October 10. This was *not* the party gathering that had been approved, on Stalin's proposal, at the CC session of October 5; only twelve CC members were present, with no delegates from the Petrograd and Moscow party organizations as in Stalin's proposal. The impetus for the October 10 session undoubtedly originated with Lenin and enjoyed Sverdlov's full support. For the first time since July, Lenin (still in danger of arrest) attended, together with Trotsky, Zinoviev, Kamenev, Stalin, and Sverdlov—the real power center of the party—joined by Uritsky, Dzerzhinsky, Kollontai, Bubnov, Sokol'nikov, and Lomov (Oppokov).[35]

Sverdlov, as chairman, led off with a rapid but concise survey of the political situation in the army on the Rumanian, Lithuanian, and Minsk and northern fronts. Lenin then took the floor, to speak on the current situation, or, more accurately, to urge in the strongest terms that the party commit itself to an armed insurrection in the immediate future. "The majority of the population," Lenin argued,

> is now behind us. Politically the situation is completely ripe for a transfer of power.

After discussion, primarily on the urgent need for technical preparation, the CC, by a vote of 10 to 2, adopted the following resolution:

> Recognizing that an armed uprising is inevitable and that its time has come, the CC proposes that all organizations of the Party be guided by this and from this point of view consider and decide all practical questions (Congress of Soviets of the Northern Region, the removal of troops from Peter [Petrograd], actions of the Muscovites and Minskites, etc.).

By their statements at the meeting and by their subsequent conduct, Kamenev and Zinoviev identified themselves as the two members who voted against the resolution. Stalin can thus be identified as one of the majority who voted in favor of an early uprising. His reward took the form of inclusion in the seven-man Political Bureau, which was "to provide political leadership in the days ahead."

Was the Political Bureau a forerunner of the later policy-making Politburo? Trotsky denies it:

> The new institution, however, turned out completely impracticable. Lenin and Zinoviev were still in hiding; Zinoviev, moreover, continued to wage a struggle against the insurrection, and so did Kamenev. The political bureau in its October membership never once assembled, and it was soon simply forgotten—as were other organizations created ad hoc in the whirlpool of events.[36]

Deutscher disagrees:

> Thus the institution that was eventually to tower mightily above state, party, and revolution was called into being.

But he adds,

> The Political Bureau was unable to fulfill the task assigned to it. Zinoviev and Kamenev refused to submit to the decision on the insurrection and did their utmost to achieve its reversal. Lenin went back into hiding and could not take part in the day-to-day preparations.[37]

Fainsod adopts a more positive attitude:

> With the success of the insurrection, its [the Politburo's] purpose was achieved, and the PB as originally constituted passed out of existence.[38]

Leonard Schapiro states,

> There is no evidence that this precursor of the Politburo ever functioned. The organization of the uprising was in the hands of the Military Revolutionary Committee of the Petrograd Soviet, which was formed on 12 October and of which Trotsky was chairman.[39]

Setting the Date

Did the CC at its October 10 session set a date for the uprising? Deutscher affirms that it did:

> At the same session [of the CC, October 10], 20 October was fixed as the day of the insurrection.[40]

Trotsky differs:

> it was agreed that the insurrection should precede the Congress of Soviets and begin, if possible, not later than October 15th.[41]

The question of a specific date for the uprising was *not*, however, answered at the October 10 meeting of the CC, as can be seen from the fact that it was still under discussion at the next meeting of the CC, which took place on October 16.

Did Lenin Meet Stalin on October 8?

The Central Committee, at its meeting on October 3, resolved to propose to Lenin that he move (illegally) to Petrograd, "in order to make possible continuous and close contact."[42]

In the period of Stalin's dominance, Soviet historians were under orders to portray Stalin, side by side with Lenin, as the leader of the armed insurrection for which Lenin had been calling. The exact date of Lenin's return to Petrograd was a key element in this attempt to revise the history of the Bolshevik Revolution. Thus, an entry in the chronology in volume 3 of Stalin's *Works* declares under October 8:

J. V. Stalin discusses preparations for an armed uprising with V. I. Lenin who has secretly returned to Petrograd.[43]

Despite prolonged and sometimes acrimonious debate on the exact date of Lenin's return to Petrograd, however, Soviet historians have admitted that it is impossible to be precise on this key question because of irreconcilable conflicts in the memoir literature and the lack of documentary evidence. The carefully prepared "biographical chronicle" of Lenin's life, in its volume on March–October 1917, provides a concise summary of the debate on this question among Soviet historians and concludes,

Lenin *may have* returned to Petrograd on one of the days between 3 and 10 October.[44]

As to Lenin's alleged meeting with Stalin on October 8, Soviet historians in the Khrushchev era no longer accepted it. In a study of Soviet historiography on the Bolshevik Revolution, Larry Holmes writes, with regard to the period 1957–61,

No longer was Stalin given a special role in the preparation and leadership of the revolt. Stalin was converted into a non-person. The October 8 meeting between Lenin and Stalin was no longer mentioned.[45]

It would appear, therefore, that the alleged meeting between Lenin and Stalin on October 8 was an invention of Soviet historians of the Stalin era.

The earliest irrefutable date for Lenin's presence in Petrograd is October 10, the date of the session of the Central Committee which he attended in disguise.

The CC Session of October 16

Despite its historic significance, the October 10 session of the CC was too narrow, its participants were too few, to enact the definitive party resolution on the seizure of power. Originally envisioned (by Stalin and others) as an enlarged session, the October 10 meeting was actually below full strength. As Daniels has pointed out, several of those absent (Rykov, Nogin, Milyutin) would probably have voted against the proposal for an armed uprising.[46]

The need for an enlarged session of the CC led on October 16 to a meeting that included, besides members of the CC, representatives of the Executive Commission of the Petersburg Committee, the Military Organization, the Petrograd Soviet, trade unions, factory-plant committees, the Petrograd regional organization, and railway workers. (Contrary to the original plan, no representatives of the Moscow city and district committees attended.)

The purpose of the October 16 meeting is well defined by Rabinowitch:

> reassessment of the party's strategy in the face of the difficulties that had developed in implementing the call for an immediate uprising.[47]

Sverdlov chaired the session and proposed its three-point agenda: reports on the last CC meeting, short reports from representatives, and the current situation.

Lenin dominated the meeting, not only presenting its opening report on the October 10 session of the CC but also fighting successfully for the adoption of his resolution "On the Current Situation" at the meeting's conclusion, at 3:30 A.M. on October 17.

Several items in Lenin's initial presentation deserve comment. A difficult point was the relationship between the party and the masses. Lenin tried to have it both ways. On the one hand, "the masses were supporting us . . . before the Kornilov revolt":

> The Kornilov revolt itself pushed the masses even more decisively toward us.

On the other hand,

> *One cannot be guided by the mood of the masses* for it is changeable and not to be calculated; we must go by an objective analysis and assessment of the revolution.

Having thus devalued in advance any pessimistic evaluation of the party's policy based on an alleged lack of mass readiness for an armed uprising, Lenin added for good measure the international aspect:

> Certain objective facts about the international situation indicate that *in acting now we will have the whole European proletariat on our side.*

The conclusion, in Lenin's eyes, was obvious:

> A political analysis of the class struggle both in Russia and in Europe points to the need for a very determined and active policy, which can only be *an armed uprising.*[48]

To help maintain the momentum and to strengthen Lenin's position, Sverdlov led off the discussion from local representatives with an optimistic report from the Secretariat. The party, said Sverdlov, "has grown on a gigantic scale"; he gave a figure of "no fewer than 400,000" for the party's current strength. The increase in numbers was matched by an increase in influence:

> Our influence has grown in the same way, especially in the Soviet, and in the army and navy.

But the forces of counterrevolution were also growing in strength and organization. Sverdlov went on to report the mobilization of counter-revolutionary forces in the Donetsk district, in Minsk, and on the northern front.[49]

The debate that followed was more than spirited; the participants fully sensed the gravity of the party's situation. Even Stalin emerged briefly from his customary cautious silence to make a statement, leading off with the unimpeachable sentiment that "the right day must be chosen for the rising." What that day might be, however, Stalin did not say. What he had in mind evidently was a purely theoretical step:

> Why not give ourselves the chance to choose the day and the conditions so the counter-revolution has no chance to organize itself?[50]

Even that noncommittal sentiment was not original with Stalin. Molotov, speaking at a meeting of the Petersburg Committee on October 5, had made the same point more cogently:

> Our task now is not to restrain the masses but to select the most opportune moment for taking power into our own hands.[51]

Like Lenin, Stalin put his faith in the European proletariat:

> There are two lines here: one steers for the victory of the revolution and relies on Europe, the second has no faith in the revolution and reckons on being only an opposition.

Stalin argued that the revolution had already begun:

> The Petrograd Soviet has already taken its stand on the road to insurrection by refusing to sanction the withdrawal of troops. The navy has already rebelled since it has gone against Kerensky.[52]

But Stalin followed Lenin on the basic point, confirmation of the October 10 decision on preparation for an uprising. He evidently voted with the majority (19 in favor, 2 opposed, 4 abstentions) on Lenin's resolution:

> The meeting unreservedly welcomes and entirely supports the CC resolution [of October 10], calls on all [party] organizations and all workers and

soldiers to make comprehensive and intensive preparation for an armed insurrection and to support the Center created for this by the Central Committee and expresses complete confidence that the CC and the Soviet will in good time indicate the favorable moment and the appropriate methods of attack.[53]

Since the vote was recorded without the names of those participating, it is technically possible that Stalin was one of the four who abstained on Lenin's resolution. Zinoviev and Kamenev, it is clear, cast the two negative votes. But the weight of evidence indicates that Stalin followed Lenin on the basic question of preparation for an armed uprising.

Lenin's resolution called for support of "the Center created . . . by the Central Committee." Did he have in mind the seven-man Political Bureau, which the CC had established on October 10? Or did this statement anticipate an action to be taken toward the conclusion of the October 16 session in which the Military-Revolutionary "Center" was actually set up? The step was taken by the CC meeting alone (i.e., without the participation of the nonparty, non-CC delegates present at the meeting). The center was to consist of five men: Sverdlov, Stalin, Bubnov, Uritsky, and Dzerzhinsky.[54] The protocols do not record who introduced the resolution to create this body, but clearly it must have had Lenin's backing. It was to function as a component of "the Soviet Revolutionary Committee," that is, the Military Revolutionary Committee (MRC), which the Petrograd Soviet had established on October 9.

Stalin's presence on this body has lent it a prominence out of keeping with its undistinguished and unrecorded existence. As Daniels has noted,

> The center never functioned as a separate group, but the decision establishing it did serve as the factual basis for the legend proclaimed in the official history later on that Stalin was the man in charge of the uprising.[55]

The composition of the center sufficiently indicates that it could not have functioned in any really authoritative way. Uritsky, Bubnov, and Dzerzhinsky were second- or third-level party functionaries; Sverdlov and Stalin were promising but not yet dominant leaders. Trotsky's absence can be explained as the result of the provision that the center was to function as part of the MRC, which Trotsky controlled. Kamenev and Zinoviev, who had been included in the Political Bureau, had, by October 16, taken such a resolute stand against the decision for an armed uprising that they could no longer be considered for membership in a body set up to implement the decision.

Stalin's membership in the October 16 center, like his membership in the October 10 Political Bureau, was not, however, a guarantee that he would actually be allotted a prominent role in the seizure of power. It was, rather, an opportunity for him to take a leading role in a complex undertaking with enormous possibilities but also with great risks.

Most Western writers have downgraded the significance of both the Political Bureau and the Military-Revolutionary Center, pointing out that there is no documentary evidence that either body actually functioned as such. Soviet historian I. I. Mints has a point, however, when he charges that the Western views are based on a misunderstanding of the way in which the two bodies actually functioned. As Mints sees it, establishment of the bodies was simply a designation of the party figures who served as members to report for duty in the activities under way.[56] Even if one accepts Mints's point, however, the fact remains that Stalin failed to take advantage of his membership on the two committees to make his own contribution to the seizure of power. Secure in his newspaper office, out of touch with current developments, ignorant of the strategy actually being followed in the Bolshevik uprising, Stalin was the victim of his own temperament— and of the low evaluation Trotsky and Sverdlov had formed of his character and abilities.

Formation and Development of the Military Revolutionary Committee

On October 9 at a meeting of the Petrograd Soviet, Trotsky introduced a resolution calling for the creation of a "revolutionary defense committee,"

> the primary purpose of which was to become fully familiar with all information relating to the defense of the capital and to take all possible steps to arm workers in order to facilitate the revolutionary defense of Petrograd and the safety of the public from the attacks being openly prepared by military and civil Kornilovites.[57]

Trotsky's resolution was at first rejected in favor of a rival SR-Menshevik one by "a narrow margin," but this vote was reversed at "an unusually crowded and lively plenary session of the Petrograd Soviet later the same evening."

On that basis the Soviet proceeded to establish the Military Revolutionary Committee, which Rabinowitch aptly describes as "the institution used by the Bolsheviks in the following days to subvert and overthrow the Provisional Government."

Did Stalin Understand and Support Trotsky's Strategy of Insurrection?

According to Rabinowitch, Trotsky was the party's "most influential spokesman" for the strategy of linking the overthrow of the Provisional Government with the convocation and policies of the Second All-Russian Congress of Soviets.[58] Rabinowitch regards Stalin as one of "a significant number of . . . top Bolsheviks" who shared this view. Rabinowitch does not, however, provide any evidence to verify Stalin's support for the strategy devised by Trotsky and implemented under his direction. It is open to serious doubt, in fact, that Stalin did (a) fully understand and (b) effectively support this strategy. His articles and editorials during this period referred instead to an "armed uprising" of the workers and poor peasants rather than to action by the Bolshevik party. Of course, it can be argued that in his journalistic writings Stalin was helping to provide cover for the clandestine preparations under way to carry out the seizure of power. Read at their face value, however, Stalin's writings of this period call for a nationwide armed uprising in which the role of the party is either not stated at all or is restricted to the level of providing slogans and general guidance to the mass movement.

It is also true that Stalin later defended against Lenin the way in which the seizure of power was carried out in 1917, especially the prominent role assigned to the Congress of Soviets.[59] But it is doubtful that Stalin saw things so clearly at the time. Unwilling to acknowledge the leading role played by Trotsky in the seizure of power, Stalin by 1923 had convinced himself that he, Stalin, had been part of the Bolshevik leadership which, against Lenin's advice, had engineered the coup in October 1917.

Kamenev and Zinoviev Break Ranks, with Stalin's Tacit Support

Continuing his opposition to Lenin's demand for an armed uprising, Kamenev on October 18 took the grave step of publishing a statement setting forth his and Zinoviev's views in a nonparty newspaper, Maxim Gorky's *Novaya zhizn'*. Lenin's furious reaction, in a letter to the CC written on October 19, was to demand the expulsion of the two "strike-breakers" from the party.[60]

On the same day, Zinoviev wrote a brief letter to the editorial board of *Rabochii put'* in which he attempted to minimize the serious-ness of the split. "For a number of reasons," Zinoviev wrote,

> I am obliged to refrain from making a detailed analysis of this polemic now. I will only say that my real views on the subject in dispute are very far from those with which Comrade Lenin takes issue. . . . Endorsing yesterday's statement by Comrade Trotsky in the Petrograd Soviet of Workers' and Soldiers' Deputies, I think that we are quite able to close ranks and defer our disputes until circumstances are more favorable.[61]

It was Stalin's responsibility, as senior editor of *Rabochii put'*, to decide whether or not to print Zinoviev's letter. Not only did Stalin choose to print it—he added an unsigned editorial comment that endorsed it and, for good measure, criticized Lenin's letter:

> FROM THE EDITORIAL BOARD. We in our turn express the hope that with Comrade Zinoviev's statement (and also Comrade Kamenev's state-ment in the Soviet), the matter may be considered closed. The sharp tone of Comrade Lenin's article does not change the fact that, *funda-mentally, we remain of one mind.*[62]

It was with Stalin's demonstration of the spirit of "forgive and forget" fresh before their eyes that the Central Committee met on October 20.[63] With Lenin still in hiding, it fell to Trotsky to expose and condemn Stalin's untimely gesture of reconciliation. The publica-tion of Zinoviev's letter and of the unsigned editorial comment was "inadmissible," said Trotsky. Kamenev's resignation from the CC, he added, should be accepted.

Still in search of broad party unity, Stalin demurred; the protocols succinctly record his statement:

> Comrade Stalin considers that K[amenev] and Z[inoviev] will submit to CC decisions and shows that our whole position is contradictory: he maintains that expulsion from the Party is no remedy, what is needed is to preserve Party unity; he proposes that these two Comrades should be required to submit but be kept in the CC.

At this point Sokol'nikov, the junior member of the editorial board of *Rabochii put'*, could contain himself no longer. Unwilling to share responsibility for the anonymous editorial note, Sokol'nikov

> reports that he had no part in the editorial statement on the subject of Zinoviev's letter, and considers this statement a mistake.

Thus, as the result of Trotsky's insistence and Sokol'nikov's dis-claimer, Stalin stood revealed as the anonymous defender of Kamenev and Zinoviev. When a vote was taken on Kamenev's resignation from the CC, Stalin experienced a new rebuff; the vote was 5 to 3 in favor of accepting Kamenev's resignation.

Earlier in the session Stalin had proposed deferring to the next session of the CC consideration of Lenin's letter demanding the expulsion of Kamenev and Zinoviev from the party. This proposal was now formally rejected—another rebuff to Stalin. Giving further expression to its sober, determined mood, the CC then unanimously approved a proposal by Milyutin

> that not a single member of the CC should have the right to come out against decisions passed by the CC.

Although he voted for this proposal, Stalin could not help seeing it as an implied repudiation of his attempt to defend Kamenev and Zinoviev. His response was drastic: he announced his withdrawal from the editorial board of *Rabochii put'*. The CC, however, resolved that

> in view of the fact that Comrade Stalin's statement in today's issue [of *Rabochii put'*] was made in the name of the editorial board and has to be discussed by the editorial board, it is decided to pass on to the next business without discussing Comrade Stalin's statement or accepting his resignation.

Before it broke up, the CC endorsed a proposal by Trotsky that

> all our organizations can go into our revolutionary center and discuss any question of interest to them in our group there.

A few minutes later, Trotsky stressed the need for interested parties "to keep in contact with the Military Revolutionary Committee attached to the Soviet," in effect defining the MRC as the real center of action in preparation for the uprising.

Stalin's inglorious performance at the October 20 session of the CC must have left him with wounded feelings. His attempt to play the role of peacemaker had been unceremoniously rebuffed, with Trotsky figuring as his principal critic. His grand gesture of resigning as editor of *Rabochii put'* had not even merited discussion.

Setting the Agenda for the Congress of Soviets

Considering the setbacks that Stalin had sustained at the October 20 session of the CC, and having in mind his extreme touchiness, one might have expected him to miss the next session of the CC, held on October 21.[64] Surprisingly, however, Stalin not only attended the session but made a number of substantial contributions to its work.

In response to a report by Dzerzhinsky on the "complete disorganization" of the Executive Committee of the Petrograd Soviet, the CC resolved to send ten of its members to join the Executive Committee and work there; Stalin was one of the ten. But this was a sideshow of minor importance; the real business of the session was to formalize plans for the now imminent Second All-Russian Congress of Soviets. It was Stalin who defined the congress's agenda. He proposed that reports for the congress be prepared on five subjects: the war, state power, control, the national question, and the land. Sverdlov suggested that a preliminary meeting of the Bolshevik fraction of the congress was necessary and proposed that he himself, together with Stalin and Milyutin, be designated for work in the group.

Stalin then proposed that a comrade be sent to Moscow "demanding that the Moscow delegation come immediately." In preparation for their arrival, Stalin continued, it was necessary to prepare theses on the most important current issues, and he offered the following agenda:

> A report by Lenin on land, the war, and power, on workers' control, by Milyutin, on the national question, which Stalin would handle, and on the current situation, by Trotsky. To this Milyutin added an additional report on "rules of procedure," to be given by Sverdlov.

"All of this," the protocols state, was approved.

Stalin had reason to be satisfied with his performance at the October 21 session. Not only had his proposals dealing with urgent questions been accepted, but he was a member of two new gatherings, the ten-man delegation to beef up the Executive Committee of the Petrograd Soviet and the three-man group to report to the Bolshevik fraction of the Congress of Soviets. If his ego had been bruised by the rebuffs he had experienced at the October 20 session, he seems to have put that aside and returned the following day with the performance of a real party leader. The auspices were highly favorable, then, for Stalin's successful participation in the Bolshevik seizure of power. It is in this context that we must evaluate Stalin's puzzling failure at the crucial moment. The problem begins with another CC session.

Stalin and the Military Revolutionary Committee

By his selection as a member of the Military-Revolutionary Center at the October 16 session of the CC, Stalin was also added to the rapidly developing Military Revolutionary Committee. Yet in all the documentary or memoir literature on the MRC in those crucial days, there is not a single reference to Stalin's having participated in any way as an MRC functionary.

Part of the reason for his failure to act was that the CC, whose sessions Stalin attended on an irregular basis, was slow to acknowledge the importance of the MRC. Rabinowitch points out that

the published record of the Central Committee's activities during these days reveals that at its meetings scant attention was paid to the operations of the Military Revolutionary Committee; the Central Committee now devoted most of its time to internal party matters.[65]

It was in the Petrograd Soviet, however, not the CC, that the MRC originated and developed. Rabinowitch notes that

at no time during the first half of October was the question of forming a nonparty institution like the Military Revolutionary Committee ever raised in the Central Committee.[66]

Under these circumstances it is understandable that Stalin, whose views were limited to his participation in meetings of the CC and his duties as senior editor of *Rabochii put'*, should have failed to realize the significance and potential of the new nonparty body. Stalin was given plenty of opportunity to take part in the work of the MRC and thereby to play a significant role in the seizure of power, but he failed to so do.

The explanation lies partly in Stalin's own character and limitations, but equally in the evaluation of them by those directing the work, above all, Trotsky and Sverdlov. It was their failure to call on Stalin for any task connected with the uprising which sealed his fate. Lomov, a member of the MRC, later recalled a tense moment on the morning of October 24, when the Kerensky government was taking the offensive. Roused from a troubled sleep by the ringing of a telephone, Lomov heard Trotsky summon him with the words, "'Kerensky is on the offensive . . . we need everyone at Smolny.'"[67]

Everyone—except Stalin.

The CC Meets without Stalin

Early on the morning of October 24, the government launched an attack on the Bolshevik press, aimed at shutting down the Bolshevik newspapers *Soldat* and *Rabochii put'*. On Kerensky's orders a detachment of cadets and police raided the print shop, seized a bundle of the day's issue of *Rabochii put'*, and smashed some matrices. On completion of the raid, the troops sealed the entrance to the print shop and departed, leaving behind a guard.

The fact that the government's first overt action against the Bolsheviks was an attack on their press may help to explain why Stalin—

senior editor of the party organ—remained in his office at a time when most other Bolshevik leaders were assembling at Bolshevik headquarters in the Smolny for a hastily convened meeting of the CC organized by Sverdlov.

In an article published several years ago, I argued that it was probably the rebuffs Stalin suffered at the October 20 session of the CC which led to his failure to attend the crucial October 24 session and thus to miss the opportunity for making any significant contribution to the Bolshevik seizure of power.[68] In light of the protocols of the October 21 session, however, that judgment must be reconsidered. Certainly Stalin was hurt by developments at the October 20 session—his tender of resignation as editor of the party organ is sufficient proof of this. Nevertheless, he mustered sufficient courage not only to attend the next session of the CC, on October 21, but to make a number of useful contributions to its work. Thus, the evidence indicates that Stalin was able to rise above personal considerations and submerge his feelings in the common cause.

All the more puzzling, therefore, is Stalin's absence from the CC session of October 24 at which last-minute preparations and assignments for the seizure of power were made.[69] The absence of Stalin's name from the assignments is striking. Here is the list:

Bubnov—railroads
Dzerzhinsky—post and telegraph
Milyutin—food supplies
Podvoisky—observation of the Provisional Government (changed to Sverdlov, after objections by Podvoisky)
Kamenev and Vinter (Berzin)—negotiations with the Left SRs
Lomov and Nogin—information to Moscow

So far, all assignments had been to members of the CC. Sverdlov, however, in response to an urgent demand by Trotsky for establishment of a reserve headquarters at the Peter and Paul Fortress, proposed giving these tasks to Lashevich, not a member of the CC. The committee voted in favor of this proposal, adding G. I. Blagonravov, also a nonmember of the CC, and designated Sverdlov himself to exercise continuous contact with the fortress. The assignment of Lashevich and Blagonravov to a key sector of the uprising is especially striking. As Trotsky later wrote,

When the parts were being assigned to the various actors in that drama, no one mentioned Stalin or proposed any sort of appointment for him. He simply dropped out of the game.[70]

By contrast, Kamenev, for all his doubts about the uprising, *did* attend the October 24 session of the CC, showing a full awareness of its historic importance by proposing that "no CC member should be able to leave the Smolny today without special permission of the CC," a proposal that was promptly approved. Kamenev was also given an assignment: he and Vinter (Berzin) were named to negotiate with the Left SRs.

The assignment of Bolsheviks to tasks continued throughout the day on October 24 as delegates arrived for the Congress of Soviets. According to Gorodetsky,

> Arriving Bolshevik delegates were immediately included in the work of the preparation of the uprising. They talked with the leading workers of the CC and immediately received assignments.[71]

In the heat of the action, Stalin's absence went unnoticed. We should not overlook the possibility that Stalin was ignorant about what was going on. Having declined a role in the Information Bureau of October 7 and having failed to take advantage of his appointment to the Political Bureau of October 10 and the Military-Revolutionary Center of October 16, Stalin may simply have been in the dark about the whole operation. Evidence to support this judgment is provided by Stalin himself, in the form of an editorial that he contributed to the October 24 number of *Rabochii put'*. Since this editorial has attracted widespread interest among historians of the revolution, it deserves close attention.

"What Do We Need?"

The editorial that Stalin wrote for the October 24 issue of *Rabochii put'* (but that he did not sign) can be described as an orthodox Leninist analysis of the course of the revolution from February to October.[72] It was, wrote Stalin, "the workers and soldiers who overthrew the tsar in February." Unfortunately, however,

> the workers and soldiers voluntarily turned over the power to representatives of the landlords and capitalists.

That, wrote Stalin,

> was a fatal mistake on the part of the victors. And for this mistake the soldiers at the front and the peasants in the rear are now paying dearly.

As a consequence of this mistake, Stalin continued, the workers have

> "received" high prices and starvation, lockouts and unemployment.

The peasants

have "received" . . . arrests of their deputies and punitive expeditions.

The soldiers have "received"

a protracted war, which it is intended to prolong until next autumn.

Finally, said Stalin, the people have seen their hopes for an early convocation of the Constituent Assembly disappear, since

it is now obvious that the enemies are preparing to torpedo it outright.

What is to be done? "This mistake must be rectified at once." Echoing Lenin's urgent appeals, Stalin warned,

The time has come when further procrastination is fraught with disaster for the whole course of the revolution.

Therefore,

The present government of landlords and capitalists must be replaced by a new government, a government of workers and peasants.

The present impostor government which was not elected by the people and which is not accountable to the people must be replaced by a government recognized by the people, elected by the representatives of the workers, soldiers and peasants, and accountable to their representatives.

The Kishkin-Konovalov government should be replaced by a government of the Soviets of Workers', Soldiers' and Peasants' Deputies. [Nikolai Kishkin was minister of the interior in the Provisional Government. Alexander Konovalov was deputy premier and minister of industry.]

On the key question, how this is to be done, Stalin sketched the outlines of an organized but peaceful popular uprising. He urged his readers

to muster all your forces, rise up as one man, organize meetings and elect your delegations and, through them, lay your demands before the Congress of Soviets which opens tomorrow in the Smolny.

Stalin brushed aside the idea that there might be risks or uncertainties in such a course of action:

If you all act solidly and staunchly no one will dare to resist the will of the people. The stronger and the more organized and powerful your action, the more peacefully will the old government make way for the new. And then the whole country will boldly and firmly march forward to the conquest of peace for the people, land for the peasants, and bread and work for the starving.

Stalin closed by repeating his basic view:

> A new government must come into power, a government elected by the Soviets, recallable by the Soviets and accountable to the Soviets.
>
> Only such a government can ensure the timely convocation of the Constituent Assembly.

Stalin's October 24 editorial shows that he had absorbed some of Lenin's sense of urgency, but it demonstrates equally clearly that he had failed to grasp Lenin's acceptance of the fact that a Bolshevik seizure of power in the name of the soviets would almost certainly lead to a prolonged and bitter civil war. There was no hint in Stalin's editorial that the use of armed force would be necessary to conquer power and to defend it. Nor was there the slightest sign of recognition that the Bolsheviks, aided by the Left SRs, could achieve victory by timely action in the exercise of what Lenin called "the art of insurrection."

So far out of line with reality, in fact, was Stalin's October 24 editorial that few Western historians believe that it was intended to be taken at face value. Rabinowitch, for example, sees Stalin's editorial as being squarely in line with Bolshevik policy:

> The continuing emphasis of the Bolshevik Central Committee and the Military Revolutionary Committee on the role of the Congress of Soviets in *completing* the task of subverting the Provisional Government and creating a revolutionary soviet regime was nowhere more clearly reflected than in the lead editorial prepared by Stalin for the edition of *Rabochii put'* which reached the streets some time after midday on October 24.[73]

Stalin, however, said nothing about "completing" the task of subverting the Provisional Government; for him, the entire action was to consist of "organiz[ing] the workers," "elect[ing] your delegates" and "lay[ing] your demands before the Congress of Soviets."

For Deutscher, the defensive spirit of the editorial was part of "the cautious camouflage of the insurrection."[74] In the late Stalin period, according to Holmes, Stalin's editorial

> was regarded [by Soviet historians] as an appeal to the populace to begin the revolt. According to historians, Stalin convoked the TsK [CC], which then ordered the VRK [MRC] to begin the revolt.

During the brief period of the anti-Stalin campaign, Soviet historians belatedly recognized that the editorial did not reflect favorably on Stalin's role. According to Holmes,

Historians [i.e., Soviet historians] not only complained that previous [Soviet] historiography exaggerated Stalin's positive contribution, but also asserted that Stalin was one of the key opponents to Lenin's plan for a socialist revolution. Stalin's October 24 article . . . was termed anti-Leninist. Directly refuting Stalinist historiography, it was asserted that the article did not call for revolution but appealed for peaceful transfer of power to Soviets.[75]

Stalin Speaks to the Bolshevik Fraction

Stalin did not spend the entire day on October 24 at his editorial office. In the afternoon, together with Trotsky, he attended a meeting of the newly arrived Bolshevik delegates to the forthcoming Second Congress of Soviets. No exact record of what he said on that occasion has been preserved, but fortunately one of the delegates, a certain Zhakov, attended the meeting and shortly thereafter summarized it in a letter that was later published in *Proletarskaia revoliutsiia*.

As reported by Zhakov, both Stalin and Trotsky emphasized the defensive character of the strategy being pursued by the Military Revolutionary Committee. According to Zhakov,

Stalin gave a speech about the latest reports available to the CC (RSDLP). From the front they're coming over to us. One Latvian regiment came over to us, [but was] detained. [There is] wavering in the Provisional Government. Today at 5–6 o'clock [they] are sending [someone] for negotiations.

. . . the CC of the Party of SRs asked what is the purpose of the Military Revolutionary Committee—uprising or defense of order? If the former, we will recall [our representatives]. (In the Committee Left-SRs are active.) We of course replied, order, defense. They left their [people in the committee]. Sailors arrested 50 junkers. *In the Military Revolutionary Committee there are two tendencies* (1) *immediate armed uprising,* (2) *first, to gather forces. The CC RSDLP supports the latter.* The [cruiser] *Aurora* has asked whether to fire on attempts to raise the bridge. We recommended not firing. In any case the bridge will be ours, and the Troitsky bridge will be defended. There is mutiny among the junkers and the armed troops. We have special weapons for beating off the armored troops. *Rabochii put'* is being set up. The telephones so far are not ours. (Within two minutes news was received that an armored troop soldier, posted by the government at the Central Station, is a Bolshevik, and the telephones have come over to the side of the government.) The post office is ours. Two regiments are coming from the front to help us. The bicycle troops called from the front to subdue us have sent a delegation with a Bolshevik resolution and are asking whether to come to our aid or to return to the front.[76]

Thanks to Zhakov's brief summary, we have a fairly clear picture of Stalin's state of mind and fund of information on the afternoon of October 24. By this time, evidently, Stalin was aware that widespread action was under way aimed at subverting the Provisional Government. Stalin's remarks point to the conclusion, however, that his information was gleaned principally from the CC; his data on the MRC's actions and policies are second-hand, reflecting a CC point of view rather than one based on first-hand experience. It is also clear that by the afternoon of the twenty-fourth Stalin had come to the Smolny and was trying to keep abreast of the rapidly changing situation. He showed no awareness, however, of the fact that the CC had held a meeting earlier in the day, or that specific assignments in support of the uprising had been made to other members of the CC. These impressions are reinforced by one of the rare glimpses available of Stalin's mood at this time.

On the Eve

According to Anna Allilueva, Stalin came back to his apartment on the evening of October 24 in a jubilant mood. She quotes him as saying,

> "Yes, everything is ready. Tomorrow we act. All city districts are in our hands. We will seize power."[77]

Allilueva's testimony is valuable, even if we discount her ability years later to recall Stalin's exact words. What she reports is in general agreement with other evidence, including Zhakov's letter.

In the official record, the Bolshevik Central Committee meeting on the morning of October 24 was the last to be held before the seizure of power. Recently, however, Ye. A. Lutsky, a Soviet historian, has advanced the claim that an unscheduled meeting of the CC took place at Bolshevik headquarters in the Smolny on the night of October 24/25. Lutsky recognizes that no official protocol of such a meeting has been found, and he candidly admits that the evidence for it comes either from unpublished archival sources or from memoirs published as late as 1957.[78] Nevertheless, the case he makes deserves serious consideration, not least because of its bearing on Stalin's role in the seizure of power.

Lutsky names the hours from 2 to 5 A.M. on October 25 as the time of the meeting. He believes ten members of the CC were present, including Lenin, Zinoviev, Kamenev, Trotsky, and Stalin. Missing were all but one member of the Military-Revolutionary Center—

Bubnov, Dzerzhinsky, Sverdlov, and Uritsky. The odd man out (or in) was Stalin. The other members of the center, in Lutsky's words, "were occupied with organizational-operational matters arising out of the armed uprising." Stalin's presence at the meeting in the Smolny therefore constitutes further proof that he had been assigned no part in the action to overthrow the Provisional Government.

Reports on the current status of the uprising, according to Lutsky, constituted part of the work of the session, but its main function was to plan for the establishment of the new government. Following a proposal advanced earlier by Lenin, the meeting adopted the title, "Worker-Peasant Government." The old term "minister" for a cabinet member carried too many associations with the old regime. In its place Lenin proposed "commissar," in part because it had been used by the Paris Commune. Although Lutsky does not say so, it was Trotsky who suggested adding "people's." The executive of the new government, accordingly, would be styled "the Council [Soviet] of People's Commissars." Trotsky remembered Lenin's delight: "That's splendid; smells terribly of revolution."[79] To no one's surprise, Lenin agreed to head the new regime.

Recognizing that peasant support would be vital, the meeting gave top priority to drafting a "Decree on the Land," using the SR land program as the basis. According to Lutsky, that action concluded the session.

Not all Stalin's biographers consider his inactivity a problem; Tucker, for example, passes over it in silence, while Ulam offers the ingenious explanation that Stalin's assigned task was precisely *not* to expose himself to arrest by taking an active part in the uprising but to remain in the background, as part of a reserve party center, ready to take responsibility in case the insurrection misfired.[80]

Of all Stalin's Western biographers, it was Deutscher who felt most acutely the need to rationalize and explain Stalin's absence from the action on October 24. Deutscher writes,

> It is not possible to find any alternative explanation for Stalin's absence or inactivity at the headquarters during the rising. But the queer and undeniable fact remains.[81]

The Soviet historian Gorodetsky faults Stalin for his "mistaken" position on the twenty-fourth, as manifested by the editorial "What Do We Need?" and by his emphasis on the defensive aspect of the MRC in his speech to the Bolshevik fraction that afternoon.[82] But Gorodetsky makes no attempt to explain Stalin's misfire. Can a satisfactory answer be found to the question that puzzled Deutscher? Part of the answer, as I have indicated, lies not in Stalin himself but in the failure by others, notably Trotsky and Sverdlov, to bring him actively into the preparation and execution of the uprising.

Yet Stalin had behaved well in the July Crisis and had effectively shared with Sverdlov direction of the Sixth Party Congress. Thus, Stalin's record included a number of positive aspects. Sverdlov was too objective in his evaluation of a party comrade's capabilities, in any case, to let personal feelings block his use of each individual's capacities in the way best calculated to advance the party's cause. In October, Sverdlov either personally sponsored or acquiesced in the designation by others of Stalin's assignment to a number of potentially important party bodies, the Political Bureau of October 10 and the Military-Revolutionary Center of October 16 being the most significant. It was up to Stalin, however, to grasp his opportunity and join his comrades in the challenging task at hand. This he conspicuously failed to do, just as he failed to attend the decisive October 24 meeting of the CC. Neither Sverdlov nor Trotsky thought highly enough of Stalin to make certain of his attendance. Their failure to notify Stalin of the October 24 session can be reckoned among the basic factors accounting for the "queer and undeniable fact" that puzzled Deutscher.

What about Stalin's own evaluation of the situation and his place in it? Can the hurt feelings generated by the October 20 CC session provide all or part of the answer? In my 1977 article I laid emphasis on that factor, using the protocol of the CC session of October 20 as my principal basis, while recognizing that other factors were involved.

The chief obstacle to acceptance of the "hurt feelings" explanation is that Stalin not only attended the next session, on October 21, but virtually dominated it. If one triangulates three clusters of data—the protocol of the October 21 session, Stalin's October 24 editorial, "What Do We Need?" and his speech to the Bolshevik fraction on the afternoon of October 24—a different explanation emerges. In this reading we have Stalin rebounding from the, for him, highly unsatisfactory session of October 20 by coming back on the following day with a positive program for moving closer to the seizure of power. First, he outlined the agenda for a series of reports by Bolshevik leaders at the forthcoming Congress of Soviets. A little later he filled in the blanks by naming specific party leaders, including Lenin and Trotsky, to deliver reports, with Stalin himself taking responsibility for the national question.

At the same session the CC members showed their regard for Stalin by naming him to two new groups: a detachment of prominent party figures charged with strengthening the Executive Committee of the Petrograd Soviet and a three-man group (Sverdlov, Stalin, and

Milyutin) designated to speak to the incoming Bolshevik delegates to the Congress of Soviets. (Later, this was changed—Sverdlov and Milyutin dropped out, and Trotsky joined Stalin in addressing the delegates.)

On the basis of these data a hypothesis can be established along the following lines: Stalin, by the afternoon of October 24, and possibly a few hours earlier, had become aware of the existence of the Military Revolutionary Committee. He had not, however, grasped the fact that the MRC, acting in close cooperation with the CC and the MO, had assumed responsibility for carrying out the uprising. For Stalin, as his speech to the delegates on the afternoon of October 24 shows, the MRC's activities were defensive. The uprising was to be a genuine mass action, with workers and soldiers meeting, electing representatives, and laying their demands before the Congress of Soviets, which would take power without encountering effective resistance from the Provisional Government.

Stalin, in this reading, believed that he had done his duty by his constructive suggestions at the October 21 CC session and by his programmatic editorial in the October 24 issue of *Rabochii put'*. Having failed to report for an assignment, Stalin remained unaware of the direction being taken by the process of subverting the Provisional Government. He felt no need, therefore, to check in at the Smolny after the October 21 CC session. His failure to attend the meeting on the morning of October 24 was the result of Sverdlov's bypassing Stalin in calling the meeting; Stalin's own lack of initiative which kept him from checking in at party headquarters; and his mistaken belief that the uprising was to be carried through on October 25 by action of the masses. It is conceivable that Sverdlov welcomed Stalin's ignorance of the real strategy. Sverdlov may have realized that an espousal by Stalin of the vision of a mass armed uprising could serve as camouflage for the strategy actually being employed. In this reading, Stalin served unwittingly as part of the cover plan.

Stalin was by no means stupid, but he sometimes had difficulty in grasping a new situation. Capable of committing a blunder the first time a new challenge faced him, Stalin learned from experience. His best accomplishments were those in which he acted deliberately but forcefully in a situation that he thoroughly understood as the result of prior experience. The Bolshevik seizure of power was a once-and-for-all operation in which there was no opportunity for a slow learner like Stalin to attend a dress rehearsal in preparation for the actual event. Thus, the Bolshevik Revolution was an operation in which Stalin was at a disadvantage. No single factor determined the outcome; it was the interaction of subjective elements, a low evaluation of Stalin's capacities by others, and a modicum of sheer chance (a casual visit to the Smolny on the morning of October 24 would have done the trick) which sealed Stalin's fate.

What could be more ignominious for a man who claimed to be one of the party's top leaders (and who already dreamed of being its sole leader) than to have missed the great, never-to-recur, moment of truth, the seizure of power? Acres of print, tidal waves of ink (and blood), would be needed before Stalin could feel comfortable in the belief that his failure to lead the revolution in 1917 had been blotted out of men's memories forever.

7 / / C O D A

Why, finally, did Stalin miss the October Revolution? The simplest answer, and one that contains perhaps 75 percent of the truth, is that the Bolshevik seizure of power was a team effort, and Stalin was not a team player. If one adds that he was not perceived to be a team player by those who organized and directed the operation, one can add another 5 percent to the probability of our thesis.

To move still closer to a full explanation of Stalin's default, one must shift one's attention from Stalin as an individual and focus on two complex clusters of data which helped shape the events in which he was involved: the structure of power at the time of the October Revolution and the nature of Lenin's contribution to the Bolshevik victory.

The Structure of Power Immediately Preceding the Bolshevik Revolution

The structure of Bolshevik and Soviet power in Petrograd on the eve of the October Revolution was unique in Bolshevik history.

Take first the party itself and its official policy-making body, the Central Committee. In the final three and a half weeks of October 1917, the CC was torn by internal dissension arising out of Lenin's demand for an immediate uprising and the varied responses to this demand by other members of the CC. Lenin's two most articulate opponents were Kamenev and Zinoviev, hitherto among his most trusted and reliable supporters.

The CC's inner policy-making body, the *uzkii sostav*, had ceased to function—its final recorded session took place on August 23. Lenin, the party's recognized leader, remained in hiding until the final week in October and during much of that time was forced to convey his views to the CC in the form of directives and letters. The only regular sessions of the CC he attended in person prior to the seizure of power were those of October 10 and 16.

The point is not that Lenin was not providing leadership—he was, and to an increasingly urgent degree, wielding his most powerful weapon, his pen. But there was a great difference between Lenin present and Lenin absent.

For Stalin, the rapid changes in the locus of power in the party—the eclipse of the *uzkii sostav*, the shift by Kamenev and Zinoviev to outright opposition, Lenin's absence from Petrograd, the rise of Trotsky—created a situation in which it became increasingly difficult for him to find a solid footing. How little Stalin understood what was taking place is revealed by his unsigned editorial note in *Rabochii put'* for October 20, in which he deplored the sharpness of Lenin's attack on the two "strike-breakers" and asserted that "basically we [including Kamenev and Zinoviev] remain of one mind."[1]

By his own decisions and actions, arising out of his customary sense of caution when confronted with a new challenge, Stalin took no part in the work of the two bodies that played leading roles in the seizure of power—the Military Revolutionary Committee (MRC), set up by the Petrograd Soviet under Trotsky's direction, and the Bolshevik Military Organization (MO), which functioned as a manpower reservoir for the MRC, but with which Stalin had broken his close ties by his high-handed behavior in mid-August. Aware though he certainly was by October 24 of the MRC's existence, and with the path open to him of taking an active part in its operations if he so desired, Stalin failed to grasp the potential inherent in the MRC's rapid expansion and bold assertiveness. On Stalin's part were caution and distrust, on the MRC and MO's side a concentration on immediate tasks which left little room for concern lest Stalin miss out on the fun.

Lenin's Contributions to the Bolshevik Victory

After Stalin's death and Khrushchev's attack on his "cult of personality," Soviet historians and their masters on the Communist Party Central Committee were faced with a serious problem: in rewriting party history, including the history of the October Revolution, what figure should take the central position hitherto occupied by Stalin as Lenin's right-hand man, in official party histories during the years of Stalin's dominance? Should they rehabilitate Trotsky and accord him a position roughly equivalent to his true historical importance, or should they continue to deny his pivotal role in the seizure of power?

The party's answer was clear and unequivocal: Trotsky's posthumous disgrace as an enemy of the party, if not an unperson, was to continue, and his true stature in the events of October was to be denied as fervently as it had been under Stalin. To do otherwise, the party ideologists must have felt, would be to risk undermining the party's claim to power based in part on its monopoly of historical interpretation of the revolution.

The downgrading of Stalin's role and the continued denial of Trotsky's importance left the party ideologists no choice but to enlarge the role of Lenin. In post-1956 party history, therefore, Lenin's figure, already a commanding one before 1956, was inflated to superhuman proportions.[2] Not only did Lenin, in the new Soviet historiography, provide the impetus and the theoretical basis for Bolshevik strategy, but he was also given credit for the day-to-day preparations for Bolshevik victory, including detailed masterminding of the strategy that led the Bolsheviks to power.

To overcome the awkward absence of contemporary documentation that would support this inflation of Lenin's status, surviving veterans of the revolution were encouraged to rewrite their memoirs and reminiscences, assigning a central position to Lenin and ignoring or denying the role played by Trotsky. One of the survivors, Podvoisky, proved to be especially suited to this kind of revisionism, publishing new memoirs in which Lenin's steady and sure guidance of the MRC's operation was prominently featured.[3] Soviet historians of the revolution, led by Academician I. I. Mints, made their contribution in the form of monographs and collections of documents in which Trotsky's name was either absent or denigrated.[4] Mints then cited his own editorial work as proof that Trotsky had played no significant role as leader of the MRC.[5]

It is regrettable that Soviet historians took this path rather than candidly admitting past errors and reevaluating the situation confronting the party in October 1917. The effort to assign total credit for Bolshevik strategy to Lenin suffered from serious weaknesses and condemned Soviet historians to propagate a version of the revolution which cannot be brought into accord with the facts.

An insurmountable obstacle to accepting the "Lenin did it all" interpretation is the impassioned letter he wrote to the CC on the eve of the seizure of power, late on October 24, 1917, in which he expressed his agonized fear that nothing was being done to overthrow the Provisional Government and that the chance of victory was being blindly thrown away—this at a time when the Military Revolutionary Committee was well on its way to nailing down a total triumph over the decrepit Kerensky government.[6] If Lenin had been personally directing the operations of the MRC, it is inconceivable that he would have written the letter dated the evening of October 24. Only a man gripped by an almost physical sense of doom could have written that anguished appeal for action.

It is probable that Stalin made a significant contribution to Lenin's befuddlement. Since mid-July Stalin had served as one of the liaison agents charged with keeping the party leader informed on the current state of affairs. A Stalin out of touch with the fast-breaking drama of insurrection on October 24 was a poor source of information for Lenin.

Another reason for doubting the "Lenin did it all" interpretation is that the strategy advocated by Lenin—a nationwide armed uprising—was not the form taken by events. What actually took place was a well-coordinated seizure of power in the nation's capital, followed at varying intervals of time in Moscow and other urban centers throughout the Russian Empire. This is not to deny the importance of the peasant revolt and the army mutiny, which provided the indispensable background for the power shift in Petrograd. But peasant revolt and army mutiny were ongoing processes, not a sudden, sharp explosion in late October.

The task set for Soviet historians by party ideologists is an almost impossible one. On the one hand, they must portray Lenin as the dominant figure in the seizure of power. On the other hand, they are required to show Trotsky as an evil-minded spoilsport who nearly wrecked Lenin's strategy by his insistence on timing the insurrection to coincide with the convening of the Second Congress of Soviets. For Lenin, waiting for the Congress of Soviets was a betrayal of the party's revolutionary mission—delay could be fatal, botching a unique opportunity. Yet without Trotsky's insistence on timing the action to occur at the same time as the congress, the events of October would have lacked any significance broader than that of a minority party's effort to seize power at the moment of the existing government's mortal weakness.

Lenin was wrong in mid-July when he asserted that a military–right-wing dictatorship had been established, at a time when the Kerensky government was staggering from one disaster—the political crisis and the failure of the offensive—to another, the Kornilov mutiny. Having made a faulty analysis in July, Lenin advocated a strategy for the party—a nationwide armed uprising—which was equally faulty. (It was their well-founded distrust of this strategy which sparked Zinoviev's and Kamenev's break with Lenin in October.)

Logically, Lenin should have revised his strategy at the end of August when the clash between Kerensky and Kornilov revealed the weakness of the government and its loss of control over the army. Lenin immediately saw the party's opportunity, but he continued to speak in terms of an armed uprising when existing conditions made possible a much more direct attack on the Provisional Government.

Lenin's miscalculation in mid-July was linked with his general view of the soviets. Unlike Trotsky, Lenin never had the experience of serving in a soviet. His attitude toward the soviets was purely instrumental: in his view they were tools to be picked up or discarded as political conditions changed. He had little sense of their appeal to workers and soldiers, for whom they provided a deeply satisfying mode of expressing their aspirations in the ongoing revolution.

Although Lenin changed his concept of the soviets' role in early September, he still failed to see the way in which they could be linked with a Bolshevik drive for power. Tacitly discarding the right-wing–military dictatorship construct of mid-July, Lenin still spoke in terms of a nation-wide armed uprising at a time when the Provisional Government needed merely a well-coordinated push to stagger to its fall.

Lenin's Positive Contribution

Lenin's contribution to the Bolshevik victory, nevertheless, was decisive on two counts. First, by tirelessly demanding that the party prepare itself for the seizure of power, Lenin supplied a sense of drive which could not be ignored. Under the enormous pressure of his impassioned call for immediate action, his old leadership team split asunder—Kamenev and Zinoviev came out in open opposition, and Stalin wavered. Had it not been for the energy and enthusiasm of a new pair of leaders, Sverdlov and Trotsky, Lenin's urgent appeals could not have been translated into action. Stalin, meanwhile, sought his bearings in the power structure of an earlier, less hectic time. His move to shield Zinoviev from Lenin's wrath, together with his unsuccessful attempt to blunt the edge of Kamenev's proffered resignation from the Central Committee, shows how little he understood the new situation.

Paradoxically, however, Lenin's second vital contribution to the Bolshevik triumph was his provision of the myth of armed uprising to transform the seizure of power into one of Marxism's most revered and potent symbols. Because of the timing of the action—not merely the convening of the All-Russian Second Congress of Soviets but also the breakdown of discipline in the army, the tacit support of the Petrograd workers, the rapid deepening and spreading of the peasant revolt—the necessary conditions were present in which party spokesmen could maintain that what took place on October 24–25 in Petrograd was in fact the armed uprising that Lenin had been demanding.

The consequences of this situation for Stalin were far from favorable. By October 24 he had come to accept an armed uprising as the next item on the party's agenda; in his October 24 editorial he provided his own interpretation of the Leninist vision. Since Lenin neglected, however, to alter his strategic goal to correspond to the altered "current situation," Stalin was left rudderless and adrift. Lenin's position in the party and in history was immeasurably strengthened by the apparent coincidence between his strategic vision and the epoch-making events of October 25, 1917, notwithstanding the fact that the seizure of power took place at a time and under circumstances not of his choosing. Lacking Lenin's stature and vision, Stalin could not so easily surmount his own shortcomings. In the future he would always be dogged by a sense of having somehow missed the revolution.

The Implications for Stalin's Later Career

Does it really matter that Stalin missed the revolution? A good case can be made, as Tucker has shown, for viewing Stalin as an up-and-coming party official whose contribution to the overall success of Bolshevik policies in 1917 was creditable if not outstanding.[7] Granted the merits of Tucker's defense of Stalin's record in 1917, that record was nowhere near what Stalin's own sense of destiny was to demand. A number of consequences followed from Stalin's perception of the inadequacies of his performance in 1917.

First, and a necessary precondition for any further progress toward a more satisfying record, was to discredit, defeat, and destroy the image of Trotsky as one of the principal architects of Bolshevik victory coequal with Lenin. That task, not too difficult, given Trotsky's blunders and underestimation of Stalin, was completed by 1929, when Trotsky, stripped of his power, was deported. Like Banquo's ghost, however, Trotsky refused to lie down and die, and it took Stalin another eleven years finally to destroy him and silence his accusing voice.

A much more difficult problem for Stalin was to rewrite the history of the revolution in his own terms. In a sense, Stalin never solved this problem. The general outlines of the history of the revolution were too well established to provide an opportunity for the kind of reconstruction which would have been needed. Even in the party history written on his orders in the late 1930s—the famous "Short Course"—Stalin and his stooge-historians failed to create a plausible image of Stalin as Lenin's coequal leader of the Bolshevik party in 1917. Something more was needed—the demonstration that Stalin was capable of planning and directing a revolution even more sweeping, even more fundamental than Lenin's 1917 triumph.

The "revolution from above," which Stalin directed in the 1930s—the collectivization of agriculture, the construction of a heavy industrial base, and the profound social transformation that accompanied these shifts—was, among other things, Stalin's demonstration that he, even more than Lenin and far outclassing Trotsky, was capable of "making a revolution." Yet there was more to Stalin's "second revolution."

For Stalin there still remained the unacceptable presence of witnesses from 1917 who knew the hollowness of his claim to having played a leading role in the revolution. Among the motives that led Stalin to unleash the Great Purge, in which Old Bolsheviks were a prominent category of victims, this urge to destroy and silence awkward witnesses was prominent. The sadistic intensity with which Stalin pursued and destroyed those who failed to "remember" his role as he wanted it portrayed grew directly out of his bitter memories of his missteps and shortcomings in 1917.

Ultimately, then, it was Stalin's self-perceived failures in 1917 which helped drive him to the heights and depths of his own revolution, out of which emerged a new society, a new Communist party, and a new nation.

Note: While this book was in press, A. M. Sovokin published an article, "V. I. Lenin in the Days of October" (*Voprosy istorii KPSS*, 1987, no. 4), which can best be described as the latest "Lenin did it all" interpretation of the October Revolution. Stalin is not directly mentioned, but his concept of "creative Marxism" is applied three times to Lenin. A 1953 article by Podvoisky is cited in support of the assertion that Lenin personally directed the uprising, and Trotsky is portrayed as its evil genius. Soviet historians will have to do better than this.

NOTES

Letters at the end of each note refer to sections in the Bibliography.

Chapter I: March

1. Haupt and Marie, 179 (H).
2. Tucker, 159 (F).
3. *VI KPSS*, 1962, no. 3:143 (E).
4. Ulam, 132, 134–135 (F).
5. Tucker, 163 (F).
6. Medvedev, 7 (F); Tucker, 160–61 (F).
7. *VI KPSS*, 1962, no. 3:143 (E).
8. MELI, 31 (F).
9. Trotsky, 197 (F).
10. Deutscher, 127 (F).
11. Baikalov, 118 (H), cited by Tucker, 161 (F).
12. Trotsky, 187 (F).
13. Deutscher, 132 (F).
14. Ulam, 135 (F).
15. Smith, 330 (F).
16. Souvarine, 151 (F).
17. Daniels, *Red October*, 28 (G). For an extensive treatment of Muranov's career, see Daniels, *Conscience*, 41, 49, 393 (G).
18. Chamberlin 1:115 (G).
19. Tucker, 119 (F).
20. Carr 1:74 (G).

21. Mints 2:42 (G).
22. *Works* 3:1–3 (C).
23. Carr 1:75 (G).
24. Deutscher, 132–33 (F).
25. *Works* 3:4–9 (C). Italics in the original.
26. Trotsky, 289 (F).
27. *Works* 3:30–33 (C).
28. *Works* 3:10–11.
29. Deutscher, 182 (F).
30. Trotsky, *School,* 191 (E).
31. Sukhanov, *Zapiski* 2:265 (G); Sukhanov, *Record,* 230 (G).
32. Tucker, 178–79 (F).
33. *Works* 3:12–16 (C). Italics in the original.
34. Lenin, *Soch.* 20:13–47 (D).
35. *Works* 2:439 (C).
36. Moskalev, 186 (I).
37. Deutscher, 124 (F).
38. Tucker, 157 (F).
39. Lenin, *PSS* 48:101 (D).
40. Lenin, *PSS* 48:161.
41. Lenin, *PSS* 48:131.
42. Lenin, *PSS* 48:132–33.
43. Lenin, *PSS* 48:141–42.
44. Shlyapnikov, *Kanun* 2:137–38, 187 (H), cited in Gankin and Fisher, 207 n. 114 (E).
45. *Works* 3:17–21, 25–30 (C).
46. Trotsky, 189 (F); Trotsky, *History* 3:53 (G).
47. *Works* 3:25 (C).
48. *Works* 3:30–33.
49. *Works* 3:36.
50. *Works* 3:31.
51. *Works* 3:22–24.
52. Longley, 68–69 (I).
53. Deutscher, 134 (F).
54. Djilas, 114 (H).
55. *VI KPSS,* 1962, no. 5:111–12 (E); Trotsky, *School,* 236–39 (E).
56. McNeal, *Resolutions* 1:210 (E).
57. Ulam, 132 (F).
58. Trotsky, *School,* 274 (E).
59. *VI KPSS,* 1962, no. 3:145–47 (E).
60. Alliluev, 110 (H).

Chapter 2: April

1. Raskol'nikov, 1925, 54 (H); Rabinowitch, *Prelude,* 37 (G).
2. Raskol'nikov, 1964, 63–64 (H); Smith, 332 (F).

3. Sukhanov, *Zapiski* 3:26–27 (G). See also Carr 1:77–78 (G).
4. Yaroslavsky, 94 (F). See also the chronology in *Works* 3:440 (C).
5. *Lenin: Biography*, 299 (I).
6. *Lenin: Biog. khronika* 4:55 (A).
7. Smith, 332 (F).
8. Trotsky, 194 (F).
9. Lenin, *Soch.* 20:109–45 (D).
10. *April Crisis*, 15–16 (E).
11. Tucker, 168 (F).
12. Yaroslavsky, 94 (F).
13. Lenin, *Soch.* 20:38 (D).
14. *Works* 3:34–35 (C).
15. *Works* 3:36–38.
16. Lenin, *CW* 24:135 (D).
17. *Works* 3:39–40.
18. *Works* 3:41–45.
19. Protocols in *Seventh Conference*, 7–60 (E).
20. Trotsky, 200 (F).
21. McNeal, *Resolutions* 1:214 (E).
22. Rabinowitch, *Prelude*, 44 (G).
23. Lenin, *PSS* 31:309–11 (D); McNeal, *Resolutions* 1:216 (E).
24. Trotsky, 206 (F).
25. Anikeev, 31 (E).
26. Lenin, *CW* 24:227 (D).
27. *Seventh Conference*, vii (E).
28. *Seventh Conference*, 66.
29. *Seventh Conference*, 78–86.
30. *Seventh Conference*, 78–86.
31. *Works* 3:42 (C).
32. *Seventh Conference*, 103–5 (E).
33. Trotsky, 201 (F).
34. *Seventh Conference*, 105–7 (E).
35. *Seventh Conference*, 108–10.
36. *Seventh Conference*, 112.
37. *Works* 3:46–50 (C).
38. Gopner, 52 (H).
39. *Seventh Conference*, 207–8 (E).
40. Anikeev, 26–53 (E).
41. *Seventh Conference*, 228 (E).
42. *Seventh Conference*, 322.
43. *Seventh Conference*, 322, note. On the telegram to Michael Romanov, see Trotsky, 181 (F).
44. *Seventh Conference*, 322 (E).
45. *Seventh Conference*, 323, note.
46. *Seventh Conference*, 323.
47. *Seventh Conference*, 323.
48. *Seventh Conference*, 323.

49. Deutscher, 142–43 (F).
50. Ulam, 141 (F).
51. Payne, 180 (F).
52. Trotsky, 202 (F).
53. Trotsky, 202.
54. *Seventh Conference*, 324 (E).
55. *Seventh Conference*, 119.
56. *CPSU in Resolutions* 1:446 (E).
57. *Seventh Conference*, 370 n. 208 (E).
58. *Works* 3:52–58 (C).
59. McNeal, *Resolutions* 1:225 (E).
60. *Works* 3:58 (C).
61. *Seventh Conference*, 213–15 (E).
62. *Seventh Conference*, 282–83.
63. Lenin, *Soch.* 20:312 (D).
64. *Seventh Conference*, 219–22 (E).
65. *Seventh Conference*, 222–24.
66. *Seventh Conference*, 224–26.
67. *Works* 3:59 (C).
68. Tovstukha, 67–68 (F).
69. Lenin, *Soch.* 16 (1930):291; 21 (1931):569 (D).
70. Fainsod (1953), 154 (I); Fainsod (1963), 178 (I); Hough and Fainsod, 129 (I).
71. *ES* (1953), 2:688 (B); *MSE* (1954), 7:340 (B); *ES* (1964), 2:224 (B).
72. *SIE* 11 (1968), col. 2725 (B); *BSE* 20 (1975):215 (B).
73. *CC Protocols*, 155 (E); *CC Minutes*, 162 (E).
74. *CC Protocols*, 166; *CC Minutes*, 172. Italics added. I am indebted to the late Charles Duval for calling this passage to my attention.
75. Yaroslavsky, 96 (F).

Chapter 3: May–June

1. Lenin, *CW* 24:314–528 (D).
2. Trotsky, 205–6 (F).
3. Trotsky, 207.
4. Deutscher, 143–44 (F).
5. Tucker, 179 (F).
6. Ulam, 142 (F).
7. Smith, 333 (F).
8. Souvarine, 167 (F).
9. *Works* 3:166–67 (C).
10. *Works* 3:67–69.
11. *Works* 3:70–83.
12. *Works* 3:61–66.

13. Lenin, *CW* 25:28 (D).
14. Lenin, *CW* 24:362-63.
15. Balabanoff, 120 (H).
16. Trotsky, *School*, 5 (E).
17. Deutscher, *PA*, 154 (I).
18. Sukhanov, *Record*, 340 (G).
19. Lenin, *CW* 24:421 (D).
20. *Leninskii sbornik*, no. 4:300 (D).
21. Lenin, *CW* 24:432 (D); Deutscher, *PA*, 255-56 (I).
22. *Leninskii sbornik*, no. 4:303 (D).
23. Balabanoff, 127 (H).
24. Lenin, *CW* 24:523-24 (D).
25. Deutscher, *PA*, 340 (I).
26. Trotsky, 206 (F).
27. Balabanoff, 127-28 (H).
28. Chamberlin 1:156 (G).
29. *First Legal PK*, 96-102 (E).
30. Rabinowitch, *Prelude*, 45 (G).
31. Rabinowitch, *Prelude*, 51.
32. Lenin, *CW* 24:445-48 (D).
33. Ulam, 143 (F).
34. Lenin, *CW* 25:20 (D).
35. MELI, 35 (F).
36. *June Demonstration*, 486 (E).
37. Rabinowitch, *Prelude*, 60 (G).
38. Chamberlin 1:161 (G).
39. Chamberlin 1:161.
40. *June Demonstration*, 494-95, 611-12 (E).
41. Rabinowitch, *Prelude*, 76 (G).
42. Rabinowitch, *Prelude*, 72.
43. Chamberlin 1:162 (G).
44. Rabinowitch, *Prelude*, 97 (G).
45. Sovokin, 1966, 62 (I).
46. Rabinowitch, *Prelude*, 80 (G).
47. Revised text in *Works* 3:101-4 (C).
48. Rabinowitch, *Prelude*, 64 (G).
49. Anikeev, 34 (E).
50. Rabinowitch, *Prelude*, 72 (G).
51. *June Demonstration*, 515 (E); Rabinowitch, *Prelude*, 102 (G).
52. *Works* 3:92-94 (C). Italics in the original.
53. *Works* 3:84-91.
54. Rabinowitch, *Prelude*, 122 (G).
55. Stalin's report has not been published. See McNeal, *Works*, 48 (A).
56. Mints 2:404 (G).
57. Lenin, *CW* 25:109-11 (D). Italics in the original.
58. *Works* 3:105-9 (C).

Chapter 4: July

1. *Works* 3:169–70 (C).
2. Rabinowitch, *Prelude*, 121–22 (G).
3. Rabinowitch, *Prelude*, 137–38, citing Nevsky, 29–30 (H).
4. Rabinowitch, *Prelude*, 137.
5. Raskol'nikov, 1925, 1982 (H).
6. Raskol'nikov, 1982, 143.
7. Rabinowitch, *Prelude*, 182 (G).
8. Raskol'nikov, 1982, 208 (H).
9. Rabinowitch, *Prelude*, 201–2 (G), citing Sukhanov, *Record*, 479–81 (G).
10. Rabinowitch, *Prelude*, 179.
11. Rabinowitch, *Prelude*, 277, citing Graf, 232 (H).
12. Rabinowitch, *Prelude*, 178.
13. Lenin, *Soch.* 21:9–10 (D).
14. Rabinowitch, *Prelude*, 172–73 (G).
15. *Works* 3:175–76 (C).
16. Rabinowitch, *Prelude*, 201 (G).
17. Rabinowitch, *Prelude*, 207.
18. *Works* 3:117 (C); Mints 2:609 (G).
19. Rabinowitch, *Prelude*, 215 (G), citing Il'in-Zhenevsky, 82 (H).
20. Rabinowitch, *Prelude*, 216–17.
21. Trotsky, 213 (F).
22. *Lenin: Biog. khronika* 4:282 (A).
23. Trotsky, 212 (F).
24. "S podlinym verno," "Ia uveren," and "Shtrikhi."
25. *Stalin: Sbornik statei* (I).
26. Tucker, 472 (F).
27. Levine, 409 (F).
28. Bedny, *PSS* 12:79–84 (I).
29. Hyde, 94–95 (F).
30. Trotsky, 209–10 (F).
31. Souvarine, 167 (F).
32. Ulam, 144 (F).
33. Smith, 333 (F).
34. Hingley, 89 (F).
35. Hyde, 131 (F).
36. De Jonge, 100 (F).
37. Tucker (F) has called attention to Bedny's insight (see 470–71).
38. Trotsky, 213 (F).
39. *Sixth Congress*, 36 (E).
40. Lenin, *CW* 25:176–78 (D).
41. Sovokin, "Enlarged Meeting," 128 (I).
42. *Leninskii sbornik*, no. 4 (D).
43. Sovokin, "Enlarged Meeting," 128 (I).
44. McNeal, *Resolutions* 4:246–47 (E).
45. *Konferentsii*, 52–88 (E).

46. *Works* 3:114 (C).
47. *Works* 3:118; Elov, 94 (H).
48. *Works* 3:120; Elov, 98.
49. Elov, 98.
50. *Works* 3:121–29 (C).
51. *Works* 3:127–28. Italics added.
52. *Konferentsii*, 68 (E). Italics added. See also Elov, 109 (H).
53. Elov, 110; *Konferentsii*, 68.
54. *Works* 3:129 (C); *Konferentsii*, 68–69.
55. *Konferentsii*, 17. In the protocols the second point is illegible, but I agree with Sovokin, "Enlarged Meeting," 129 (I), that it can be restored on the basis of Lenin's article, "The Political Situation."
56. *Konferentsii*, 165 (E).
57. *Konferentsii*, 78.
58. Lenin, *Soch.* 10–17 (D).
59. *Works* 6:340–41 (C).
60. *On the Paths to October*, 99 (C).
61. *On the Paths to October*, 101–5.
62. *Works* 3:160–62 (C).
63. Trotsky, 214 (F).
64. *Lenin: Biog. khronika* 4:304 (A).
65. Lenin, *CW* 25:194–207 (D).
66. *Works* 3:155–57 (C).
67. *Sixth Congress*, 285–86 (E).
68. *Works* 6:53–55 (C).
69. *Sixth Congress*, 14–20 (E).
70. *On the Paths to October*, 87–95 (C).
71. *Works* 3:166–79 (C).
72. *Sixth Congress*, 148 (E).
73. *Sixth Congress*, 277.
74. *Sixth Congress*, 17.
75. *Sixth Congress*, 17.
76. *Sixth Congress*, 17.
77. *Sixth Congress*, 277.
78. *Sixth Congress*, 18–19
79. *Sixth Congress*, 19–20.
80. *Sixth Congress*, 20.
81. *Works* 3:179 (C).
82. *Sixth Congress*, 23 (E).
83. *Sixth Congress*, 28.
84. *Sixth Congress*, 462.
85. *Sixth Congress*, 23.
86. *Sixth Congress*, 26.
87. *Works* 3:179 (C).
88. *Works* 3:180.
89. *Works* 3:187.
90. *Sixth Congress*, 20 (E).

91. *Sixth Congress*, 37.
92. *Sixth Congress*, 419n.139.
93. Sovokin, "Resolution," 14n. 27 (I).
94. *Sixth Congress*, 104–5 (E).
95. *Sixth Congress*, 110.
96. Sovokin, "Resolution," 24 (I).
97. *Sixth Congress*, 110–14 (E).
98. *Sixth Congress*, 285. Italics added.
99. *Sixth Congress*, 118–19.
100. *Sixth Congress*, 121–22.
101. *Sixth Congress*, 149.
102. *Sixth Congress*, 147–50 (Kharitonov), 150–55 (Milyutin).
103. *Sixth Congress*, 166–78.
104. Sovokin, "Resolution," 9–25 (I).
105. *Sixth Congress*, 241–51 (E).
106. *Sixth Congress*, 254.
107. *Sixth Congress*, 250.
108. *Sixth Congress*, 251.
109. *Sixth Congress*, 252.
110. *Sixth Congress*, 439n. 229.
111. *History of the CPSU*, vol. 3, pt.1, p. 197 (I).

Chapter 5: August

1. Trotsky, 222 (F).
2. Trotsky, 223.
3. Trotsky, 222.
4. Deutscher, 156 (F).
5. *CC Protocols*, 3–5 (E).
6. *CC Protocols*, 6–7.
7. Ulam, 150 (F).
8. *CC Protocols*, 13 (E).
9. *CC Protocols*, 4.
10. *CC Protocols*, 26–27.
11. Trotsky, 223 (F).
12. Deutscher, 155 (F).
13. *CC Protocols*, 3 (E).
14. *CC Protocols*, 13.
15. *CC Protocols*, 37–38.
16. *CC Protocols*, 36.
17. *CC Protocols*, 37–38.
18. *CC Protocols*, 37.
19. Rabinowitch, *Bolsheviks*, 161–62 (G).
20. Rabinowitch, *Bolsheviks*, 164.
21. *Works* 3:377–81 (C).
22. *CC Protocols*, 32 (E).

23. Rabinowitch, *Bolsheviks*, 345n. 2 (G).
24. Lenin, *PSS* 34:248-56 (D).
25. Trotsky, 222 (F).
26. *CC Protocols*, 20 (E).
27. *CC Protocols*, 26-27. Italics in the original.
28. *CC Protocols*, 22-23.
29. *Works* 3:215-20 (C).
30. *Works* 3:279.
31. Lenin, *CW* 25:249-50 (D). Italics in the original.
32. Lenin, *CW* 25:286. Italics in the original.
33. Lenin, *CW* 25:289. Italics added.
34. Lenin, *CW* 25:289. Italics in the original.
35. Lenin, *CW* 25:289. Italics added.

Chapter 6: September–October

1. *Works* 3:278 (C). Italics added.
2. *Works* 3:288.
3. *Works* 3:242.
4. Lenin, *CW* 25:290-300 (D).
5. *CC Protocols*, 43-45 (E).
6. *CC Protocols*, 42.
7. *Lenin: Biog. khronika* 4:350 (A).
8. *CC Protocols*, 56-57 (E).
9. *CC Protocols*, 58-62.
10. *CC Protocols*, 55.
11. Daniels, *Red October*, 53-54 (G).
12. Deutscher, 158 (F).
13. *CC Protocols*, 55 (E).
14. *CC Protocols*, 52.
15. Yaroslavsky, 102 (F).
16. *Works* 3:448-49 (C). Italics added.
17. Trotsky, 226-27 (F).
18. Deutscher, 159 (F).
19. Medvedev, 10 (F).
20. *Lenin: Biog. khronika* 4:352 (A).
21. *CC Protocols*, 63-64 (E).
22. *CC Protocols*, 65.
23. *CC Protocols*, 242n.100.
24. Lenin, *Soch.* 21:49 (D).
25. *CC Protocols*, 65 (E).
26. *CC Protocols*, 66-67.
27. *CC Protocols*, 69-70.
28. *CC Protocols*, 263n. 107.
29. *CC Protocols*, 76. The protocols speak of "Moscow and Peter workers." I assume they mean "party workers."

30. Gorodetsky, 1957, 30 (I).
31. CC *Protocols*, 76 (E).
32. CC *Protocols*, 80.
33. Trotsky, 228 (F).
34. Rabinowitch, *Bolsheviks*, 201 (G).
35. CC *Protocols*, 83-86 (E).
36. Trotsky, *History* 3:155; 371 (G).
37. Deutscher, 163 (F).
38. Fainsod, 1963, 307 (I).
39. Schapiro, 175 (I).
40. Deutscher, 163 (F).
41. Trotsky, *History* 3:155-56 (G).
42. CC *Protocols*, 74 (E).
43. *Works* 3:422 (C).
44. *Lenin: Biog. khronika* 4:373 (A). Italics added.
45. Holmes, 356 (I).
46. Daniels, *Conscience*, 457 (G).
47. Rabinowitch, *Bolsheviks*, 219 (G).
48. CC *Protocols*, 93-94 (E). Italics added.
49. CC *Protocols*, 94.
50. CC *Protocols*, 100.
51. *First Legal PK*, 303 (E), cited in Rabinowitch, *Bolsheviks*, 200 (G).
52. CC *Protocols*, 100 (E).
53. CC *Protocols*, 104; CC *Minutes*, 108 (E).
54. CC *Protocols*, 104; CC *Minutes*, 109.
55. Daniels, *Conscience*, 61 (G).
56. Mints 2:1007.
57. Rabinowitch, *Bolsheviks*, 232 (G).
58. Rabinowitch, *Bolsheviks*, 224-25.
59. *Soch.* 4:317 (C).
60. CC *Protocols*, 109 (E).
61. CC *Protocols*, 114.
62. CC *Protocols*, 115. Italics added.
63. CC *Protocols*, 106-8.
64. CC *Protocols*, 117-18.
65. Rabinowitch, *Bolsheviks*, 239 (G).
66. Rabinowitch, *Bolsheviks*, 252-53.
67. Rabinowitch, *Bolsheviks*, 249.
68. Slusser, 405-16 (I).
69. CC *Protocols*, 119-21 (E).
70. Trotsky, *School*, 234 (E).
71. Gorodetsky, 1957, 41 (I).
72. *Works* 3:414-17 (C).
73. Rabinowitch, *Bolsheviks*, 157 (G). Italics added.
74. Deutscher, 118 (F).
75. Holmes, 270, 437, and 514n. 94 (I).
76. Zhakov, 88-93 (H). Italics added.

77. Allilueva, 61 (H), cited by Smith, 374 (F).
78. Lutsky, "Session" (I).
79. Trotsky, *Life*, 290 (H).
80. Ulam, 154 (F).
81. Deutscher, 167 (F).
82. Gorodetsky, 1957, 3 (I). See also Gorodetsky, *Rozhdenie*, 98–99 (G).

Chapter 7: Coda

1. *CC Protocols*, 115 (E).
2. See, for example, the chronology in the article "Great October Socialist Revolution," *SIE* 3:58–63 (B).
3. Podvoisky (H).
4. Mints 2:1007, citing *MRC* (E).
5. Mints 2:1007 (G).
6. Lenin, *PSS* 34:435–36 (D).
7. Tucker, 179–80 (F).

BIBLIOGRAPHY
AND LIST OF
SHORT TITLES

A. Bibliographies and Chronologies

Lenin: Biog. khronika   *Vladimir Il'ich Lenin: Biograficheskaia khronika, 1870–1924.* 12 vols. Moscow: Izdatel'stvo politicheskoi literatury, 1973–82.

McNeal, *Works*   McNeal, Robert H., comp. *Stalin's Works: An Annotated Bibliography.* Stanford: Stanford University Press, 1967.

B. Reference Works and Encyclopedias

BSE   *Bol'shaia sovetskaia entsiklopediia.* 3d ed. vols. Moscow.

ES (1953)   *Entsiklopedicheskii slovar'.* 3 vols. Moscow, 1953–55.

ES (1964)   *Entsiklopedicheskii slovar' v dvukh tomakh.* 2 vols. Moscow, 1964.

Granat   *Entsiklopedicheskii slovar' Russkogo bibliograficheskogo instituta Granata: Deiateli Soiuza sovetskikh sotsialisti-*

	cheskikh respublik i Oktiabr'skoi revoliutsii (Avtobiografii i biografii). Moscow, 1927–29.
MSE	*Malaia sovetskaia entsiklopediia.* 3d ed. 10 vols. Moscow.
SIE	*Sovetskaia istoricheskaia entsiklopediia.* 16 vols. Moscow, 1961–76.

C. Writings by Stalin

On the Paths to October	Stalin, I.V. *Na putiakh k Oktiabriu.* Moscow: Gosizdat, 1924.
Soch.	Stalin, I.V. *Sochineniya.* 13 vols. Moscow: Gospolitizdat, 1946–51.
Works	Stalin, J.V. *Works.* 12 vols. Moscow: Foreign Languages Publishing House, 1952–55.

D. Writings by Lenin

Lenin, *CW*	Lenin, V. I. *Collected Works.* London: Lawrence & Wishart, 1960–.
Lenin, *PSS*	Lenin, V. I. *Polnoe Sobranie Sochinenii.* 5th ed. 54 vols. Moscow, 1959–65.
Lenin, *Soch.*	Lenin, V. I. *Sochineniia.* 3d ed. 30 vols. Moscow, 1928–32.
Leninskii sbornik	*Leninskii sbornik.* No. 1, Moscow: Gosizdat, 1924. No. 4, Moscow: Gosizdat, 1925. No. 7, Moscow: Gosizdat, 1928.

E. Documentary Publications

Anikeev, V. V. *Deiatel'nost' TsK RSDRP (b) v 1917 godu. (Khronika Sobytii).* Moscow: "Mysl Izdatel'stvo," 1969.

Anikeev, V. V. "Dokumenty Tsentral'nogo partiinogo arkhiva o deiatel'nosti partii v period podgotovkoi Oktiabria." *Voprosy istorii KPSS,* 1966, no. 11:122–27.

Anikeev, V. V. *Dokumenty Velikogo Oktiabria: Istoriograficheskii ocherk.* Moscow: Politizdat, 1977.

Anikeev   Anikeev, V. V. "Protokoly Tsentral'nogo Komiteta RSDRP (b): Mart–Oktiabr' 1917 g." In *Istochnikove-*

denie Istorii Velikogo Oktiabria (Moscow, 1977), 26–53.

CC Minutes

The Bolsheviks and the October Revolution: Minutes of the Central Committee of the Russian Social-Democratic Party (Bolsheviks), August 1917–February 1918. London: Pluto Press, 1974.

Gankin and Fisher

Gankin, O. H., and Fisher, H. H. *The Bolsheviks and the World War.* Stanford: Stanford University Press, 1940.

CPSU in Resolutions

Kommunisticheskaia partiia Sovetskogo soliuza v rezoliutsiiakh i resheniiakh s''ezdov, konferentsii i plenumov TsK, 1898–1954. 7th ed. 4 vols. Moscow: Gospolitizdat, 1954.

McNeal, Resolutions

McNeal, Robert H., general editor. *Resolutions and Decisions of the Communist Party of the Soviet Union.* 4 vols. Toronto: University of Toronto Press, 1974.

Vol. 2. Elwood, Ralph Carter, ed., *The Russian Social-Democratic Labour Party, 1898–October 1917.* Toronto: University of Toronto Press, 1974.

MRC

Petrogradskii voenno-revoliutsionnyi komitet. Dokumenty i materialy v trëkh tomakh. 3 vols. Moscow: Izdatel'stvo "Nauka," 1966–67.

First Legal PK

Pervyi legal'nyi Peterburgskii komitet bol'shevikov v 1917 godu. Moscow and Leningrad: Gosizdat, 1927.

VI KPSS, 1962, no. 3

"Protokoly i rezoliutsii Biuro TsK RSDRP (b) (Mart 1917 g.)." *Voprosy istorii KPSS,* 1962, no. 3:134–57.

CC Protocols

Protokoly tsentral'nogo komiteta RSDRP (b), Avgust 1917–Fevral' 1918. Moscow: Gosizdat politicheskoi literatury, 1958.

VI KPSS, 1962, no. 5

"Protokoly vserossiiskogo (martovskogo) soveshchaniia partiinykh rabotnikov (27 marta–2 aprelia 1917 g.)," *Voprosy istorii KPSS,* 1962, no. 5:112, and no. 6:139–40.

April Crisis

Revoliutsionnoe dvizhenie v Rossii v aprele 1917 g: Aprel'skii krizis. Moscow: Izdatel'stvo Akademii nauk SSSR, 1958.

June Demonstration

Revoliutsionnoe dvizhenie v Rossii v mae–iiune 1917 g: Iiun'skaia demonstratsia. Moscow: Izdatel'stvo Akademii nauk SSSR, 1959.

July Crisis

Revoliutsionnoe dvizhenie v Rossii v iiule 1917 g: Iiul'skii krizis. Moscow: Izdatel'stvo Akademii nauk SSSR, 1958.

Seventh Conference

Sed'maia (aprel'skaia) vserossiiskaia konferentsiia

	RSDRP (bol'shevikov). Petrogradskaia obshchegorodskaia konferentsiia RSDRP (bol'shevikov) aprel' 1917 goda: Protokoly. Moscow: Gospolitizdat, 1958.
Sixth Congress	*Shestoi s"ezd RSDRP (bol'shevikov) Avgust 1917 goda: Protokoly.* Moscow: Gospolitizdat, 1958.
Trotsky, School	Trotsky, Leon. *The Stalin School of Falsification.* 3d ed. New York: Pathfinder Press, 1971.
Konferentsii	*Vtoraia i tret'ia petrogradskie obshchegorodskie konferentsii bol'shevikov v iule i oktiabre 1917 g: Protokoly i materialy.* Moscow and Leningrad: Gosizdat, 1927.

F. Biographies of Stalin

Barbusse	Barbusse, Henri. *Stalin: A New World Seen through One Man.* New York: Macmillan, 1935.
De Jonge	De Jonge, Alex. *Stalin and the Shaping of the Soviet Union.* New York: Morrow, 1986.
Deutscher	Deutscher, Isaac. *Stalin: A Political Biography.* 2d ed. New York: Oxford University Press, 1967.
Hingley	Hingley, Ronald. *Joseph Stalin: Man and Legend.* New York: McGraw-Hill, 1974.
Hyde	Hyde, H. Montgomery. *Stalin: The History of a Dictator.* New York: Farrar, Straus, & Giroux, 1971.
Levine	Levine, Isaac Don. *Stalin.* New York: Cosmopolitan Book Corp., 1931.
Lyons	Lyons, Eugene. *Stalin, Czar of All the Russias.* Philadelphia: Lippincott, 1940.
Medvedev	Medvedev, Roy A. *Let History Judge.* New York: Knopf, 1971.
MELI	Moscow. Marx-Engels-Lenin Institute. *Joseph Stalin: A Political Biography.* New York: International Publishers, 1949.
Payne	Payne, Robert. *The Rise and Fall of Stalin.* New York: Simon & Schuster, 1965.
Smith	Smith, Edward Ellis. *The Young Stalin: The Early Years of an Elusive Revolutionary.* New York: Farrar, Straus, & Giroux, 1967.
Souvarine	Souvarine, Boris. *Stalin: A Critical Survey of Bolshevism.* New York: Alliance Book Corp., Longmans, Green, 1939.

Tovstukha   Tovstukha, I. "Joseph Stalin." In Haupt and Marie (H), 65–68.

Trotsky   Trotsky, Leon. *Stalin, An Appraisal of the Man and His Influence.* New York: Harper & Bros., 1941.

Tucker   Tucker, Robert C. *Stalin as Revolutionary: A Study in History and Personality.* New York: Norton, 1973.

Ulam   Ulam, Adam B. *Stalin: The Man and His Era.* New York: Viking Press, 1973.

Yaroslavsky   Yaroslavsky, E. *Landmarks in the Life of Stalin.* Moscow: Foreign Languages Publishing House, 1940.

G. Histories of the Russian Revolution

Carr   Carr, E. H. *The Bolshevik Revolution.* 3 vols. New York: Macmillan, 1951–53.

Chamberlin   Chamberlin, W. H. *The Russian Revolution, 1917–23.* 2 vols. New York: Macmillan, 1935.

Daniels, *Conscience*   Daniels, Robert V. *The Conscience of the Revolution: Communist Opposition in Soviet Russia.* Cambridge: Harvard University Press, 1965.

Daniels, *Red October*   Daniels, Robert V. *Red October: The Bolshevik Revolution of 1917.* New York: Scribner, 1967.

Gorodetsky, *Rozhdenie*   Gorodetskii, Ye. N. *Rozhdenie sovetskogo gosudarstva, 1917–1918 gg.* Moscow: Izdatel'stvo "Nauka," 1965.

Mints   Mints, I. I. *Istoriia Velikogo Oktiabria v trëkh tomakh.* 3 vols. Moscow: Izdatel'stvo "Nauka," 1968.

Rabinowitch, *Bolsheviks*   Rabinowitch, Alexander. *The Bolsheviks Come to Power: The Revolution of 1917 in Petrograd.* New York: Norton, 1976.

Rabinowitch, *Prelude*   Rabinowitch, Alexander. *Prelude to Revolution: The Petrograd Bolsheviks and the July 1917 Uprising.* Bloomington: Indiana University Press, 1968.

Sukhanov, *Record*   Sukhanov, N. N. (pseudonym of N. N. Himmer). *The Russian Revolution, 1917: A Personal Record.* 2 vols. New York: Harper & Row, 1962. Edited, translated, and abridged by Joel Carmichael from *Zapiski.*

Sukhanov, *Zapiski*   Sukhanov, N. N. *Zapiski o revoliutsii.* 7 vols. Berlin: Grzhebin, 1922–23.

Trotsky, *History*   Trotsky, Leon. *The History of the Russian Revolution.* 3 vols. New York: Simon & Schuster, 1932–33.

BIBLIOGRAPHY

H. Memoirs

Alliluev   Alliluev, Sergei. *Proidënnyi put'*. Moscow: OGIZ, 1946.

Allilueva   Allilueva, A. S. *Vospominaniia*. Moscow: Sovetskii pisatel', 1946.

Baikalov   Baikalov, A. "Moi vstrechi s Osipom Dzhugashvili," *Vozrozhdenie*. Paris, March–April, 1950.

Balabanoff   Balabanoff, Angelica. *Impressions of Lenin*. Ann Arbor: University of Michigan Press, 1964.

Djilas   Djilas, Milovan. *Conversations with Stalin*. New York: Harcourt, Brace & World, 1962.

Elov   Elov, B. "Posle iiul'skikh sobytii," *Krasnaia letopis,'* 1923, no. 7:95–127.

Gopner   Gopner, S. I. "Martovskie i aprel'skie dni 1917 goda (iz vospominaniia uchastnika oktiabr'skoi revoliutsii)," *Voprosy istorii*, 1957, no. 3:42–52.

Graf   Graf, Tatiana. "V iiul'skie dni 1917 g." *Krasnaia letopis'*, 1932, no. 5–6.

Haupt and Marie   Haupt, Georges, and Marie, Jean-Jacques. *Makers of the Russian Revolution*. Ithaca: Cornell University Press, 1974.

Il'in-Zhenevsky   Il'in-Zhenevskii, A. F. *Ot fevralia k zakhvatu vlasti: Vospominaniia o 1917 g.* Leningrad: Priboi, 1927.

Il'in-Genevsky, A. F. *From the February to the October Revolution, 1917*. London: Modern Books, 1931.

Ivanov   Ivanov, Boris I. Unpublished memoirs, cited by Medvedev (F), 6–7.

Nevsky   Nevskii, V. I. "V oktiabre: beglye zametki pamiati," *Katorga i ssylka*, 1932, no. 11–12:96–97.

Podvoisky   Podvoiskii, N. I. *God, 1917*. Moscow: Gospolitizdat, 1958.

Raskol'nikov, 1925   Raskol'nikov, F. F. *Kronshtadt i Piter v 1917 goda*. Moscow and Leningrad: Gosizdat, 1925.

Raskol'nikov, 1982   Annotated translation, *Kronstadt and Petrograd in 1917*. London: New Parks Publications, 1982.

Raskol'nikov, 1964   Raskol'nikov, F. *Na boevykh postakh*. Moscow: Voenizdat, 1964.

Shlyapnikov, *Kanun*   Shliapnikov, A. G. *Kanun semnadtsatoga Goda*. 2 vols. Moscow and Petrograd: Gosizdat, 1923.

Shlyapnikov, *1917*   Shliapnikov, A. G. *Semnadtsatyi god.* 4 vols. Moscow and Leningrad, 1925–31.

Shveitser   Shveitser, Vera. *Stalin v turukhanskoi ssylke: Vospominaniia podpol'shchika.* Moscow, 1940.

Trotsky, *Life*   Trotsky, Leon. *My Life: An Attempt at an Autobiography.* New York: Scribner, 1931.

Vereshchak   Vereshchak, S. "Stalin v tiur'me: Vospominaniia politicheskogo zakliuchennogo." *Dni*, Jan. 22 and 24, 1928.

Zhakov   "Pis'mo M. Zhakova k Vasil'chenkoe," *Proletarskaia revoliutsiia*, 1922, no. 10:88–93.

I. Secondary Studies

Books

Deutscher, *PA*   Deutscher, Isaac. *The Prophet Armed: Trotsky, 1879–1921.* London: Oxford University Press, 1954.

Fainsod, 1953   Fainsod, Merle. *How Russia Is Ruled.* Cambridge: Harvard University Press, 1953.

Fainsod, 1963   Revised edition, 1963.

Holmes   Holmes, Larry Eugene. "Soviet Historical Studies of 1917 Bolshevik Activity in Petrograd." Ph.D. diss., University of Kansas, 1968.

Hough and Fainsod   Hough, Jerry F., and Fainsod, Merle. *How the Soviet Union Is Governed.* Cambridge: Harvard University Press, 1979.

Lenin: Biography   *Vladimir Il'ich Lenin: Biografiia.* Moscow: Gosizdat politicheskoi literatury, 1960. 2d ed., 1963; 3d ed., 1967.

History of the CPSU   *Istoriia Kommunisticheskoi partii Sovetskogo Soiuza v shesti tomakh.* Moscow: Izdatel'stvo politicheskoi literatury, 1964–.

Moskalev   Moskalev, M. A. *Russkoe biuro bol'shevistskoi partii: 1912–Mart 1917 g.* Moscow: Gospolitizdat, 1947.

                        Moskalev, M. A. *Biuro tsentral'nogo komiteta RSDRP v Rossii, Avgust 1903–Mart 1917.* Moscow: Izdatel'stvo politicheskoi literatury, 1964.

Schapiro   Schapiro, Leonard. *The Communist Party of the Soviet*

Union. 2d ed., rev. and enl. London: Methuen, in association with Eyre and Spottiswood, 1970.

Articles and Short Works

Bedny, *PSS*	Bednyi, Demian (pseudonym of Ye. A. Pridvorov). *Polnoe sobranie sochinenii.* 19 vols. Moscow and Leningrad: Gosizdat, 1928–33.
	Bednyi, Demian. *Sobranie sochinenii v vos'mi tomakh.* 8 vols. Moscow: Izdatel'stvo "Khudozhestvennaia literatura," 1965.
	Bednyi, Demian. *Stikhotvorenie.* Leningrad: Sovetskii pisatel', 1949.
Gorodetsky, 1957	Gorodetskii, Ye. N. "Iz istorii oktiabr'skogo vooruzhennogo vosstaniia i II vserossiiskogo s" ezda sovetov," *Voprosy istorii,* 1957, no. 10:23–48.
Longley	Longley, D. A. "The Divisions in the Bolshevik Party in March 1917." *Soviet Studies* 14, no. 1 (1972):61–76.
Lutsky, "Session"	Lutskii, Ye. A. "Zasedanie TsK RSDRP (b), noch'iu 24–25 oktiabria 1917 g." *Voprosy istorii KPSS,* 1986, no. 11:81–90. See also Lutsky's earlier article, "Memuarnye istochniki o zasedanii TsK RSDRP (b) 24–25 oktiabria 1917 g," *Sovetskie arkhivy,* no. 4: 1980, 26–31.
Slusser	Slusser, Robert M. "On the Question of Stalin's Role in the Bolshevik Revolution," *Canadian Slavonic Papers* 19, no. 4 (1977):405–16.
Sovokin, 1966	Sovokin, A. M. "K istorii iiun'skoi demonstratsii 1917 g," *Voprosy istorii KPSS,* 1966, no. 5:45–54.
Sovokin, "Enlarged Meeting"	Sovokin, A. M. "Rasshirennoe soveshchanie TsK RSDRP (b), 13–14 iiulia 1917 g," *Voprosy istorii KPSS,* 1959, no. 4:125–38.
Sovokin, "Resolution"	Sovokin, A. M. "Rezoliutsiia VI s"ezda partii 'O politicheskom polozhenii'." In *Istochnikovedenie istorii Velikogo Oktiabria* (Moscow, 1977), 9–25.
Stalin: Sbornik statei	*Stalin: Sbornik statei k piatidesiatiletiia so dnia rozhdeniia.* Moscow and Leningrad, 1930.

INDEX OF NAMES

Note: Entries for Lenin and Stalin are limited to their writings.

INDEX

INDEX

INDEX

Library of Congress Cataloging-in-Publication Data

Slusser, Robert M.
  Stalin in October.

  Bibliography: p.
  Includes index.
  1. Stalin, Joseph, 1879–1953. 2. Revolutionists—
Soviet Union—Biography. 3. Soviet Union—History—
Revolution, 1917–1921. I. Title.
DK268.S8S48 1987   947.084'2'0924 [B]   87-3666
ISBN 0-8018-3457-0
      0-8018-4112-7 (pbk.)

Designed by Chris L. Smith
Composed by BG Composition, Inc. in Goudy Old Style with display lines in Gill Sans
Printed by the Maple Press Company